Styles of Learning
and Teaching

To Dorothy

Styles of Learning and Teaching

*An Integrated Outline of Educational Psychology
for Students, Teachers, and Lecturers*

Noel Entwistle

*Bell Professor of Education
University of Edinburgh*

David Fulton Publishers

London

Copyright © 1988 by David Fulton Publishers Ltd.,
Reprinted April 1983
Reprinted November 1986
Reprinted June 1988
Reprinted July 1990

British Library Cataloguing in Publication Data:

Entwistle, N.J. (Noel James), *1936*
    Styles in learning and teaching: an
    integrated outline of educational
    psychology for students, teachers and
    lecturers.
    1. Educational psychology
    I. Title
    370.15

    ISBN 1-85346-104-0

Printed and bound in Great Britain

Contents

Preface

This book is, in a sense, a text-book of educational psychology designed mainly for those with little previous knowledge of the subject. But it is not a conventional text-book. It breaks with tradition in several ways. To begin with it does not cover the whole area which normally defines educational psychology. It concentrates instead on those aspects which are most directly applicable to understanding the processes related to learning intellectual skills and acquiring knowledge. Also the book does not aim to provide a detailed coverage; it is deliberately selective in the topics which are covered. The main aim is to present an outline, or perhaps an overview, of current ideas in educational psychology in the hope of providing a more coherent picture of what otherwise tends to be a rather fragmentary set of topics drawn from mainstream psychology. Read in conjunction with more conventional text-books, this overview should provide a good guide to the recent literature.

Two other important differences will be found in the way topics are treated. Instead of looking for implications for teaching within each topic, the aim of the major part of the book is to build up a coherent framework within which to understand the learning process. Once that framework is established, and justified from several areas of psychological research, the final section tries to point out implications for the teacher and the student. The rationale behind this approach is explained in the first chapter.

Another difference lies in the emphasis placed on learning in higher education. Although this approach has the added advantage of making this introduction to educational psychology suitable for lecturers in colleges or universities, its main purpose is to look at learning first from the point of view of the learner. By starting with research into the everyday learning of adults, and encouraging introspection, it is hoped to show how theories relate to personal experience. The involvement of the reader in a 'learning experiment', based on recent research into how students learn, is intended to enhance awareness of factors associated with success and failure in higher education. As alertness to personal strengths and weaknesses in learning is a characteristic of most successful students, it is anticipated that this emphasis on research into higher education will foster more effective study methods.

A feature of the book is the use of a series of STOP and THINK sections which are intended to provoke a more active interaction with the ideas being presented. This feature is, in a sense, the embodiment of one aspect of the model of the learning process developed in Part II.

Although it is hoped that lecturers will find sections of the book particularly relevant to their work, the main audience is teachers and those intending to become teachers. Part III presents an introduction to some of the important concepts and ideas from educational psychology and educational research which underpin everyday classroom learning.

The first part of the title 'Styles of Learning and Teaching' is perhaps too specific for a book which aims to provide an overview of a substantial range of topics affecting learning — memory, intellectual abilities, cognitive development, motivation, and personality. But this title has been chosen to indicate the stance taken. To indicate the importance placed on individual differences in both student and teacher in determining the outcomes of learning. These differences clearly have a quantitative aspect — the strength of the memory, the level of ability, the stage of development. But the use of the term 'style of learning' is intended to draw attention to the importance of qualitative differences in the approaches to, and processes of, learning. People differ in the ways they prefer to think, or study, or teach. And these differences have implications for learning which have not previously been fully considered.

The style of writing adopted is intended to avoid unnecessary difficulties in comprehension. Technical terms from the jargon of educational psychology have to be used, but these are defined from the outset. Topics are introduced in a way which should allow beginners to follow the later arguments, but these are often followed through to a deep level by introducing results from illustrative research studies in some detail. Thus, although the book can be seen as introductory, it cannot be said to be elementary. There is, in fact, a rather rapid shift in the level of difficulty in some sections. But this can be seen, in part, as a deliberate intellectual challenge to the reader. Learning should, of course, be made as interesting as possible. It does not follow, however, that it should be made uniformly easy. It could be argued, on the contrary, that learning should be made difficult enough to force the student to grapple with complex abstract ideas. Indeed Whitehead, in his essays on *The Aims of Education,* endorsed the importance of confronting students with such difficulty.

'Whenever a text-book is written of real educational worth, you may be quite certain that some reviewer will say that it will be difficult to teach from it. Of course it will be difficult to teach from it. If it were easy, the book ought to be burned; for it cannot be educational. In education, as elsewhere, the broad primrose path leads to a nasty place.'

Whether this book will have any such 'real educational worth' will depend on how successful it is in achieving its main aims. The intention is to help readers to consider critically their own ways of learning and thinking, to understand a model of the learning process and the evidence from which it has been derived, to grasp the significance of the main psychological factors affecting learning, and finally to derive for themselves implications for their own teaching.

If the book proves to be useful in this way, it will be due in no small measure to the many people who have contributed to it, by commenting on chapters or by discussing the ideas it contains. I should like particularly to thank Ann Floyd, Ference Marton, John Nisbet, Lennart Svensson, Johanna Turner, and my wife, Dorothy, all of whom read the whole manuscript and made many valuable suggestions. I am also grateful to Geoffrey Brown, Charles Desforges, Maureen Hanley, Philip Levy, Edwin Peel, Kjell Raaheim, and Alec Ross for their comments on individual chapters. The burden of preparing the final typescript has been shared between Pamela Gordon and Maureen Reith: their sustained efforts and unfailing accuracy are much appreciated.

Edinburgh, 1980   NOEL ENTWISTLE

PART I

Introduction to Educational Psychology

CHAPTER 1

Objectivity and Sensitivity

The intention of this book is to introduce and analyse some of the important concepts and ideas from educational psychology which help us to understand how students and pupils learn. Part II contains detailed reports of some very recent work on the styles and strategies used by students in tackling their academic work. These chapters are placed early in the book for two reasons. First, the results of this research have produced a model of learning processes which provides a framework within which to examine other areas of educational psychology. That framework helps us to see coherence in what might otherwise seem, in Part III, to be a series of disconnected areas of psychological research. The second reason for starting with students is that an examination of adult learning provides an opportunity for introspection by the reader, and hence a way of seeing links between theories of learning and the 'real world' of everyday experience.

The book contains several recurrent themes which indicate the stance taken by the author. There is an acknowledged emphasis on those aims of education which relate to cognitive development, the acquisition of knowledge and skills. This emphasis has been introduced as a way of limiting coverage, rather than as a protest against recent educational ideas which put more stress on the social purposes of schooling. It is not being suggested that the social setting of learning, or the home background of pupils, are irrelevant: nor that the social and emotional development of pupils should be ignored. It *is* being argued that we should think very seriously about how to be more effective in achieving those educational objectives which relate to intellectual development. And the model of learning developed here is limited to psychological aspects of education — to a description of the learning process in terms mainly of the individual characteristics of the learner and teacher, with a bias towards the more complex forms of learning.

The theme which develops out of this concern with intellectual development comes from an examination of one important concept in educational psychology — intelligence. The traditional view of intelligence limited it to logical thinking. Recent developments in education have emphasized appeals to pupils' imagination. But analyses of the structure of the intellect point up three distinct components: memory, logical reasoning, and imaginative thinking. In education, the importance of all three should be recognized. Each has its value in different types of learning. An over-emphasis on 'creativity' in school learning may be as damaging to some pupils, as an excessive stress on memorization may be to others. At certain stages in learning, hard repetitive 'slog' may be essential. And some pupils may, in fact, take more easily to rote learning than to coping with reasoning and understanding. This book contains a plea not to devalue any of the ways of thinking which are part of our normal mental processes, and evidence to substantiate that plea.

The emphasis on intellectual aims does not imply a lack of interest in non-cognitive factors associated with learning. In fact the second major theme in the book reflects a belief in the importance of recognizing individual differences not just in ability, but also in personality and motivation. It is argued that fundamental differences in personality affect our *styles* of learning — our preferred ways of thinking. And that our approaches to teaching reflect previous experiences with learning. We teach as we prefer to learn. Stemming from this is perhaps the most insistent message derived from the research literature. There can be no single 'right' way to study or 'best' way to teach. People differ so much in intellectual abilities, attitudes, and personality that they adopt characteristically different approaches to learning, to teaching, to conducting research, or to writing a book. No one of these approaches could be 'right' for more than a small proportion of people. Yet many teachers and educationalists still proclaim the overriding merits of one particular philosophy of teaching, and roundly denounce the alternatives. Why should that be? We shall argue that a teacher's strong preference for one or other teaching approach — say formal rather than informal — is a reflection of his own learning style and personality. In one way that is not unreasonable: he may teach best using that approach. But best for whom? Presumably only for those pupils or students who share the teacher's own style of learning. For many others that way of presenting knowledge may create unnecessary difficulties.

The final recurrent theme is the importance in learning of *activity:* learning should not be simply a passive process of absorbing predigested knowledge. In higher education, learning should involve many activities; memorizing where necessary, but also relating new information to old, linking theoretical ideas or academic knowledge to personal experience wherever possible, adopting a critical stance to other people's ideas, and evaluating evidence with caution. The book itself has thus been designed to provoke such activities. The ideas developed in the first three parts of the book are more theoretical than practical, yet the ultimate purpose of the book is to show how useful these ideas can be in thinking about education. Thus the reader is encouraged to seek those connections out of his own experience as he reads, by thinking actively about possible implications of the research evidence and theories being introduced.

The book also seeks to provoke activity and personal involvement through the use of a 'learning experiment' and 'STOP AND THINK' sections. The learning experiment is a way of promoting introspection about the reader's own ways of learning, and also serves as an introduction to a particular series of research studies. The 'STOP AND THINK' sections invite the reader to think ahead of the text, to consider issues, and to relate to personal experience. Some readers may find these sections useful, others may consider them an annoying interruption to the developing argument. From what has already been said such differences are to be expected and the reader must decide whether or not to take time to think about these questions. The intention is simply to assist in developing an active, critical approach to reading. But in the end the reader's own questions will be more useful than those provided in the text.

Psychology applied to education

Psychology was originally the study of the human mind, later it included the study of behaviour, and then widened its scope still further to cover the behaviour of animals. Out of this wide reach of academic psychology, only those parts with the clearest relevance to education are to be discussed. The definition of 'relevance' is, however, necessarily somewhat subjective; the particular topics selected depend on the focus already outlined. And the way these topics are treated also depends on the connection that is seen between psychology and education. Does psychology produce laws from which direct solutions to educational problems can be derived? Is the link between psychology and education as strong as, for example, that between physics and engineering?

In the early years of this century there was great optimism about the practical value of psychology. For example, James Ward, a Cambridge professor at the turn of the century, argued for the logical inevitability of a strong link between psychology and education.

'It is not hard to show in a general way that a science of education is theoretically possible, and that such a science must be based on psychology and the cognate sciences. To show this we have, indeed, only to consider that the educator works, or rather ought to work, upon a growing mind, with a definite purpose of attaining an end in view. For unless we maintain that the growth of mind follows no law; or, to put it otherwise, unless it be maintained that systematic observation of the growth of (say) a hundred minds would disclose no uniformities; and unless, further, it can be maintained that for the attainment of a definite end there are no definite means, we must allow that if the teacher knows what he wants to do there must be a scientific way of doing it' (Ward, 1926, page 1).

The logic is impeccable — but the assumptions are dubious, and attempts at establishing general laws which explain the growth of mind have proved more difficult than Ward imagined. The weakness in the assumptions could be deduced from the previous section. There are many reasons why we should *not* expect general laws of learning, when individuals, content, and context are all so different. Nevertheless many psychologists have pursued this line of enquiry, looking for general scientific laws of behaviour, and have publicized their implications for education. Students and teachers have viewed the relevance of those implications from mainstream psychology with increasing doubt. By the 1950s the search for scientific laws of behaviour had taken psychologists far away from the interests of educators. Attempts to extrapolate from evidence on pigeons and rats to teaching strategies in the classroom opened up a serious 'credibility gap'. Stimulus-response psychology still has its value in explaining certain aspects of human behaviour, but it does not provide the most appropriate standpoint from which to consider the intellectual components of the educational process.

The link between psychology and education is still an important one, but it is not as direct as is often thought. Psychology should affect the way teachers think about their work, but it cannot provide specific solutions to the day-to-day problems teachers face. The famous American philosopher and psychologist, William James, argued against a direct link between psychology and teaching.

'You make a great, a very great mistake, if you think that psychology, being the science of mind's laws, is something from which you can deduce definite programmes and schemes and methods of instruction for immediate classroom use. Psychology is a science, and teaching is an art; and sciences never generate arts directly out of themselves. An intermediary inventive mind must make the application, by using its originality' (James, 1899, pages 23-24.)

This is an appeal to match objectivity with sensitivity in moving from theory or research findings to classroom applications.

James Ward made a similar point about the necessity for the teacher to interact with psychological ideas by drawing on practical experience of teaching situations.

'The teacher who has a fair knowledge of psychology can see the "why" and "wherefore" of any (educational) theory that is offered him, can even to a large extent make his own theory, or, at any rate, intelligently apply and, by and by, supplement out of his own experience the theory with which he starts' (Ward, 1926, page 9).

Both Ward and James expected simple laws of learning to emerge from the study of thinking and behaviour. The splintering, since then, of psychology into disparate sections providing contrasting, and even contradictory, explanations of learning and thinking has made it difficult for teachers to be sure what it is that psychology can offer. Often it is expected that a theory of learning will be a panacea, that a single approach to teaching will solve all our educational problems. And some psychologists have reinforced this expectation by arguing strongly for an approach which is in harmony with their own view of learning.

There is now a growing belief that psychological and educational research improve practice, not in the direct way that physics can affect engineering, but in an indirect way by changing the way practical situations are interpreted — by making teachers more aware of aspects of the teaching/learning process which previously had perhaps passed unnoticed. The influence of 'tradition' in education is strong, even where that tradition is called 'progressive'. Research and theory can be used to examine the strengths and weaknesses of whatever has become the 'accepted' approach. Its effect can be compared with the way philosophy has been used to challenge established ideas.

'What is characteristic of philosophy is the piercing of that dead crust of tradition and convention, the breaking of those fetters which bind us to inherited preconceptions, so as to attain a new and broader way of looking at things.... . What is decisive is a new way of seeing and, what goes with it, the will to transform...' (Waismann, 1968, page 32).

The Plowden Report (1967) emphasized the point that theory, and the searching analysis which goes with it, had a value for teachers.

'What is immediately needed is that teachers should bring to bear on their day to day problems, astringent intellectual strutiny' (paragraph 550).

The teacher is bombarded in the classroom by an enormous amount of information. Research findings and theoretical ideas can suggest ways of interpreting that information in potentially more useful ways. It provides a language (concepts) and a grammar (models) to consider the rationale for many aspects of educational practice. Even an empirical psychologist such as Cronbach (1975) is now acknowledging the limited extent to which psychological research can provide 'facts' which will be of direct, and immediate, value in making practical decisions.

'Though enduring systematic theories about man in society are not likely to be achieved, systematic inquiry can realistically hope to make two contributions. One reasonable aspiration is to assess local events accurately, to improve short-run control... . The other reasonable aspiration is to develop explanatory concepts, concepts that will help people use their heads' (page 126).

Thus the links between psychology and education are seen to be indirect. We cannot expect immediate implications for educational practice in each and every theory or piece of research. However the indirect effects *are* valuable. A study of educational psychology provides a precise language with which to discuss practical issues. It provides evidence about, for example, the outcomes of specific types of teaching or learning which helps to move away from personal impression towards demonstrably valid ideas. But most of all it challenges the teacher and the learner to re-examine accepted ways of thinking about the educational process.

The whole structure of this book has been affected by the assumption of an indirect link between research evidence and educational practice. Instead of attempting to spell out at each stage the educational implications of every psychological theory or research finding, it is considered more important to build up a coherent theoretical framework first of all. Then, in the final chapter of the book, some of the possible implications are explored. But these implications are provided only as illustrations of the ways in which ideas from psychology and educational research may guide the teacher's thinking. The important implications are seen as essentially personal and idiosyncratic. Teachers are expected to reinterpret the model of learning developed in this book in terms of their own situation and experience. If the theories are not thoroughly understood, if they lack personal relevance, or if they do not speak to the individual teacher, then their value to that teacher is negligible.

Educational psychology and educational research

Psychology is the study of mind and behaviour. Educational psychology is that part of the parent discipline which has relevance to education. In practice the term 'educational psychology' has been used in two senses. It may be used to define a body of knowledge and experience used by educational psychologists in their clinical work with children referred to them. The emphasis then is on the diagnosis and treatment of symptoms of illness, psychological disturbance, or educational backwardness. But 'educational psychology' can also be used to describe a broader body of knowledge which provides concepts and ideas derived from mainstream psychology and from educational research, so as to illuminate the work of the teacher. It is in this latter sense that this book provides 'an integrative outline of educational psychology'.

The concepts and ideas in educational psychology have been developed from a vast range of empirical studies. Generally its theories are developed out of the results of investigations into the learning of young people, either in the classroom or taking part in controlled experiments in a psychological laboratory. But the context within which data are collected also reflects an important difference in intention, or focus of interest, between the psychologist and someone whose primary concern is education.

The educational research worker usually draws his evidence directly from the classroom. His intention is to describe and to understand educational processes and outcomes, either using concepts and measurement techniques drawn from another discipline (such as psychology) or trying to refine the concepts and explanations used by the teacher themselves. The closer the description keeps to the classroom situation, the easier it will be to interpret the findings: the relevance to the teacher should be clear. The more the research worker draws on explanatory concepts alien to the teacher, or sets up an experiment which constrains the normal learning activities of pupils, the greater the subsequent problems in assessing the educational significance. The findings may have to be translated back into a normal classroom setting, and in so doing the evidence loses its conviction. Extrapolation from one context to another weakens the argument being developed.

A distinction between education and psychology in terms of *level of analysis* is important. Teachers and educational research workers seek explanations of pupils' behaviour in everyday terms of, for example, teaching methods or children's attributes, such as intelligence or personality. Psychologists are more interested in fundamental explanations of general phenomena, such as the workings of the memory or the physiological bases of motivation. This level of analysis may typically involve the use of more narrowly defined technical terms and the examination of the human being as a responding organism. The distinction is not really as sharp as this, but it has been presented in this way to point up a difference in intention which often exists between the educationalist and the psychologist and which can lead to profound disagreement about the appropriateness of alternative explanations of children's behaviour.

While evidence drawn from educational research has the advantage of relevance and immediacy, it also has at least two considerable weaknesses. In trying to describe the behaviour of pupils in a natural setting, it is difficult to tease out which aspects of the situation are most important. A series of controlled experiments, as we shall see in the next chapter, can provide more convincing evidence of which are the central features or causes of sequences of behaviour. The other weakness is that studies carried out in the classroom normally examine *accepted practice*. They do not allow us to determine what might be better approaches to teaching and learning, except in a very limited way. It is rarely possible to make drastic changes in the classroom to find out what might happen. Psychological experiments do not have the same restriction. They allow much more freedom systematically to vary certain aspects of the learning situation, and to explore the effects of novel approaches to instruction derived from an examination of *fundamental psychological processes*.

The stance taken in this book is that educational research and psychology provide complementary sets of ideas from which a sound understanding of important aspects of education can be developed. From a combination of evidence drawn directly from educational settings, and indirectly by extrapolation from the results of carefully controlled experiments, a more satisfactory theoretical rationale can be developed. But that rationale, as we have said before, cannot provide ready-made answers for teachers, and even a deep understanding of theories in educational psychology depends for its value on active attempts to examine ideas and research findings in ways which bring personal relevance to them. The theories need to be reinterpreted in relation to experience of classroom reality.

What counts as research evidence

So far the stress has been on empirical research as the source of explanations of learning. We have already pointed out that applications of research findings depend on the professional sensitivity of teachers. But this may undervalue the potential contribution of the teacher to developing a fuller understanding of classroom learning. It assumes that such knowledge can only be sound if it emerges from the findings of empirical research. Yet there is considerable doubt, even among research workers, about the relative importance of empirical research and intuition from practical experience, in developing valid knowledge about human behaviour. Should the term 'educational research' be reserved for the objective, quantitative approach, or used more widely?

STOP and THINK

● What do you see as the strengths of deriving knowledge about learning from scientific studies?

● What might a practising teacher contribute that would not already be contained in the findings from empirical research? Could such contributions be called 'educational research'?

In an article in the *Encyclopedia of Educational Research*, Kerlinger (1969) is quite clear that 'educational research' has to be limited to the objective, precise, quantitative approach. He states unequivocally that

'Educational research is social scientific research applied to educational problems... *Science* is a misused and misunderstood word. It is not an activity whose purpose is to amass facts, nor does it have a primary concern for improving the world and mankind's lot, though it may often help to do this. Its basic aim is to discover or invent general explanations of natural events.... Nomothetic means 'law-making'. A nomothetic science is one that seeks to establish laws or generalisations. In contrast, what has been called idiographic science studies unique or singular events. Idiographic means 'describing things', singular things.... Very bluntly put, there is no such thing as scientific research that is idiographic — by definition. And most educational research is and has to be scientific because we want the behavioural laws discovered to be applicable, ideally, to whole classes or sets of individuals and settings' (pages 1127-1128).

The opposite point of view has been presented by Bantock (1961) who queries whether it is sensible to follow the research strategies of the physical sciences at all. He argues that the phenomena of social science cannot be treated as if they were just more complicated physical events. Human behaviour cannot be understood simply by external observations: there *is* an important place for intuition. The understanding of social events

'necessitates at least an imaginative projection into what the phenomena concerned mean, a meaning which can only come fully from inside the activity to be studied... 'a sympathetic understanding of our fellow men, of finding a meaning in their activities, of grasping intuitively how they feel, what their plans are, what they are driving at... (although) intuition works better when controlled by the known facts' (pages 168, 170).

Bantock argues that empirical educational research has failed on two counts. First, it pays too little attention to 'conceptual clarification' of the terms used to describe human behaviour. A term like 'motivation' for example, is often used in relation to a score on a particular test without taking account of the common-sense established meaning of that term. The second failing is seen as more serious: empirical research has created an artificial view of man divorced from his social setting and lacking in the powers of introspection. Bantock sees the novelist as often achieving a more convincing holistic view of the reasons why people behave as they do.

'A training in literature is of great assistance in the sensitizing of the intelligence to the complexities of social life and to the psychological reaction of individuals in social situations, in that literature uniquely affords the feel of the "whole man alive" ' (page 177).

If the novelist is accepted as being capable of providing valid and important insights into human behaviour, we should certainly expect valuable insights into classroom learning from the teacher. But the professional life of the teacher very often binds her to the classroom; her energies are directed towards the children. There is little time to analyse or systematize the ideas about learning which guide her work. But when these thoughts are recorded, can they become a form of research? Do they help us in understanding learning?

There are, of course, instances of teachers publishing their day-to-day impressions of pupils learning. One teacher who has published widely, and has become well-known for his radical ideas, is A. S. Neill who founded the experimental school 'Summerhill'. In his early days, teaching in Scotland, he contributed a column to the *Educational News*. These anecdotes were subsequently collected into *A Dominie's Log,* and contain examples of a practising teacher reflecting on the learning process.

'I once had an experience in teaching. A boy was dour and unlovable and rebellious and disobedient. I tried all ways — I regret to say I tried the tawse (belt). I was inexperienced at the time yet I hit upon the right way. One day I found he had a decided talent for drawing. I brought down some of my pen-and-ink sketches and showed him them. I gave him pictures to copy, and his interest in art grew. I won him over by interesting myself in him. He discovered that I was only human after all.

Only human!... when our scholars discover we are only human, then they like us, and then they listen to us.' (Neill, 1915, page 20).

Such ideas are a common-place of teaching, yet are rarely recorded extensively or systematically. Teachers are not required to record their impressions; but student-teachers are. To bring the Neill tradition up to date, the next section contains an extract from a student teacher* on her first period of observation recording her impressions of a modern open-plan middle school. This is followed by observations of a trouble-maker in a secondary school.

Observations of school behaviour

'It's a bit unnerving sitting down to lunch — haven't done this for years. Children, in this case ten years olds, have an uncanny knack of watching your every move — although their eyes dart away so quickly when they realize that you've sensed their watching that is barely perceptible. One slightly younger child at the table tells me that they are quiet compared to normal. I can sense that there is tension although they seem amused, rather than disturbed, at my presence... I ought to say something; they expect it, but what? It's obvious from their expressions that they expect some inane comment. The youngest girl suddenly says 'Isn't it funny how people have different voices. I mean high, low, middle...' and we start talking about sound boxes and vocal cords. One of the children obviously understands the concept. It seems just as important not to underestimate their abilities as it is not to overestimate them.... .

Spent some time with a boy in the afternoon talking about stalactites and trying to explain their formation. Eventually I went in search of a kettle, only to find a complete absence of 'fur' as Sheffield water is soft. Still it was a good try I suppose and in the end I think he'd managed to make some sense of my explanations.... .

The boy with whom I had been talking about stalactites yesterday found me today to tell me that he had had a look in his kettle at home and found some 'fur'. We also managed to find a good description of stalactites in one of the books in the reference library. He showed me a tiny little Bible that he had in his pocket and we talked about how they managed to print it.... . The amount of knowledge that one needs is amazing. Already I've read and thought about the industrial revolution quite a lot and yet I know that there will always be at least one child who will ask a question to which I do not know the answer — but that's how it should be. How can I expect to teach children, if I myself am not receptive to new ideas?.... .

This afternoon, Paul, making a model of an engine, showed a small streak of laziness. He couldn't be bothered to think his way around the problems that building his model had raised. His initial enthusiasm upon meeting a temporary block subsided almost immediately and he needed constant chivvying to think about solving the problem and even looking for things himself.... . Later he gave me a ... story that he'd started;... it was very untidy, but I felt that at least he'd tried. I gave this to two teachers and asked them what they thought. One said that it certainly wasn't good; the other said that it was very good *for him*. So how shall I assess it?.... . His spoken English is good and yet when it comes to writing it down, it all 'goes to pot'. He writes in script and I sometimes wonder if he might find things easier if he printed the words. Perhaps the effort of writing in script requires so much concentration that he then doesn't think about the sense of his sentences. Or perhaps his mind races on so fast that he misses words out. I don't know — but his apparent failure in conventional terms has led me to... (say) that he is lazy. Perhaps it would be more truthful to say that his apparent failure hurts

---

* I am grateful to Mrs. Lynn Richardson who wrote the report and to her tutor, Mr. Mabon then of Totley and Thornbridge College, (now Sheffield Polytechnic) for allowing this extract to be published.

me too much because I recognize in it a failure in myself to communicate with him, and therefore, as my own failure is harder to accept, I am prepared to take the easy way out and say that he is lazy. What a terrible admission! At least I am beginning to look at things in more depth...

* * *

The second extract describes the behaviour of a particular adolescent girl who persistently disrupted the classes she attended.

Disruptive behaviour in secondary school*

Lesson 1

English Language: 4th year (set 3). 23 pupils present; 15 boys, 8 girls.

With all pupils seated at their desks and the teacher having collected a set of books from the cupboard, Mrs. A stands at the front of the class. She says nothing but appears to be expecting the pupils to do or say something. The whole class, with some hesitation, stand up until Mrs. A appears satisfied and indicates that they can sit down again....

The text-books are distributed, and Mrs. A begins to read aloud from a story. After reading aloud for several minutes, there is a brief question and answer session. After a few reading sessions followed by questions, individual pupils are then selected to read.... After about ten minutes, some pupils remark that they have already read this section of the book. The teacher herself seems not to have noticed this, but she covers the realization with a semi-sarcastic remark that, since it has taken them four pages to realize (an exaggeration), they would just have to put up with it.

A girl arrives late after about twenty minutes into lesson time. She enters the room noisily, exclaiming 'I'm late!' and proceeds proudly to take her seat. No excuse is offered and Mrs. A does not inquire after one. The pupil, Jill, takes a seat... by the windows. She immediately begins to close the window noisily, which occasions a request from Mrs. A that she leave the window alone. To this, Jill retorts: 'It's too cold, Miss.' This 'justified' grievance has permitted her to answer back in effect, and rather than be drawn, Mrs. A avoids a potential issue and continues with the lesson. The late-comer Jill now sits at right angles to the desk (as a sign of triumph or defiance perhaps?) and throughout the remainder of the lesson engages in sporadic but frequent conversation with the girl behind and with others across the room....

Disruptive chatter among some of the boys in the class causes the teacher to halt the lesson and threaten them with a withdrawal of permission to leave early for swimming.... This threat creates some consternation among pupils which is taken up noisily by the late-comer Jill. As a result, Mrs. A returns to the lesson theme by asking Jill to continue with the reading. The girl does so, and is obviously a competent reader. However, she reads in a manner obviously affected to provide amusement for other members of the class. When she has finished reading, Mrs. A announces that the class will do some writing, which is greeted with cries of distress and remarks to the effect that they did not possess their exercise books (which was true in some cases). However, the remainder of the lesson does consist largely of the pupils writing about the story they have been reading....

* from Sharp (1978, pages 117-121, 138-140, 142).

(The same class was observed on several subsequent occasions and records of the types of disruptive behaviour displayed by the pupils were made.)

After these initial observations had progressed for about three weeks, a questionnaire and a sociometric instrument (to measure the relative popularity of pupils) were administered... , supplemented by obtaining anonymous essays... and individual interviews... .

Drawing upon all these sources — observational records, questionnaire data, sociometric data, essay and interview material — we attempted to examine in greater depth the nature of classroom dissent... .

(The analysis explored examples of different types of dissent and used case studies from the interview transcripts to exemplify three categories — dissent as a way of demonstrating social status among other pupils, as an individual protest and assertion of independence, and as an indication of perhaps justified dissatisfaction over certain aspects of the school experience.)

At a superficial level, the most usual answer given by pupils as a reason for dissenting behaviour was 'boredom'. Like many teachers perhaps, I had always treated this response with a certain amount of scepticism and sought to elicit further clarification of what was 'really meant' by this rather unhelpful and imprecise term. Such attempts were usually in vain: boredom remained the single term that pupils returned to in order to provide what, for them, was a self-evident explanation.

Q: Why do you think you muck about?

Barry: I don't know... for a laugh I suppose; if the lesson gets boring we just start mucking about a bit... .

Q: But you don't muck about in every lesson, do you? Why do you muck about sometimes and not others then?

Jim: Well you only muck about when you can, like.

Q: How do you mean?

Jim: In lessons where you know the work. You've time to muck about a bit there.

Q: You mean, you can afford to muck about?

Jim: ... Yes, and others can't.

Q: Well what about some of your mates who can't afford to muck about? Isn't your mucking about a bit unfair to them?

Jim: (Grins widely and 'intimates' that that is not his problem... .)

Q: Or does mucking about give you an advantage over your mates — is it a way of showing you're better than them?

Barry: (friend of Jim and of less ability): (Turns round and accusingly to Jim) Yes, that's right, isn't it!

... Since dissent is usually a group activity, less able members of the group may feel doubly obliged to 'muck about': mucking about confirms their peer-group membership but also allows them to 'act out' the disdaining attitude towards work demands. From this they may obtain some reward from dissenting conduct, but they may also realize that the mucking about is relatively more at their expense... . Here then it appears that there exists a definite social status dimension to dissenting behaviour, but this... may well operate strategically to the benefit of some pupils and not others.

* * *

Intuition and evidence

The two extracts in the previous section are both examples of classroom observations. The first was from a student-teacher; the second was, in fact, part of a Ph.D. thesis. Why should we accept the second set of observations as research, and not the first one? Both show interesting insights into children's classroom behaviour. Where do we draw the line between professional intuition and research evidence?

The contradictory views of what counts as valid research evidence expressed by Kerlinger and Bantock may, to some extent, be resolved by using a broader definition of educational research.

> 'Educational research consists in careful, systematic attempts to understand the educational process and, through understanding, to improve its efficiency' (Nisbet and Entwistle, 1973, page 113).

Explicit in this definition is the emphasis on a careful, systematic approach which echoes a descriptive term used by Cronbach and Suppes (1969) — 'disciplined inquiry'. It is worth quoting their explanation of this term at length, as it indicates some of the important distinctions between systematic studies and personal anecdotes in trying to understand educational processes.

> 'In discussing disciplined inquiry... we give no narrow definition to the term. Too many writers seem to limit the term 'research' to quantitative empirical inquiry. While much has been and will be learned from social surveys, measurements, and controlled experiments, the study of education requires non-quantitative as well as quantitative techniques. Naturalistic observation, for example, has tended to fall into disuse, though it is a significant form of disciplined inquiry... .
>
> An inquiry generally sets out to answer a rather narrowly defined question. The specific findings of such enquiries are usually less important than the conceptualizations they generate... . (Furthermore) disciplined inquiry has a quality that distinguishes it from other sources of opinion and belief. The disciplined inquiry is conducted and reported in such a way that the argument can be painstakingly examined. The report does not depend for its appeal on the eloquence of the writer or on any surface plausibility. The argument is not justified by anecdotes or casually assembled fragments of evidence. Scholars in each field have developed traditional questions that serve as touchstones to separate sound argument from incomplete or questionable argument. Among other things the mathematician asks about axioms, the historian about the authenticity of documents, the experimental scientist about verifiability of observations. Whatever the character of a study, if it is disciplined the investigator has anticipated the traditional questions that are pertinent. He institutes controls at each step of information collecting and reasoning to avoid sources of error to which these questions refer. If the errors cannot be eliminated,

he takes them into account by discussing the margin for error in his conclusions. Thus the report of a disciplined inquiry has a texture that displays the raw materials entering the argument and the logical processes by which they were compressed and rearranged to make the conclusion credible.... .

Disciplined inquiry does not necessarily follow well-established, formal procedures. Some of the most excellent inquiry is free-ranging and speculative in its initial stages, trying what might seem to be bizarre combinations of ideas and procedures, or restlessly casting about for ideas. There was nothing systematic, for instance, in Ventris' procedure for breaking the code of the Mycenaean script Linear B; the style of the inquiry was one of following hunches. But there was discipline in the checking of the hunches and in organizing the report so that any qualified reader could accept or reject the argument. Binet's inquiry into intelligence was not greatly different. He had some vague ideas about the nature of intellect, but the indicators whose possible usefulness he explored ranged from rote memory to palmistry. His success came from this openmindedness and from his relentless self-criticisms, together with his convincing exposition of the reasons for the scale he finally proposed.... .

It is scarcely necessary to remark that not all conclusions of disciplined inquiry are true. Each investigation is limited by its methods, and the consensus of the best-informed members of a discipline is limited by the state of the art. In the most traditional academic fields conceptualizations and theories are continually being debated, and even factual conclusions are altered from time to time.

A disciplined inquiry does have an internal consistency that requires colleagues to take findings seriously, even when they disagree with them. A scholarly report is considerably more than a print-out of speculations, preconceptions, and wish-fulfilling observations. It nourishes thought. Indeed, the fact that it invites and rewards close examination is the mark of worthy inquiry.... .

The success of academic men in breaking old intellectual bounds and inventing fresh concepts results from the fact that they value the process of inquiry at least as much as they value its fruits. They are trained in specialized techniques of observation and analysis. Instruments refine the judgement of the observer, statistical models to weed out chance effects, mathematical models, canons of documentation, and formal criteria of acceptable definition, constitute the technology of inquiry. But far more fundamental to disciplined inquiry is its central attitude, which places a premium on objectivity and evidential test' (Cronbach and Suppes, 1969, pages 14-18).

Returning to the earlier definition of educational research, it can be seen that the research worker is seeking to reach an understanding of the educational process which has demonstrable, rather than solely personal, validity. By following the precepts of disciplined inquiry outlined by Cronbach and Suppes, the wider applicability of the findings can be demonstrated, and also the limits of their generality. The great weakness of relying on professional experience alone in trying to understand educational processes is that it is usually unsystematic and relies mainly on subjective experience and intuition. As the philosopher Karl Popper (1957) once remarked somewhat tartly:

'Intuition prevents some people from even imagining that anybody could possibly dislike chocolate.'

Teachers' insights may be valuable. They can contribute to valid knowledge about learning, particularly where the teacher is able to see the experience of learning through the pupil's eyes. The extracts from both A. S. Neill and the student-teacher both have this quality of understanding. But these are both personal responses in which principles of learning remain imbedded in a specific event. Such insights are often the starting points for later systematic, disciplined inquiry, but do not give us confidence in their validity.

Ideas born of experience alone may not be research, but they *are* part of the 'traditional wisdom' of the teaching profession. They contribute to a form of knowledge which is recognized by teachers and administrators, and which contributes to decisions about the future of education. If the ideas generated by research contradict that 'traditional wisdom', we cannot immediately assume that research findings must be right. Social science research, while potentially providing objective knowledge, often fails to do so either through deficiences in the research design, or from the sheer complexity of the total learning situation in schools. Research findings have greater objectivity and more demonstrable validity. Professional experience has the immediacy of personal experience and may show greater human sensitivity. Taken together they provide a safer basis for seeking solutions to classroom problems and improving the efficiency of the educational process.

This book concentrates on research findings; the reader is asked to provide the experiences to generate personal meaning. Later chapters explore evidence derived from disciplined inquiry in educational psychology which is directed towards a better understanding of how pupils and students learn. Before presenting this evidence, however, it is necessary to summarize some of the ways in which such evidence is collected — to indicate the specialized techniques of observation and analysis used in disciplined inquiry in this particular field. It also seemed useful to remind readers that empirical research is not the only source of useful ideas about learning. There is a long history of philosophical discussion about intellectual capabilities. Modern theories sometimes prove to be little more than refinements, or more precise restatements, of age-old ideas about learning.

STOP and THINK

● Each chapter has a summary, but before reading the summary it would probably be useful to think back over the chapter and decide for yourself which aspects you consider important, and how the argument has developed so far.

18

Summary

It is argued that the theories and empirical evidence from psychology and educational research are likely to have only an indirect effect on educational practice. They do not provide immediate solutions to practical problems. But their indirect effect is still important, through alerting teachers and educationalists to new ways of conceptualising the learning process. Some general implications can be derived from research findings, but the more important implications are more likely to come from the teacher's own understanding of psychological ideas.

Evidence in educational psychology comes from two main sources — mainstream psychology and educational research. These sources represent different levels of explanation, depending on the focus of interest either in fundamental psychological processes or what happens in classrooms. Explanations derived from these two approaches are best treated as complementary views from different perspectives. Similarly, different approaches to research — the scientific and the humanistic — both contribute valid ways of conceptualizing human learning. The main strength of the research evidence is that it is based on systematic, disciplined enquiry which carries with it greater potential for general, rather than personal validity. On the other hand, research evidence needs to be set alongside professional experience in trying to gain a better understanding of classroom learning. Improvements in educational practice depend on sensitive interpretation and application of both the more objective, codified forms of knowledge contained in psychology theory, and the traditional wisdom of the teacher.

CHAPTER 2

Evidence from Educational Research and Psychology

Research evidence has its strengths; it also has its limitations. Before leading on to the main part of the book where the results of empirical research are used to develop a model of the learning process, it is important to outline the main approaches to research in educational psychology. It is also possible to outline a general strategy towards carrying out research into education. Indicating stages through which many research studies pass over-emphasizes the logical aspects of scientific procedures, at the expense of the imaginative, but it does illustrate the careful, systematic approach — the disciplined enquiry — which leads to greater objectivity and more demonstrable validity in considering educational issues.

Stages in educational research

The starting point of most research is a *problem*. It may first be perceived in a vague, general way, but the research worker will try to narrow it down to a series of precise questions on which evidence can be obtained. The next step is generally to *review the literature* to determine what is already known about these questions and what methods other researchers have adopted in their studies. The results of previous studies will often allow definite hypotheses to be put forward. These hypotheses convert the original questions into the type of answers expected. Of course, it is not always possible, or desirable, to anticipate the outcome of the study in this way. The review of the literature may do no more than suggest useful approaches to be adopted.

   Measurement is at the heart of most empirical studies, although this may also take the form of systematically recorded observations of behaviour. If the evidence is to be considered objective, other research workers will have to be able to repeat (replicate) the study and obtain similar findings. The method of measurement thus must be carefully described and full details given of any tests or instruments used. In educational and psychological research, tests are commonly used. In assessing the appropriateness of a test, two characteristics should be carefully examined. First the reliability of the test and then its validity.

The reliability of a test can be considered as an indication of the consistency of the test — whether or not the same sets of scores or codings would be obtained if the test were given on successive occasions to the same people. Unreliability can be created, for example, by weaknesses in the construction of the test, by subjective marking or coding, or by imprecise instructions for use which lead to variations in the way the test is administered on different occasions. The reliability of a test is often described by two indices (correlation coefficients); one refers to the internal consistency of the items which make up the scale, (whether they are assessing the same characteristic), and the other (test-retest reliability) indicates the extent to which scores on one occasion agree with scores on a later occasion.

The validity of a test is more difficult to assess. This is an index of the extent to which the test measures what it is intended to measure. Evidence of validity can come from an inspection of the items to see whether they fully represent the characteristic being assessed (content validity). It can also come from indications that scores faithfully mirror known differences between people, or from comparisons between the test and another test of established validity (construct validity). The point being made here is that unless the methods of measurement applied are both reliable and valid, little confidence can be placed in the evidence subsequently presented.

Another crucial feature in the design of empirical studies is *sampling* — the use of only a proportion of the whole group to represent that group. A teacher who wants to know the reading age of a child, or even the range of reading ages in the class does not have to face this problem. She is interested in a specific child or class. But research workers look for generalizations. They want to draw conclusions which apply to a whole category of children or to provide explanations which will hold true in many classroom situations. Then careful sampling becomes essential. To be absolutely sure about any finding, we should have to test every person involved in the generalization. This is, of course, impracticable. But close approximations to the results which would be obtained from the whole population can be achieved by using a representative sample. The difficulty lies in ensuring that the sample chosen *is* representative. In social science research it is very difficult to obtain truly representative samples and often results are reported on groups who volunteered, or who happened to be there at the time (opportunity samples). Details about the procedures necessary to achieve satisfactory samples go beyond the scope of this book and are readily available elsewhere (Nisbet and Entwistle, 1970; Borg and Gall, 1979; Mouly, 1978). But it must be recognized that unless a sample has been carefully chosen and can be demonstrated to be reasonably representative, the conclusions of that investigation should be treated with caution.

The final steps in an empirical study generally involve *statistical analysis* and a statement of the conclusions and implications. Judgement about the appropriateness of the form of statistical analysis requires considerable technical knowledge, but it is often possible for conclusions and implications to be examined critically even without such knowledge. To what extent are the conclusions justified by the findings? Does the author try to generalize more than the method of sampling allows? Are there alternative explanations of the findings which have been ignored? Are the implications realistic; do they take account of the 'real world' situation and provide a satisfying account of it? Does the author present the findings in a cautious way, or is there a suggestion of special pleading or personal involvement in demonstrating one particular outcome? (For a fuller set of questions, see Entwistle and Nisbet, 1972).

Educational research is full of pitfalls for the unwary and it is probably safe to say that no study is perfect. Most studies contain weaknesses created by compromises forced on the investigator by limited time or resources, or by restrictions imposed by schools or colleges who have their main responsibility to their students, not to the researcher. Yet there is still considerable strength in well-designed empirical research when contrasted with personal experience or 'traditional wisdom' taken on their own.

These, then, are the various stages often found in research studies in educational psychology, but there are still characteristic differences in the way they are used in the specific types of research that are commonly used, namely case studies, surveys, and experiments.

Case studies

Much of the early work in psychology was based on sets of detailed case studies built up by psychotherapists in the process of treating people with various forms of mental illness or psychological difficulty. By writing up the record of each interview shortly afterwards, psychiatrists such as Freud and Jung were able to assemble data about human personality. Examining both changes and consistency in behaviour, dreams, ways of thinking and attitudes, theories to explain these observations gradually emerged and made a great impact on the growth of psychology.

The case study has important advantages. It enables the totality of phenomena to be observed — the behaviour of a person in everyday life, or the way an institution or a class operates. The main weaknesses are that the sample size is inevitably small and that consistencies and contrasts have to be discovered within the recorded data, which is rich, but also idiosyncratic. The case records of any two patients or institutions will rarely cover the same aspects, and so strict comparisons are difficult. The analysis of such data depends on the judgement of the psychologist: it is difficult to prove to others that the interpretation is warranted.

However, it is possible to extend the strengths of case studies to research where some strictly comparable data are recorded for a substantial number of people or institutions. It is also possible to promote deliberate contrasts by a careful selection of cases on the basis of prior information. There is, however, always a tension between the attempt to ensure comparability between cases and the necessity to leave sufficient freedom for the expression of normal behaviour, uninhibited by the method of data collection. Besides improving comparability and controlling contrasts, it is also necessary to check the agreement between different researchers in making interpretations of the data.

This procedure can be likened to that used by social anthropologists who observe, make careful records, and then generate theories to explain similarities and differences between primitive societies. Used cautiously, and supplemented by more objective measurements, case studies can be a valuable form of evidence. They have become increasingly important recently as an antidote to the narrowly focussed, but more objective, procedures which have been used extensively in psychology and educational research for many years.

Surveys

The term 'survey' is often associated with opinion polls or with the consumer surveys which seek reactions to commercial products. Often the data is collected by questionnaire or interview, but this is not the main characteristic of a survey. In essence it is a study which involves collecting information about a representative sample in the situation as it *normally exists*. In education, surveys have been conducted on such varying topics as the attitudes of fifth-formers to continuing their education, the standards of reading in primary schools, the relationships between 'A' level grades and degree performance, and the extent to which intelligence and creativity can be considered as separate dimensions.

Sampling follows the lines discussed already, aiming at obtaining representative groups from which generalizations can be made. Often survey samples are large, involving hundreds of schools and many thousands of pupils. The size depends on the number and variety of analyses of sub-groups which are required. It may be necessary, for example, to contrast the attitudes of boys and girls, of 15-year-olds and 10-year-olds, of able and less able children, and every combination of these. In this illustration there are already eight sub-groups and to be confident about any differences between them, each sub-group might well have to contain 100 individuals to cover an appropriate range of schools.

Because surveys typically try to take account of several aspects of the educational situation simultaneously, it is usual for the results to involve many variables. If, for example, the study was concerned with identifying factors associated with academic success, a major problem would be to determine which variable had the most important effect. We might find that a test of verbal reasoning and a test of English comprehension were most closely associated with end of term examination performance. But these tests would themselves be closely inter-related, and both of them would also be associated with indices of social class. Complex multivariate statistical techniques, such as factor analysis or multiple regression, are used to isolate the most important variables, but interpretation of the findings is still problematical.

The main weakness of the survey procedure is the lack of control over both the situation and the variables included. The survey is also like a still photograph. It portrays the situation at one point in time and so the relationships established can be evidence of no more than concomitant variation — that certain values on one variable tend to be associated with particular values on another. Yet we are usually more interested in determining causality — which variable is *responsible* for changes in another. And an experiment is likely to provide better evidence of causality.

Experiments

It is very difficult to establish causality, but when one event is invariably *followed* by another this can be taken as strong evidence of a causal link. Even in a longitudinal or follow-up study, which is a survey carried out on more than one occasion, the lack of control over variables makes it difficult to establish causality. In an experiment the situation is controlled so that, in the simplest case, different treatments are given to equivalent groups and the outcomes are compared.

This approach has been likened to research in agriculture, where, say, the yield of wheat treated by different chemicals, but grown under identical conditions, is compared. In psychology the simplest experiment would involve controlling every variable except two — an independent variable, which is systematically varied, and a dependent variable, which is thought to be affected by the other one. For example, in a learning experiment, students might be asked to learn a list of words and the number they could recall (dependent variable) might be examined after different periods of time (independent variable).

An important feature of many experiments is the creation of 'matched' groups. In other words two or more samples are selected which are as closely similar as possible. If, then, the two groups are given different 'treatment', changes after the experiment can be attributed to the different treatments.

A similar example in education might be the effects of different methods of teaching spelling. In one such experiment Hazel Smith (1975) used several contrasting teaching approaches (the independent variable).

'Words were presented either in context or in list form, and the method of learning involved studying either the whole word, the "hard spot" or the individual letters of each spelling' (page 68).

Each method was presented with tape recorded pronunciation of words and programmed learning materials. The whole sample of 359 ten-year-old children from ten primary classes worked through the different methods. A separate analysis was carried out for children from manual and non-manual social classes. After the experiment, a spelling test was administered (dependent variable), and analyses examined the relationship between method of presentation and accuracy of spelling. The conclusion reached was that

'Within the limits of this investigation, the best systematic approach to the learning of spellings seems to be one which presented the words in context and which used the whole word method of learning. Indications were that the manual social class group benefited more than the non-manual group from being given a structured approach' (Smith, 1975, page 71).

In one sense this is an unusual experiment, as it was conducted in a natural setting. Most psychological experiments are carried out in a laboratory, where much closer control over the conditions can be ensured. Another characteristic aspect of experiments is that a whole series of studies may be carried out, varying aspects of the situation systematically one by one to establish which treatment or variable is most important, and how the different variables interact. It is only with tight control over the situation, and a narrow focus on certain aspects of it, that inferences can be made with any certainty. Yet that control and narrowness of focus is also a major weakness when it comes to looking for educational implications. The laboratory setting is artificial, and often the type of learning required is at best oversimplified and at worst trivialized. Neisser (1976) has recently criticized the traditional approaches used in experiments on learning, arguing that

'studies of human memory using lists of nonsense syllables have not been helpful in explaining school learning or everyday remembering.... . (Indeed) this is a restrained understatement; nonsense-syllable learning is probably the archetype of psychological irrelevance' (pages 33 and 49).

Neisser does, however, add that recent research is moving away from such irrelevance.

'Where formerly it was thought that rote-memory experiments would yield fundamental principles applicable elsewhere, the same methods are now used to study skills and strategies learned in the world and brought to the laboratory by the subject' (page 48).

It is thus essential that the research design maintains 'ecological validity' — the experimental conditions should parallel those in the natural setting as far as possible. But experiments also run into another problem when the focus is narrowed. By concentrating on only parts of the whole situation, variables which are crucial in the real situation may be ignored.

Bronowski (1978) described the dilemma faced by any science as it tries to abstract a part from the whole to examine it more closely.

'I believe that every event in the world is connected to every other event. But you cannot carry on science on the supposition that you are going to be able to connect every event with every other event.... It is, therefore, an essential part of the methodology of science to divide the world for any experiment into what we regard as relevant and what we regard, for purposes of that experiment, as irrelevant.

We make a cut. We put the experiment, if you like, into a box. Now the moment we do that, we do violence to the connections in the world...; any cut you make at all is a convenient simplification. But in essence it is a distortion, and you are now decoding only a part of the total.... So it is natural that your decoding cannot be (wholly) right' (pages 58-59, 69).

Convergence of evidence: an illustration

There is, in a sense, an essential incompatibility between the survey and the experiment, and between both of these and the case study approach. The case study is likely to rely much less on measurement and much more on impression, but it generally tries to examine the whole, rather than the parts. The survey uses measurement to look at many aspects of the situation simultaneously, while an experiment abstracts key features to examine them sequentially often in an unrealistic setting. The strengths of the three approaches are potentially complementary, yet there has been a tendency for research traditions to be established which emphasize one or other of these procedures, to the virtual exclusion of the others. The use of case studies by the psychoanalysts has already been mentioned. In educational psychology the research on individual differences, such as the investigations of intelligence, has used almost exclusively the survey approach in which batteries of tests have been given to large samples of students and factor analyses used to investigate the structure of the intellect. In contrast, research on learning has used experimental designs with small carefully selected samples. Almost as an accident of this approach, learning theorists have concentrated on the general process of learning and have neglected the influence of individual differences (see Cronbach, 1957).

In educational research it is particularly important to use the complementary strengths both of different research strategies and of different methods of collecting data. Few studies manage to achieve an entirely satisfactory balance, but some have used an interesting variety of approaches. As an example, we shall look in some detail at a study by Bennett (1976) which attracted a good deal of publicity. The title of the report was *Teaching Styles and Pupil Progress,* and its findings added fuel to the controversy on the relative merits of traditional and progressive teaching methods in primary schools.

Formal and informal primary teaching

Bennett's study set out to examine the progress in basic skills made by pupils in formal and informal primary school classrooms. The research design initially followed a survey approach. First a census of all the teachers in the top two primary classes in Cumbria and Lancashire was carried out with a questionnaire which asked about the way classrooms were organized, about discipline, marking, time-tabling and the curriculum. The questionnaire thus contained a large number of variables describing the similarities and differences between classrooms. Teachers giving similar patterns of answers were grouped together. From this 'cluster' analysis, twelve types of teaching style were identified ranging from extremely formal to extremely informal. Seven of these styles were then selected for further investigation, but later the groups were merged into three — formal, mixed, and informal methods.

The main question being asked was 'Do teaching styles result in differential pupil progress?' To answer this question 'requires a research design which allows for a follow-up of samples of pupils over an extended period of time during which they experience differing teaching approaches. By testing at the beginning and end of this period, progress can be assessed and differential effects, if any, can be established.'

> 'A quasi-experimental design was adopted... (which) involved the selection of thirty-seven teachers to represent (the)... types isolated in the teacher typology.... The teachers selected were in each case those whose profiles most closely matched... the type description.... This selection procedure gave a pupil sample of approximately 400 per general teaching style' (Bennett, 1976, pages 79-80).

The author then goes on to describe the attainment and personality tests given at the beginning and end of the school year and later presents evidence that children in formal classrooms had made greater progress in reading, English, and mathematics than those in informal classrooms. The relative improvements in reading scores of children at different initial levels in formal and informal classrooms are shown in Table 2.1.

Thus the initial survey provided the information from which the effects of distinctive experimental treatments could be examined. But what followed

Table 2.1. Reading attainment scores after one school year by initial score, sex, and teaching style

Initial reading score	Teaching style			
	Formal		Informal	
	Boys	Girls	Boys	Girls
Above 110	123.2	121.4	116.6	120.8
(N)	(58)	(55)	(37)	(40)
109–90	106.8	107.0	104.0	102.8
(N)	(80)	(81)	(62)	(77)
Below 89	88.7	93.4	92.1	91.0
(N)	(36)	(25)	(53)	(52)

(Adapted from Bennett, 1976, page 85.)

may be better described as a follow-up study applying survey techniques to three contrasting classroom environments. The research retains all the characteristics of the survey — a realistic setting, a large sample, numerous variables and multivariate analyses. The study has been criticized for failing to control for variables other than teaching style. For example, no information was given on the experience of the teachers (did the more experienced teachers use formal methods?), or on the social class of the children (could parental encouragement have been a factor in the differential progress?). The emphasis in this study was on representative sampling, rather than on creating matched groups. The research workers concentrated on selecting groups of teachers who represented as closely as possible the teaching styles identified in the cluster analysis. To match teachers on other variables would have weakened the close resemblance of the questionnaire profiles of all the teachers within the defined groups. This is a good example of the dilemmas which face educational researchers. Whichever choice had been made, the decision would have been open to criticism, and problems would have arisen in interpreting the findings.

Although most of the critics of this study (see, for example, Gray and Satterley, 1976) have concentrated on the lack of experimental control or on the interpretation of data on changes in attainment, Bennett based his arguments on two other types of evidence — another survey using systematic observation of classroom behaviour and a case study of an atypical informal teacher (Bennett and Entwistle, 1976).

In the observation study carried out by Barbara Wade, and reported in full more recently (Wade, 1979), the classroom behaviour of pupils was observed in formal and informal teaching situations. The number of times a child indulged in various categories of behaviour was recorded for 101 pupils at three levels of attainment. Comparisons between children at the extremes of attainment showed that:

'high achievers (in reading) engaged in 21 per cent more work activity overall. They did twice as much reading, twice as much computation, but slightly less writing. They have slightly less social interaction with fellow pupils, be it work related or social. They move around the class less' (Bennett, 1976, page 114).

It was also clear that more time was spent on work-related activities in formal than in informal classes, and less time was spent on preparation for work or in social interaction. On the other hand children in formal classes spent more time in watching other pupils and in fidgeting (see Table 2.2).

Another important piece of evidence presented by Bennett was his case study of the one informal teacher whose class made as much progress as most of the formal classes. This teacher had ten years' experience and, while creating an informal atmosphere and relying on individual worksheets rather than text-books, she spent as much time as the formal teachers on mathematics and English. She had also built up a large stock of teaching materials and had her own system of records to keep a check on pupils' progress.

Table 2.2. Percentage[a] of overall recorded activities spent on work-related and other activities in formal and informal classrooms by achievement level

Pupil activities		Formal		Informal	
		Hi ach ($N = 23$)	Lo ach ($N = 9$)	Hi ach ($N = 9$)	Lo ach ($N = 26$)
Related to work	Preparation, waiting	2.3	3.4	4.2	4.4
	Actual work	41.7	37.6	32.6	32.1
	Pupil interaction	6.5	8.0	8.7	10.4
	Teacher interaction	3.8	4.2	1.9	2.8
	Watching teacher	12.5	12.1	10.2	8.9
Other Activities	Play or disruptive	2.3	4.9	5.3	6.5
	Watching other pupils	9.5	15.2	6.8	8.2
	Moving around class	2.3	3.8	2.7	4.9
	Fidgeting	17.5	19.7	11.4	16.3

[a] Based on the average number of items of behaviour recorded for the four sub-groups (263.5), calculated from Bennett (1976), Appendix D

Note: the columns do not add up to the same total, or to 100%, for two reasons: not all categories have been included, and the average number of items of behaviour was used rather than the actual total for each sub-group. The average was used to facilitate comparisons between all four sub-groups in terms of the relative incidence of the different types of behaviour.

When Bennett's book was published there was a great public outcry from each extreme of opinion. The traditionalists welcomed the findings and some even urged the prohibition of informal methods, while 'progressive' educationalists vied with each other to find reasons why the results should be ignored. But both sets of extremists concentrated on the simplest interpretation — that children in formal schools appeared to have made more progress in basic skills. Yet Table 2.1 showed, for example, that while the bright boys did much better in the formal classroom, the less able boys were making more progress in the informal classrooms. Bennett has been accused of advocating a return to formal methods. His conclusion was not as simple as that. By drawing together the converging threads of evidence from attainment tests, pupil activities, and the case study, Bennett concluded

'The central factor emerging from this study is that a degree of teacher direction is necessary, and that this direction needs to be carefully planned, and the learning experiences provided need to be clearly sequenced and structured...
It seems less than useful for a teacher to stand by and leave a child alone in his inquiries hoping that something will happen' (Bennett, 1976, page 162).

Thus Bennett's criticism is not of informal teaching in itself, but of the 'laissez-faire' approach of some informal teachers who do not provide sufficient guidance and structure.

How should research evidence of this type be used by teachers and administrators? The simple answer is 'with caution'. First, technical assessment of the research is necessary. Do any weaknesses invalidate the conclusions? Then the generality of the findings has to be challenged. Would similar results have been found in other parts of the country? Nevertheless the importance of this *type* of research is twofold. It provides additional evidence to weigh against professional opinion. And it encourages teachers to look again at established practice with a more critical eye. Research should not be expected, in itself, to show teachers what to do in the classroom. Taken in this way, Bennett's book and more recent studies which reach similar conclusions, challenge primary teachers to re-examine *some* of the assumptions about the effects of informal approaches to education. Such research should not, however, be used to argue against the whole progressive education movement.

This extended illustration was intended to show the way in which different approaches to research, and different types of data, are used to build up an argument about an important educational issue. If part of the evidence is used out of context, a false impression may be created. Given the difficulties in carrying out research, and the complexities of classroom learning, we should be cautious in drawing firm conclusions from a single study. In science a single crucial experiment may change the whole way of thinking about a topic. In education we have to look, not for a single definitive study, but for *convergence* in results from several studies and from different types of data; and for *consensus* in the views of practising teachers who have considered the implications of the findings.

The interplay between research evidence and personal experience in building up a model of the learning process is a continuing theme in this book. Although this chapter has stressed the value of empirical evidence from well-designed studies, and most of the ideas on educational psychology have come from this type of research, the next chapter shows the insights that can be obtained from careful consideration of personal experience and introspection. It provides an historical introduction both to the research on study strategies described in Part II, and to the chapters on memory and intellectual abilities in Part III.

Summary

Empirical research studies can provide useful evidence on educational issues, but only if the studies have been carefully designed and executed. The measurements used have to be derived from reliable and valid instruments. The sample must be representative of the wider group to which the findings are to be applied. And the research report should be impartial and limited to the direct implications of the study.

Three common approaches to educational and psychological research can be identified — case studies, surveys, and experiments. Each approach has both strengths and weaknesses, but they can sometimes be combined with great advantage. The *case study* enables the individual person or institution to be examined in great detail, often providing a fuller and more realistic picture than any other method of research. However, the data collected are generally based on small samples, and create difficulties in analysing and making strict comparisons. To some extent the findings are subjective and intuitive; they may still be useful, but it is difficult to be sure. *Surveys* enable more objective information to be collected about large representative samples. The results often provide definite descriptions of important aspects of the educational scene, for example, the percentage of teachers in Lancashire and Cumbria who adopt particular teaching styles. Surveys are much less effective in showing what might cause the differences identified. *Experiments* which allow control of both situation and important variables, and which often include a series of steps from which successive inferences can be made, are more likely to lead to evidence of causality. The main weaknesses of experiments are, however, that the situation may be artificial and the number of variables too small to cover the complexities of the educational setting. Dividing reality up into segments which can be controlled experimentally strengthen the inferences which can be made from the results, but, somewhat paradoxically, weakens the link between those results and the holistic view of the real world from which the experiment has been extracted.

Given the weaknesses in social science data, and the problems in drawing inferences from them, it is important not to rely on the results of a single study, or even on a single research approach. Bennett's study of informal and formal primary schools illustrates both the problems in drawing conclusions from survey data and the value in combining different types of data — test scores, observations of pupil behaviour, and a case study of an individual teacher. Taken in conjunction with the results of other similar studies, and weighed against the professional experience of teachers, such research evidence has considerable value. The interplay between objective evidence and sensitive interpretation from personal experience is a continuing theme in the book.

CHAPTER 3

Introspection in
Thinking About Thinking

The early philosopher-psychologists relied heavily on introspection and personal experience in considering how we think, and in giving advice on studying or suggestions for improving education. But it would be wrong to give the impression that the evidence they used was necessarily weak or that the conclusions they reached were entirely false. By skilful questioning and by careful observation, the early philosophers from at least the time of the Egyptians and early Greeks built up impressive evidence about thought processes, with which they speculated about the intellectual powers of man. The application of rigorous logic to cumulative introspective accounts led to useful insights into that most human characteristic — self-consciousness.

By the end of the last century philosophers had built up a substantial body of evidence on thought processes, but it has tended to be ignored by the later experimental psychologists. Of course many of the early ideas on thinking have proved inadequate. Empirical evidence *is* important, and can provide a more solid basis from which to develop theories. But that evidence must be drawn from the same type of everyday thinking which the philosophers tackled. Too often psychologists have shied away from the complexity of such thinking and become fascinated by one particular restricted facet of thought processes. In itself this procedure of narrowing down the problem to manageable proportions is understandable and appropriate. What is wrong is to go on to suggest that such findings have any necessary relevance to everyday thinking. That may or may not be true. Both Brownowski and Bantock have pointed out the dangers in carrying out scientific investigations without seeing their restricted applicability.

It is impossible to provide any useful introduction to the ideas of the early psychologists by writing a short overview. Their style of writing is an essential component in understanding their way of thinking. This chapter and the 'Bridge' which follows, thus present substantial extracts from four writers which are presented in an order which parallels the organization of the book as a whole. The earliest extract is an example of the type of advice given to students by an experienced academic, and anticipates some of the discussion of approaches and styles in student learning to be introduced in Part II. Then the following extracts provide illustrations of the way early psychologists wrote about three apparently distinct types of thinking — associative, analytic, and productive. Echoes of their ideas will be found throughout Part III, but particularly in Chapter 7 where similar categories have been used to describe the outcomes of empirical research studies. Above all, these extracts challenge the student to become more aware of his own processes of studying and thinking. Although the style of language may be unfamiliar, the ideas retain their cogency and value. Thinking is a crucial part of studying which is nowadays rarely explicitly taught.

The first extract comes from a book written by Isaac Watts (1674-1748) and published in 1741. Watts is probably best known as the writer of such hymns as 'When I survey the Wondrous Cross' and 'O God, our help in ages past', but he was also well known in his own time as a philosopher and scholar. In this extract he is drawing on his experience as a student and scholar to provide a guide to 'The Improvement of the Mind'. The five methods of improvement which Watts outlines are observation, instruction, reading, conversation, and meditation.

Isaac Watts*: The Improvement of the Mind

Approaches to studying

> Though observation and instruction, reading and conversation, may furnish us with many ideas of men and things, yet it is our own meditation and the labour of our own thoughts that must form our judgement of things. Our own thoughts should join or disjoin these ideas in a proposition for ourselves: it is our mind that must judge for ourselves concerning the agreement or disagreement of ideas, and form propositions of truth out of them. Reading and conversation may acquaint us with many truths and with many arguments to support them, but it is our own study and reasoning that must determine whether these proposition are true, and whether these arguments are just and solid.... . It is meditation and study that transfers and conveys the notions and sentiments of others to ourselves, so as to make them properly our own. It is our own judgement upon them, as well as our memory of them that makes them become our own property.... .
>
> By a survey of these things we may justly conclude that he who spends all his time in hearing lectures or poring upon books, without observation, meditation, or converse, will have but a mere historical knowledge of learning, and be able only to tell what others have known or said on the subject: he that lets all his time flow away in conversation without due observation, reading, or study, will gain but a slight and superficial knowledge, which will be in danger of vanishing with the voice of the speaker: and he that confines himself merely to his closet and his own narrow observation of things, and is taught only by his own solitary thoughts, without instruction by lectures, readings, or free conversation, will be

*Extracts taken from *The Improvement of the Mind* published by Gale and Curtis in 1810 (pages 26-27, 34-39, 120, 122, 126-127, 146, and 152-153).

in danger of a narrow spirit, a vain conceit of himself, and an unreasonable contempt of others; and after all he will obtain but a very limited and imperfect view and knowledge of things, and he will seldom learn how to make that knowledge useful.

These five methods of improvement should be pursued jointly, and go hand in hand, where our circumstances are so happy to find opportunity and conveniency to enjoy them all; though I must give my opinion that two of them, viz. reading and meditation, should employ much more of our time than public lectures, or conversation and discourse. As for observation, we may be always acquiring knowledge that way; whether we are alone or in company.

Of books and reading

Books of importance of any kind, and especially complete treatises on any subject, should be first read in a more general and cursory manner, to learn a little what the treatise promises, and what you may expect from the writer's manner and skill. And for this end, I would advise always that the preface be read, and a survey taken of the table of contents, if there be one, before the first survey of the book. By this means you will not only be better fitted to give the book the first reading, but you will be much assisted in your second perusal of it, which should be done with greater attention and deliberation, and you will learn with more ease and readiness what the author pretends to teach. In your reading, mark what is new or unknown to you before, and review those chapters, pages, or paragraphs. Unless a reader has an uncommon and most retentive memory, I may venture to affirm, that there is scarce any book or chapter worth reading once, that is not worthy of a second perusal. At least to take a careful review of all the lines or paragraphs which you marked, and make a recollection of the sections which you thought truly valuable.

There is another reason also why I would choose to take a superficial and cursory survey of a book, before I sit down to read it, and dwell upon it with studious attention, and that is, there may be several difficulties in it which we cannot easily understand and conquer at the first reading for want of a fuller comprehension of the author's whole scheme. And therefore in such treatises, we should not stay till we master every difficulty at the first perusal; for perhaps many of these would appear to be solved when we have proceeded further in that book, or would vanish of themselves upon a second reading.

What we cannot reach and penetrate at first, may be noted down as a matter of after-consideration and inquiry, if the pages that follow do not happen to strike a complete light on those which went before.... Remember that your business in reading... is not merely to know the opinion of the author or speaker, for this is but the mere knowledge of history: but your chief business is to consider whether their opinions are right or no, and to improve your own solid knowledge on that subject by meditation on the themes of their writing or discourse....

Let this therefore be your practice, especially after you have gone through one course of any science in your academical studies; if a writer on that subject maintains the same sentiments as you do, yet if he does not explain his ideas or prove the positions well, mark the faults or defects, and endeavour to do it better, either in the margin of your book, or rather in some papers of your own, or at least let it be done in your private meditations....

Other things, also, of the like nature may be usefully practised with regard to the authors which you read, viz. If the method of a book be irregular, reduce it into form by a little analysis of your own, or by hints in the margin: if those things are heaped together which should be separated, you may wisely distinguish and divide them: if several things relating to the same subject are scattered up and down separately through the treatise, you may bring them all to one view by references; or if the matter of a book be really valuable and deserving, you may throw it into a better method, reduce it to a more logical scheme, or abridge it into a lesser form: all these practices will have a tendency both to advance your skill in logic, and method, to improve your judgement in general, and to give you a fuller survey of that subject in particular. When you have finished the treatise with all your observations upon it, recollect and determine what real improvements you have made by reading that author. . . .

Shall I be so free as to assure my younger friends, from my own experience, that these methods of reading will cost some pains in the first years of your study, and especially in the first authors which you peruse in any science, or on any particular subject: but the profit will richly compensate the pains. And in the following years of life, after you have read a few valuable books on any special subject in this manner, it will be very easy to read others of the same kind, because you will not usually find very much new matter in them which you have not already examined. . . .

By pursuing books in the manner I have described, you will make all your reading subservient not only to the enlargement of your treasures of knowledge, but also to the improvement of your reasoning powers.

There are many who read with constancy and diligence, and yet make no advances in true knowledge by it. They are delighted with the notions which they read or hear, as they would be with stories that are told, but they do not weigh them in their minds as in a just balance, in order to determine their truth or falsehood; they make no observations upon them, or inferences from them. Perhaps their eye slides over the pages, or the words slide over their ears, and vanish like a rhapsody of evening tales, or the shadow of a cloud flying over a green field in a summer's day.

Or if they review them sufficiently to fix them in their remembrance, it is merely with a design to tell the tale over again, and shew what men of learning they are. Thus they dream out their days in a course of reading, without real advantage. As a man may be eating all day, and for want of digestion is never nourished; so these endless readers may cram themselves in vain with intellectual food, and without real improvement of their minds, for want of digesting it by proper reflections.

Be diligent therefore in observing these directions. Enter into the sense and arguments of the authors you read; examine all their proofs, and then judge of the truth or falsehood of their opinions; and thereby you shall not only gain a rich increase of your understanding, by those truths which the author teaches, when you see them well supported, but you shall acquire also by degrees a habit of judging justly, and of reasoning well, in imitation of the good writer whose works you peruse.

This is laborious indeed, and the mind is backward to undergo the fatigue of weighing every argument, and tracing everything to its original. It is much less labour to take all things upon trust: believing is much easier than arguing. . . .

I confess those whose reading is designed only to fit them for much talk, and little knowledge, may content themselves to run over their authors in such a sudden and trifling way: they may devour libraries in this manner, yet be poor reasoners at last, and have no solid wisdom or true learning. The traveller who walks on fair and softly in a course that points right, and examines every turning before he ventures upon it, will come sooner and safer to his journey's end, than he who runs through every lane he meets, though he gallops full speed all the day. The man of much reading, and a large retentive memory, but without meditation, may become in the sense of the world a knowing man; and if he converse much with the antients, he may attain the same of learning too; but he spends his days afar off from wisdom and true judgement, and possesses very little of the substantial riches of the mind. . . .

Of study or meditation

In the beginning of your application to any new subject, be not too uneasy under present difficulties that occur, nor too importunate and impatient for answers and solutions to any questions that arise. Perhaps a little more study, a little further acquaintance with the subject, a little time and experience will solve those difficulties; untie the knot, and make your doubts vanish: especially if you are under the instruction of a tutor, he can inform you that your inquiries are perhaps too early and that you have not yet learned those principles upon which the solution of such a difficulty depends.

Do not expect to arrive at certainty in every subject which you pursue. There are a hundred things wherein we mortals in this dark and imperfect state must be content with probability, where our best light and reasonings will reach no further. We must balance arguments as justly as we can, and where we cannot find weight enough on either side to determine the scale, with sovereign force and assurance, we must content ourselves perhaps with a small preponderation. This will give us a probable opinion, and those probabilities are sufficient for the daily determination of a thousand actions in human life, and many times even in matters of religion. . . .

Though we should always be ready to change our sentiments of things upon just conviction of their falsehood, yet there is not the same necessity of changing our accustomed methods of reading or study and practice, even though we have not been led at first into the happiest method. Our thought may be true, though we may have hit upon an improper order of thinking. Truth does not always depend upon the most convenient method. There may be a certain form and order in which we have long accustomed ourselves to range our ideas and notions, which may be best for us now, though it was not originally best in itself. The inconveniences of changing may be much greater than the conveniences we could obtain by a new method. . . .

Of enlarging the capacity of the mind

There are three things which in an especial manner go to make up that amplitude or capacity of mind, which is one of the noblest characters belonging to the understanding:

1. When the mind is ready to take in great and sublime ideas without pain or difficulty.
2. When the mind is free to receive new and strange ideas, upon just evidence, without great surprise or aversion.
3. When the mind is able to conceive or survey many ideas at once without confusion, and to form a true judgement derived from that exclusive survey.

The person who wants either of these characters, may in that respect be said to have a narrow genius... (yet) it is often found that a fine genius has but a feeble memory. For where the genius is bright, and the imagination vivid, the power and memory may be too much neglected and lose its improvement. An active fancy readily wanders over a multitude of objects, and is continually entertaining itself with new flying images; it runs through a number of new scenes or new pages with pleasure, but without due attention, and seldom suffers itself to dwell long enough upon any one of them, to make a deep impression thereof upon the mind, and commit it to lasting remembrance. This is one plain and obvious reason why there are some persons of very bright parts and active spirits, who have but short and narrow powers of remembrance; for having riches of their own, they are not solicitous to borrow.

And as such a quick and various fancy and invention may be some hindrance to the attention and memory, so a mind of a good retentive ability, and which is ever crowding its memory with things which it learns and reads continually, may prevent, restrain, and cram the invention itself. Some persons who have been blest by nature with sagacity, and no contemptible genius, have too often forbid the exercise of it, by tying themselves down to the memory of the volumes they have read, and the sentiments of other men contained in them.

Where the memory has been almost constantly employing itself in scraping together new acquirements, and where there has not been a judgement sufficient to distinguish what things were fit to be recommended and treasured up in the memory, and what things were idle, useless, or needless, the mind has been filled with a wrteched heap and hotch-potch of words or ideas, and the soul may be said to have had large possessions, but no true riches . . . .

(Among the rules for improving the memory, the importance of clear understanding and systematic presentation should be stressed.)

Clear and distinct apprehension of the things which we commit to memory, is necessary in order to make them stick and dwell there. If ye would remember words, or learn the names of persons or things, we should have them recommended to our memory by clear and distinct pronounciation, spelling or writing. If we would treasure up the ideas of things, notions, propositions, arguments, and sciences, these should be recommended also to our memory by a clear and distinct perception of them. Faint glimmering and confused ideas will vanish like images seen in twilight. Every thing which we learn should be conveyed to the understanding in the plainest expressions, without any ambiguity, that we may not mistake what we desire to remember. This is a general rule whether we would employ the memory about words or things, though it must be confest that mere sounds and words are much harder to get by heart than the knowledge of things and real images.

For this reason take heed (as I have often before warned) that you do not take up with words instead of things, nor mere sounds instead of real sentiments and ideas. Many a lad forgets what has been taught him merely because he never well understood it: he never clearly and distinctly took in the meaning of those sounds and syllables which he was required to get by heart . . . .

(Finally) method and regularity in the things we commit to memory, is necessary in order to make them take more effectual possession of the mind, and abide there long. As much as systematical learning is decried by some vain and humorous triflers of the age, it is certainly the happiest way to furnish the mind with a variety of knowledge.

Whatsoever you would trust to your memory, let it be disposed in a proper method, connected well together, and referred to distinct and particular heads of classes, both general and particular. An apothecary's boy will much sooner learn all the medicines in his master's shop, when they are ranged in boxes or on shelves according to their distinct natures, whether herbs, drugs, or minerals, whether leaves or roots, whether chymical or galenical preparations, whether simple or compound, etc., and when they are placed in some order according to their nature, their fluidity, or their consistence, etc., phials, bottles, gallipots, cases, drawers, etc., so the genealogy of a family is more easily learnt when you begin at some great grandfather as the root, and distinguish the stock, the large boughs, the lesser branches, the twigs, and the buds, till you come down to the present infants of the house. And indeed all sorts of arts and sciences taught in a method something of this kind are more happily committed to the mind or memory.

* * * * *

The next extract comes from one of the earliest psychologists — William James. He was born in 1842 and had a brother, Henry, who was an equally famous novelist. William James approaches psychology as a philosopher: he used introspection and wide reading to provide the data for his rigorous logical analyses. In 1890 William James published his most famous book, *The Principles of Psychology,* which in its 'Briefer Version' became the main text-book for successive generations of students, and is still considered one of the most readable psychology books ever written. The following extract is from a series of lectures given to teachers which summarized some of his main ideas. The book was published in 1899 and shows the importance William James placed on the association of ideas in explaining how we think.

William James*: Connections in the memory

Association of ideas

'... In each of us, when awake (and often when asleep),... there is a stream, a succession of states, or waves, or fields (or of whatever you please to call them), of knowledge, of feeling, of desire, of deliberation, etc., that constantly pass and repass, and that constitute our inner life. ... Consciousness is (thus) an ever-flowing stream of objects, feelings, and impulsive tendencies... Its phases or pulses are like so many fields or waves, each field or wave having usually its central point of liveliest attention, in the shape of the most prominent object in our thought, while all round this lies a margin of other objects more dimly realized, together with the margin of emotional and active tendencies which the whole entails. Describing the mind thus in fluid terms, we cling as close as possible to nature. At first sight, it might seem as if, in the fluidity of these successive waves, everything is indeterminate. But inspection shows that each wave has a constitution which can be to some degree explained by the constitution of the waves just passed away. And this relation of the wave to its predecessors is expressed by the two fundamental 'laws of association', so-called, of which the first is named the law of contiguity, the second that of similarity.

The Law of Contiguity tells us that objects thought of in the coming wave are such as in some previous experience were *next* to the objects represented in the wave that is passing away. The vanishing objects were once formerly their neighbours in the mind. When you recite the alphabet or your prayers, or when the sight of an object reminds you of its name, or the name reminds you of the

*Extracts taken from the 1958 re-issue of *Talks to Teachers,* published by W.W. Norton and Company, New York, pages 28, 65-67, 86-90.

object, it is through the law of contiguity that the terms are suggested to the mind.

The *Law of Similarity* says that, when contiguity fails to describe what happens, the coming objects will prove to *resemble* the going objects, even though the two were never experienced together before. In our 'flights of fancy', this is frequently the case.

If, arresting ourselves in the flow of reverie, we ask the question, 'How came we to be thinking of just this object now?' we can almost always trace its presence to some previous object which has introduced it to the mind, according to one or other of these laws. The entire routine of our memorized acquisitions, for example, is a consequence of nothing but the Law of Contiguity. The words of a poem, the formulas of trigonometry, the facts of history, the properties of material things, are all known to us as definite systems or groups of objects which cohere in an order fixed by unnumerable iterations, and of which any one part reminds us of the others. In dry prosaic minds, almost all the mental sequences flow along these lines of habitual routine repetition and suggestion.

In witty, imaginative minds, on the other hand, the routine is broken through with ease at any moment; and one field of mental objects will suggest another with which perhaps in the whole history of human thinking it had never once before been coupled. The link here is usually *analogy* between the objects successively thought of. . . .

Memory

There is no more pre-eminent example for exhibiting the fertility of the laws of association as principles of psychological analysis (than that of memory).

Nothing is easier than to show you just what I mean by this. Suppose I am silent for a moment, and then say in commanding accents: 'Remember! Recollect!' Does your faculty of memory obey the order, and reproduce any definite image for your past? Certainly not. It stands staring into vacancy, and asking, 'What kind of a thing do you wish me to remember?' It needs in short, a *cue*. But, if I say, remember the date of your birth, or remember what you had for breakfast, or remember the succession of notes in the musical scale; then your faculty of memory immediately produces the required result: the 'cue' determines its vast set of potentialities toward a particular point. And if you now look to see how this happens, you immediately perceive that the cue is something *contiguously associated* with the thing recalled. The words, 'date of my birth', have an ingrained association with a particular number, month, and year; the words, 'breakfast this morning', cut off all other lines of recall except those which lead to coffee and bacon and eggs; the words, 'musical scale' are inveterate mental neighbours of do, re, mi, fa, sol, la, etc. The laws of association govern, in fact, all the trains of our thinking which are not interrupted by sensations breaking on us from without. Whatever appears in the mind must be *introduced;* and, when introduced, it is as the associate of something already there. This is as true of what you are recollecting as it is of everything else you think of. . . .

Descending more particularly into the faculty of memory, we have to distinguish between its potential aspect as a magazine or storehouse and its actual aspect as recollection now of a particular event. Our memory contains all sorts of items which we do not now recall, but which we may recall, provided a sufficient cue be offered. Both general retention and the special recall are explained by association. An educated memory depends on an organised system of associations; and its goodness depends on two of their peculiarities: first, on the persistency of the associations;, and, second, on their number. Let us consider each of these points in turn.

First, the persistency of the associations. This gives what may be called the quality of *native retentiveness* to the individual. If, as I think we are forced to, we consider the brain to be the organic condition by which the vestiges of our experience are associated with each other, we may suppose that some brains are 'wax to receive and marble to retain'. The slightest impressions made on them abide. Names, dates, prices, anecdotes, quotations, are indelibly retained, their several elements fixedly cohering together, so that the individual soon becomes a walking cyclopaedia of information. All this may occur with no philosophic tendency in the mind, no impulse to weave the materials acquired into anything like a logical system. In the books of anecdotes, and, more recently, in the psychology books, we find recorded instances of monstrosities, as we may call them, of this desultory memory; and they are often otherwise very stupid men. It is, of course, by no means incompatible with a philosophic mind; for mental characteristics have infinite capacities for permutation. And, when both memory and philosophy combine together in one person, then indeed we have the highest sort of intellectual efficiency. Your Walter Scotts, your Leibnitzes, your Gladstones, and your Goethes, all your folio copies of mankind, belong to this type. Efficiency on a colossal scale would indeed seem to require it. For, although your philosophic or systematic mind without good desultory memory may know how to work out results and recollect where in the books to find them, the time lost in the searching process handicaps the thinker, and gives to the more ready type of individual the economic advantage.

The extreme of the contrasted type, the type with associations of small persistency, is found in those who have almost no desultory memory at all. If they are also deficient in logical and systematizing power, we call them simply feeble intellects; and no more needs to be said about them here. Their brain matter, we may imagine, is like fluid jelly, in which impressions may be easily made, but are soon closed over again, so that the brain reverts to its original indifferent state.

But it may occur here, just as in other gelatinous substances, that an impression will vibrate throughout the brain, and send waves into other parts of it. In cases of this sort, although the immediate impression may fade out quickly, it does modify the cerebral mass; for the paths it makes there may remain and become so many avenues through which the impression may be reproduced if they ever get excited again. And its liability to reproduction will depend of course upon the variety of these paths and upon the frequency with which they are used. Each path is in fact an associated process, the number of these associates becoming thus to a great degree a substitute for the independent tenacity of the original impression. As I have elsewhere written: each of the associates is a hook to which it hangs, a means to fish it up when sunk below the surface. Together they form a network of attachments by which it is woven into the entire tissue of our thought. The 'secret of a good memory' is thus the secret of forming diverse and multiple associations with every fact we care to retain. . . .

*   *   *   *   *

The next extract is from another famous early psychologist, who took a close, and practical, interest in children's education. John Dewey's ideas lie behind many of the 'activity methods' used in modern primary schools. Miller and Buckhout (1973) describe the educational system Dewey tried to reform.

'The schools Dewey had known as a boy were kept, not taught, by untrained appointees of the local politicians. Discipline was maintained by physical force. Children sat silently with their hands folded on top of their desks and listened to teacher. Occasionally they would be called to recite a lesson by rote, but no questions were tolerated. No one knew what subjects could or should be taught. The only principle that guided the choice of topics was the implicit assumption that they must not be related to the child's world outside the schoolroom — the purpose of education was to make a child appreciate a set of cultural products entirely alien to his own life' (pages 79-80).

This description could be paralleled by similar descriptions of private schools, or even public elementary schools, in Britain. Dickens' *Hard Times* provides one such example. When John Dewey came to write *How We Think* in 1910, he was struck by the contradictions he saw between the way to encourage independent critical thought and his experience of American schools. Not only did Dewey's knowledge of psychology suggest educational implications, he also tried out these ideas in his own experimental school at the University of Chicago, and became the most influential proponent of 'progressive' education in the United States.

John Dewey*: How We Think

An analysis of thinking

We shall make an analysis of the process of thinking into its steps or elementary constituents, basing the analysis upon descriptions of a number of extremely simple, but genuine, cases of reflective experience.

1. The other day when I was down town on 16th Street a clock caught my eye. I saw that the hands pointed to 12.20. This suggested I had an engagement at 124th Street, at one o'clock. I reasoned that as it had taken me an hour to come down on a surface car, I should probably be twenty minutes late if I returned the same way. I might save twenty minutes by a subway express. But was there a station near? If not, I might lose more than twenty minutes in looking for one. Then I thought of the elevated railway, and I saw there was such a line within two blocks. But where was the station? If it were several blocks above or below the street I was on, I should lose time instead of gaining it. My mind went back to the subway express as quicker than the elevated; furthermore, I remembered that it went nearer than the elevated to the part of 124th Street I wished to reach, so that time would be saved at the end of the journey. I concluded in favour of the subway, and reached my destination by one o'clock.

2. Projecting nearly horizontally from the upper deck of the ferryboat on which I daily cross the river, is a long white pole, bearing a gilded ball at its tip. It suggested a flagpole when I first saw it; its colour, shape, and gilded ball agreed with this idea, and these reasons seemed to justify me in this belief. But soon difficulties presented themselves. The pole was nearly horizontal, an unusual position for a flagpole; in the next place, there was no pulley, ring, or cord by which to attach a flag; finally, there were elsewhere two vertical staffs from which flags were occasionally flown. It seemed probable that the pole was not there for flag-flying.

---

*Extracts taken from *How We Think*, published in Boston by D.C. Heath and Co. in 1910, pages 68-78, 118-120.

I then tried to imagine all possible purposes of such a pole, and to consider for which of these it was best suited: (a) Possibly it was an ornament. But as all the ferryboats and even the tugboats carried like poles, this hypothesis was rejected. (b) Possibly it was the terminal of a wireless telegraph. But the same considerations made this improbable. Besides, the more natural place for such a terminal would be the highest part of the boat, on top of the pilot house. (c) Its purpose might be to point out the direction in which the boat is moving.

In support of this conclusion, I discovered that the pole was lower than the pilot house, so that the steersman could easily see it. Moreover, the tip was enough higher than the base, so that, from the pilot's position, it must appear to project far out in front of the boat. Moreover, the pilot being near the front of the boat, he would need some such guide as to its direction. Tugboats would also need poles for such a purpose. This hypothesis was so much more probable than the others that I accepted it. I formed the conclusion that the pole was set up for the purpose of showing the pilot the direction in which the boat pointed, to enable him to steer correctly.

3. In washing tumblers in hot soapsuds and placing them mouth downward on a plate, bubbles appeared on the outside of the mouth of the tumblers and then went inside. Why? The presence of bubbles suggest air, which I note must come from inside the tumbler. I see that the soapy water on the plate prevents escape of the air save as it may be caught in bubbles. But why should air leave the tumbler? There was no substance entering to force it out. It must have expanded. It expands by increase of heat or by decrease of pressure, or by both. Could the air have become heated after the tumbler was taken from the hot suds? Clearly not the air that was already entangled in the water. If heated air was the cause, cold air must have entered in transferring the tumblers from the suds to the plate. I test to see if this supposition is true by taking several more tumblers out. Some I shake so as to make sure of entrapping cold air in them. Some I take out holding mouth downward in order to prevent cold air from entering. Bubbles appear on the outside of every one of the former and on none of the latter. I must be right in my inference. Air from the outside must have been expanded by the heat of the tumbler, which explains the appearance of the bubbles on the outside.

But why do they then go inside? Cold contracts. The tumbler cooled and also the air inside it. Tension was removed, and hence bubbles appeared inside. To be sure of this I test by placing a cup of ice on the tumbler while the bubbles are still forming outside. They soon reverse.

These three cases have been purposely selected so as to form a series from the more rudimentary to more complicated cases of reflection. The first illustrates the kind of thinking done by everyone during the day's business, in which neither the data, nor the ways of dealing with them, take one outside the limits of everyday experience. The last furnishes a case in which neither problem nor mode of solution would have been likely to occur except to one with some prior scientific training. The second case forms a natural transition; its materials lie well within the bounds of everyday, unspecialized experience; but the problem, instead of being directly involved in the person's business, arises indirectly out of his activity, and accordingly appeals to a somewhat theoretic and impartial interest. We shall (mention) later . . . the evolution of abstract thinking out of that which is relatively practical and direct; here we are concerned only with the common elements found in all the types.

Upon examination, each instance reveals, more or less clearly, five logically distinct steps: (i) a felt difficulty; (ii) its location and definition; (iii) suggestion of possible solution; (iv) development by reasoning of the bearings of the suggestion; (v) further observation and experiment leading to its acceptance or rejection; that is, the conclusion of belief or disbelief.

Defining the difficulty

The first and second steps frequently fuse into one. The difficulty may be felt with sufficient definiteness as to set the mind at once speculating upon its probable solution, or an undefined uneasiness and shock may come first, leading only later to definite attempt to find out what is the matter. Whether the two steps are distinct or blended, there is the factor emphasized in our original account of reflection — viz. the perplexity or problem. In the first of the three cases cited, the difficulty resides in the conflict between conditions at hand and a desired and intended result, between an end and the means for reaching it. The purpose of keeping an engagement at a certain time, and the existing hour taken in connection with the location, are not congruous. The object of thinking is to introduce congruity between the two. The given conditions cannot themselves be altered; time will not go backward nor will the distance between 16th Street and 124th Street shorten itself.

Locating possible solutions

The third factor is suggestion. The situation in which the perplexity occurs calls up something not present to the senses: the present location, the thought of subway or elevated train; the stick before the eyes, the idea of a flagpole, an ornament, an apparatus for wireless telegraphy; the soap bubbles, the law of expansion of bodies through heat and of their contraction through cold. (a) Suggestion is the very heart of inference; it involves going from what is present to something absent. Hence, it is more or less speculative, adventurous. Since inference goes beyond what is actually present it involves a leap, a jump, the propriety of which cannot be absolutely warranted in advance, no matter what precautions be taken. Its control is indirect, on the one hand, involving the formation of habits of mind which are at once enterprising and cautious; and on the other hand, involving the selection and arrangement of the particular facts upon perception of which suggestion issues. (b) The suggested conclusion so far as it is not accepted but only tentatively entertained constitutes an idea. Synonyms for this are *supposition, conjecture, guess, hypothesis,* and (in elaborate cases) *theory.* Since suspended belief, or the postponement of a final conclusion pending further evidence, depends partly upon the presence of rival conjectures as to the best course to pursue or the probable explanation to favour, *cultivation of a variety of alternative suggestions* is an important factor in good thinking.

Considering the implications

The process of developing the bearings — or, as they are more technically termed, the *implications* — of any idea with respect to any problem, is termed *reasoning.* As an idea is inferred from given facts, so reasoning sets out from an idea. The *idea* of elevated road is developed into the idea of difficulty of locating station, length of time occupied on the journey, distance of station at the other end from place to be reached. In the second case, the implication of a flagpole is seen to be a vertical position; of a wireless apparatus, location on a high part of the ship and, moreover, absence from every casual tugboat; while the idea of index to direction in which the boat moves, when developed, is found to cover all the details of the case.

Reasoning has the same effect upon a suggested solution as more intimate and extensive observation has upon the original problem. Acceptance of the suggestion in its first form is prevented by looking into it more thoroughly. Conjectures that seem plausible at first sight are often found unfit or even absurd when their full consequences are traced out (using careful judgement).... .

All judgement, all reflective inference, presupposes some lack of understanding, a partial absence of meaning. We reflect in order that we may get hold of the full and adequate significance of what happens. Nevertheless, *something* must be already understood, the mind must be in possession of some meaning which it has mastered, or else thinking is impossible.... Suppose that a stone with peculiar markings has been found. What do these scratches mean? So far as the object forces the raising of this question, it is not understood; while so far as the colour and form that we see mean to us a stone, the object is understood. It is such peculiar combinations of the understood and the non-understood that provoke thought. If at the end of the inquiry, the markings are decided to mean glacial scratches, obscure, and perplexing traits have been translated into meanings already understood: namely, the moving and grinding power of large bodies of ice and the friction thus induced of one rock upon another. Something already understood in one situation has been transferred and applied to what is strange and perplexing in another, and thereby the latter has become plain and familiar, i.e. understood.... .

Our progress in genuine knowledge always consists in part in the discovery of something not understood in what had previously been taken for granted as plain, obvious, matter-of-course, and in part in the use of meanings that are directly grasped without question, as instruments for getting hold of obscure, doubtful, and perplexing meanings.... .

Corroborative evidence

The concluding and conclusive step is some kind of *experimental corroboration,* or verification, of the conjectural idea. Reasoning shows that *if* the idea be adopted, certain consequences follow. So far the conclusion is hypothetical or conditional. If we look and find present all the conditions demanded by the theory, and if we find the characteristic traits called for by rival alternatives to be lacking, the tendency to believe, to accept, is almost irresistible. Sometimes direct observation furnishes corroboration, as in the case of the pole on the boat. In other cases, as in that of the bubbles, experiment is required; that is, *conditions are deliberately arranged in accord with the requirements of an idea or hypothesis to see if the results theoretically indicated by the idea actually occur.* If it is found that the experimental results agree with the theoretical, or rationally deduced, results, and if there is reason to believe that *only* the conditions in question would yield such results, the confirmation is so strong as to induce a conclusion — at least until contrary facts shall indicate the advisability of its revision.

Observation exists at the beginning and again at the end of the process: at the beginning, to determine more definitely and precisely the nature of the difficulty to be dealt with; at the end, to test the value of some hypothetically entertained conclusion. Between those two termini of observation, we find the more distinctively *mental* aspects of the entire thought-cycle: (i) inference, the suggestion of an explanation of solution; and (ii) reasoning, the development of the bearings and implications of the suggestion. Reasoning requires some experimental observation to confirm it, while experiment can be economically and fruitfully conducted only on the basis of an idea that has been tentatively developed by reasoning.

The disciplined, or logically trained, mind — the aim of the educative process — is the mind able to judge how far each of these steps needs to be carried in any particular situation.... . (That) mind is the one that best grasps the degree of observation, forming of ideas, reasoning, and experimental testing required in any special case, and that profits the most, in future thinking, by mistakes made in the past. What is important is that the mind should be sensitive to problems and skilled in methods of attack and solution.

STOP and THINK

● Compare the extracts from William James and John Dewey. Did they present similar or contrasting views of thought processes?

● What did you see as the most important points made by each author? Did they make sense in terms of your own experience?

● Dewey stressed the importance of corroboration, as the final stage of working out a problem. To what extent did he provide evidence of trying to corroborate his own reflections and introspections on thinking as problem solving?

It is important to recognize that these two extracts have been chosen to draw attention to certain aspects of the ideas of William James and John Dewey. Their writings are so extensive that little more than a hint at their views on psychology and education could be given here. The contrast that has been emphasized by selecting these extracts is essentially between an associative view of thinking and a stress on thinking as problem solving — searching for a solution and testing it. Both authors recognize the importance of activity in thinking. James points to the importance of 'forming diverse and multiple associations with every fact we care to retain'. Dewey takes memory for granted and is considering how best to use it in solving both practical and theoretical problems by analytic thinking. His emphasis is on the 'cultivation of a variety of alternative suggestions'. These 'introspectionist' psychologists have thus drawn attention to an important distinction between learning as *memorization,* and learning which involves *active analytic thinking,* which is also found in recent educational research and experimental psychology.

How useful is it to consider the introspections of these two great thinkers of the past? If treated with caution their ideas are valuable in stimulating our thinking about more modern approaches to psychology. Which aspects seem to have continuing relevance?

The model which James uses to illustrate his views on association may now seem to be dangerously misleading. 'Some brains are "wax to receive and marble to retain" '. 'As in other gelatinous substances,... an impression will vibrate throughout the brain'. The important thing to recognize is that such a model was not intended to describe the mechanisms within the brain through which associative connections are *actually* made. It only suggests that what happens is *'as if'* it had the properties of the model. The distinction is not always recognized; models are used to illustrate, to provide practical analogies, they are rarely descriptive. But the model which James used was not so far off the mark, even as a description. Recent neurological research is establishing the way in which biochemical changes in the brain create minute electric currents which pass messages and lead to neural connections being made (see, for example, Rose, 1976).

Dewey made the educational implications of his writings clear and tried out his ideas in practice. His descriptions of thinking as a form of problem solving were paralleled by an assertion that education should aim to develop 'the disciplined, or logically trained, mind'. Pupils should thus be encouraged to follow through, in full, the implications of their ideas and to apply their conclusions to the mastery of new situations. In practice pupils were, and still are, often required to accept knowledge without question, and to remember facts and principles enunciated by accepted authorities. 'Their minds are loaded with disconnected items... without reference to a more general character which they stand for and mean'. Dewey emphasized the need for *intellectual,* not simply physical, activity in learning, and the utility of concrete reality in stimulating abstract thought. The dangers in rote learning facts and accepted principles, and in allowing school learning to become detached from the everyday world, are still with us. They are perhaps less explicit in education today than in Dewey's time, but that makes them all the more insidious in their continuing effects.

BRIDGE

A Learning Experiment

This section contains the last of the historical extracts, but presented as a bridge between Part I and Part II. This extract was written in 1945; it thus acts as a bridge in time. It introduces another type of thinking — productive thinking — which, added to associative and analytic thinking, completes the trio mentioned earlier. Finally this 'bridge passage' will serve as an introduction to a series of research studies on student learning which form the main core of Chapter 4. These studies make considerable use of students' introspections about their experiences of studying. It therefore seems sensible to present this final extract as a learning experiment — an opportunity for careful introspection about the reader's own approaches to studying.

This book is *about* learning: it is also an exercise *in* learning. Bringing the two together we have the learning experiment. The task is to read the extract through carefully and prepare yourself in your normal way for answering questions about it afterwards.

INSTRUCTIONS FOR THE EXPERIMENT

You will need up to two hours free from interruption. There are three parts to the experiment. In the next section you will find the last of the extracts. Read through the article and be ready to answer questions on it afterwards. The idea is to read as you would do normally when preparing for, say, a tutorial or test. Make notes if you like.

After reading the article take a break if you like, then fill in first the inventory (pages 57-60) and then the questionnaire (pages 61-62).

DO NOT LOOK AT EITHER THE INVENTORY OR THE
QUESTIONNAIRE BEFORE READING THE EXTRACT

Max Wertheimer*: Thinking as imaginative reconstruction

What occurs when, now and then, thinking really works productively? What happens when, now and then, thinking forges ahead? What is really going on in such a process?

If we look for answers in books, we often find apparently easy ones. But confronted by actual processes of this kind — when one has just had a creative idea, however modest the issue, when one has begun really to grasp an issue, when one has enjoyed a clean, productive process of thought — those answers often seem to cover up the real problems rather than to face them squarely. The flesh and blood of what has happened seem to be lacking in those answers.

Surely in the course of your life you have been curious about a lot of things, sometimes seriously. Have you been equally serious about what this thing called thinking may be? There are, in this world of ours, eating, thunderstorms, blossoms, crystals. Various sciences deal with them; they attempt by great effort to get real understanding, to grasp what these things really are. Are we equally serious when we ask what productive thinking is?

There are fine cases. You can find them often, even in daily life. If you have had your eyes open, you have probably encountered somewhere in your life — if nowhere else, then in children — this surprising event, the birth of a genuine idea, of a productive development, the transition from a blind attitude to understanding in a productive processs. If you have not been fortunate enough to experience it yourself, you may have encountered it in others; or you may — fascinated — have glimpsed it when reading good books.

Many are of the opinion that men do not like to think; that they will do much to avoid it; that they prefer to repeat instead. But in spite of many factors that are inimical to real thinking, that suffocate it, here and there it emerges and flourishes. And often one gets the strong impression that men, even children, long for it.

What really takes place in such processes? What happens if one really thinks, and thinks productively? What may be the decisive features and the steps? How do they come about? Whence the flash, the spark? What are the conditions, the attitudes, favorable or unfavorable to such remarkable events? What is the real difference between good and bad thinking? And in connection with all these questions: how improve thinking? your thinking? thinking itself? Suppose we were to make an inventory of basic operations in thinking — how would it look? What, basically, is at hand? Could the basic operations themselves be enlarged and improved, and thus be made more productive?

For more than two thousand years some of the best brains in philosophy, in logic, in psychology, in education, have worked hard to find real answers to these questions. The history of these efforts, the brilliant ideas brought forward, the hard work done in research and in theoretical discussion, present on the whole a rich, dramatic picture. Much has been achieved. In a large number of special questions solid contributions to understanding have been made. At the same time there is something tragic in the history of these efforts. Again and again when great thinkers compared the ready answers with actual, fine thinking, they were troubled and deeply dissatisfied — they felt that what had been done had merits, but that in fact it had perhaps not touched the core of the problem at all.

The situation is still somewhat of this kind. To be sure, many books deal with these questions as if, fundamentally, everything were settled — in one way or another. For there are basically different ideas about what thinking is, each with

*Extracts taken from *Productive Thinking* published by Harper, New York in 1945 (pages 1-3, 5-11, 14-17, 45, 46, 48-50, 56-58).

serious consequences for behavior, for education. When observing a teacher we may often realize how serious the consequences of such ideas about thinking can be.

Although there are good teachers, with a natural feeling for what genuine thinking means, the situation in schools is often not good. How teachers act, how a subject matter is taught, how textbooks are written, all this is widely determined by two traditional views about the nature of thinking: the view of traditional logic and the view of association theory. These two views have their merits. To a degree they seem adequate to certain types of thought processes, to certain jobs in thinking; but it is at least an open question whether the way in which they interpret thinking does not cause serious hindrance, an actual impairment of genuine abilities.... .

As a kind of background for the following discussions, I present first a very short characterization of the two traditional approaches. They surpass all others in the rigor and completeness with which they consider operations and establish basic concepts, standards, criteria, laws and rules. Other approaches — even if they seem at first in strong opposition to these two — often still contain as their very meat, in one way or another, precisely the operations, the rules of these two. Modern research in thinking is largely determined by one or the other, or both at the same time. I shall indicate their main lines, but shall omit some points which appear as additions of another nature and which, besides, are not clear in themselves.

Traditional logic attacked the problems in an ingenious fashion: how are we to find the main issues in the vast variety of the topics of thinking? As follows: thinking is concerned with truth. Being true or false is a quality of assertions, propositions, and only of these. The elementary form of proposition asserts or denies some predicate of a subject, in the form 'all S are P,' or 'no S is P,' or 'some are,' or 'some are not.' Propositions involve general concepts — class concepts. These are basic to all thinking. For the correctness of a proposition it is decisive that its 'intension' or 'extension' be dealt with correctly. On the basis of assertions inferences are drawn. Logic studies formal conditions under which inferences are or are not correct. Certain combinations of propositions make it possible to derive 'new', correct propositions. Such syllogisms, with their premises and their conclusions, are the crown, the very heart of traditional logic. Logic establishes the various forms of syllogism which guarantee correctness of the conclusion.

Although most of the textbook syllogisms seem barren, a kind of circle, like the classical example —

> All men are mortal
> Socrates is a man
therefore, Socrates is mortal—

there are examples of real discoveries which can in a first approach be regarded as syllogisms, as for example the discovery of the planet Neptune. But formally, basically, there seems to be no real difference between the two kinds of syllogism. The decisive characteristics and the rules are identical for both — the somewhat silly and the really sensible ones.

Traditional logic is concerned with the criteria that guarantee exactness, validity, consistency of general concepts, propositions, inferences and syllogisms. The main chapters of classical logic refer to these topics. To be sure, sometimes the rules of traditional logic remind one of an efficient police manual for regulating traffic.

If we disregard differences of terminology, controversies of a subtle nature, we may list as characteristic the following operations of traditional logic:

definition
comparison and discrimination
analysis
abstraction
generalization
forming class concepts
subsumption, etc.
forming propositions
forming inferences
forming syllogisms, etc.

These operations as conceived, defined, and utilized by the logician have been and are being taken by psychologists as subjects for investigation. As a result, we have many experimental investigations on abstraction, generalization, definition, drawing conclusions, etc.

Some psychologists would hold that a person is able to think, is intelligent, when he can carry out the operations of traditional logic correctly and easily. The inability to form general concepts, to abstract, to draw conclusions in syllogisms of certain formal types is viewed as a mental deficiency, which is determined and measured in experiments.

However, one may view classical logic, it had and has great merits:

in the decisiveness of its will to truth;
in the concentration on the basic difference between a mere assertion, a belief, and an exact judgment;
in its emphasis on the difference between hazy concepts, hazy generalizations, and exact formulations;
in the development of a host of formal criteria which are suited to testing for, and discovering mistakes, haziness in thinking such as unjustified generalization, jumping at conclusions;
in its emphasis on proof;
in the seriousness of the rules of discussion;
in the insistence on stringency and rigor in each individual step in thinking.

The system of traditional logic, as envisaged in its main lines in the *Organon* of Aristotle, was recognized as final through the centuries; elaborations were added here and there, but these did not change its main character. A new branch started at the time of the Renaissance, a development that was essential to the growth of modern science. The central point was the introduction, as fundamental, of a procedure which until then had been regarded as of minor value because of lack of complete conclusiveness. This is the procedure of induction, with its emphasis on experience and experimentation, a methodological concept which reached its greatest perfection in John Stuart Mill's famous canon of rules of induction.

The emphasis here is not on rational deduction from general propositions but on gathering facts, on studying the empirically constant connections of facts, of changes, and on observing the consequences of changes introduced into factual situations, procedures which culminate in general assumptions. Syllogisms are viewed as tools by which one can draw consequences from such hypothetical assumptions in order to test them.

It is widely believed that inductive logic adds to the classical rules and operations the emphasis on:

empirical observations
careful gathering of facts
studying problems empirically
introducing experimental methods
correlating facts
developing crucial tests

The second great theory of thinking is centered in the classical theory of associationism. Thinking is a chain of ideas (or, in more modern terms, a chain of stimuli and responses, or a chain of behavior elements). The way to understand thinking is clear: we have to study the laws governing the succession of ideas (or, in modern terms, of behavioral items). An 'idea' in classical association theory is some remnant of perception, a copy, in more modern terms, a trace of stimulations. What is the fundamental law of the succession, of the connection of these items? Answer — very elegant in its theoretical simplicity: if two items, *a* and *b,* have often occurred together, a subsequent occurrence of *a* will call forth *b* in the subject. Basically the items are connected in the way in which my friend's telephone number is connected with his name, in which nonsense syllables become reproducible when learned in a series of such syllables, or in which a dog is conditioned to respond with salivation to a certain musical sound.

Habit, past experience, in the sense of items repeated in contiguity — inertia rather than reason, are the essential factors, just as David Hume had maintained. As compared with classical associationism, this theory is now being developed in a most intricate way; but the old idea of repetition, in contiguity, is still the central feature. A leading exponent of this approach stated explicitly not long ago that the modern theory of the conditioned reflex is essentially *of the same nature* as classical associationism.

The list of operations here looks about as follows:

association, acquiring connections — bonds on the basis of repetitions
role of frequency, of recency
recall from past experience
trial and error, with chance success
learning on the basis of repeated success
acting in line with conditioned responses, and with habit

These operations and processes are now being widely studied with highly developed methods.

Many psychologists would say: ability to think is the working of associative bonds; it can be measured by the number of associations a subject has acquired, by the ease and correctness with which he learns and recalls them.

No doubt there are merits in this approach also, with regard to the subtle features at work in this kind of learning and behaving.

Both approaches had difficulties with regard to sensible, productive processes of thinking.

Consider first traditional logic. In the course of the centuries there arose again and again a deep-felt dissatisfaction with the manner in which traditional logic handles such processes. In comparison with actual, sensible, and productive processes, the topics as well as the customary examples of traditional logic often look dull, insipid, lifeless. To be sure, the treatment is rigorous enough, yet often it seems barren, boring, empty, unproductive. If one tries to describe processes of genuine thinking in terms of formal traditional logic, the result is often unsatisfactory: one has, then, a series of correct operations, but the sense of the process and what was vital, forceful, creative in it seems somehow to have evaporated in the formulations. On the other hand it is possible to have a chain of logical operations, each perfectly correct in itself, which does not form a sensible train of thought. Indeed there are people with logical training who in certain situations produce series of correct operations which, viewed as a whole, nevertheless form something akin to a flight of ideas. Training in traditional logic is not to be disparaged: it leads to stringency and rigor in each step, it contributes to critical-mindedness; but it does not, in itself, seem to give rise to productive thinking. In short, there is the danger of being empty and senseless, though exact; and there is always the difficulty with regard to real productiveness.

Realization of the latter point — among others — led in fact to the emphatic declaration by some logicians that logic, interested in correctness and validity, has nothing at all to do with factual thinking or with questions of productivity. A reason was also given for this: logic, it was said, has timeless implications and is, therefore, in principle, divorced from questions of actual thought processes which are merely factual and, of necessity, processes in time. This separation was certainly meritorious for certain problems; from a broader view, however, such assertions often look somehow like the declaration of the fox that the grapes were sour.

Similar difficulties arose in association theory: the fact that we have to distinguish between sensible thought and senseless combinations, and the difficulty in dealing with the *productive* side of thinking.

If a problem is solved by recall, by mechanical repetition of what has been drilled, by sheer chance discovery in a succession of blind trials, one would hesitate to call such a process sensible thinking; and it seems doubtful whether the piling up of such factors only, even in large numbers, can lead to an adequate picture of sensible processes.

(The distinction between productive thinking and the approaches more commonly encouraged in school work can best be illustrated by concrete examples. One such example is a problem children are often given – finding the area of a parallelogram.)

I am visiting a classroom. The teacher: 'During the last lesson we learned how to find the area of a rectangle. Do you all know it?'

The class: 'Yes.' One pupils calls out: 'The area of a rectangle is equal to the product of the two sides.' The teacher approves, then gives a number of problems with rectangles of varying sizes, which all solve readily.

'Now,' says the teacher, 'we shall go on.' He draws a parallelogram on the blackboard: 'This is called a parallelogram. A parallelogram is a plane quadrilateral the opposite sides of which are equal and parallel.'

Here a pupil raises his hand: 'Please, teacher, how long are the sides?' 'Oh, the sides may be of very different lengths,' says the teacher. 'In our case one line measures 11 inches, the other 5 inches.' 'Then the area is 5 × 11 square inches.' 'No,' answers the teacher, 'That's wrong; you will now learn how to find the area of a parallelogram.' He labels the corners a, b, c, d.

'I drop one perpendicular from the upper left corner and another perpendicular from the upper right corner.

'I extend the base line to the right.

'I label the two new points e and f.'

With the help of this figure he then proceeds to the usual proof of the theorem that the area of a parallelogram is equal to the product of the base by the altitude, establishing the equality of certain lines and angles and the congruence of the pair of triangles. In each case he states the previously learned theorem, postulate, or axiom upon which the equality or congruence is based. Finally he concludes that it has been proved that the area of a parallelogram is equal to the base times the altitude.

'You will find what I have shown you in your textbook on page 62. Do the lesson at home, repeat it carefully so that you will know it well.'

The teacher now gives a number of problems all of which require finding the areas of parallelograms of different sizes, sides and angles. This being a 'good' class, the problems are all correctly solved. Before the end of the hour the teacher assigns ten more problems of this kind for homework.

At the next meeting of the class, one day later, I am there again.

The lesson begins with the teacher calling on a pupil to demonstrate how the area of a parallelogram is found. The pupil does it exactly. One sees that he has learned the problem. The teacher whispers to me: 'And he is not the best of my pupils. Without doubt the others know it as well.' A written quiz brings good results.

Most people would say, 'This is an excellent class; the teaching goal has been reached.' But observing the class I feel uneasy, I am troubled. 'What have they learned?' I ask myself. 'Have they done any thinking at all? Have they grasped the issue? Maybe all that they have done is little more than blind repetition. To be sure, they have solved promptly the various tasks the teacher has assigned, and so they have learned something of a general character, involving some abstraction. Not only were they able to repeat word for word what the teacher said, there was easy transfer as well. But — have they grasped the issue at all? How can I clarify it? What can I *do*?'

I ask the teacher whether he will allow me to put a question to the class. 'With pleasure,' he answers, clearly proud of his class.

I go to the board and draw this figure.

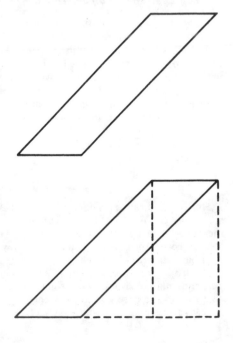

Some are obviously taken aback.

One pupil raises his hand: 'Teacher, we haven't had that yet.'

Others are busy. They have copied the figure on paper, they draw the auxiliary lines as they were taught, dropping perpendiculars from the two upper corners and extending the base line. Then they look bewildered, perplexed.

Some do not look at all unhappy; they write firmly below their drawing: 'The area is equal to the base times the altitude' — a correct subsumption, but perhaps an entirely blind one. When asked whether they can show it to be true in this case, they too become perplexed.

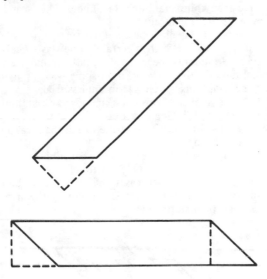

With still others it is entirely different. Their faces brighten, they smile and draw the following lines in the figure, or they turn their papers through 45°, and do it.

The teacher, observing that only a minority of the pupils has mastered the problem, says to me with some indignation: 'You certainly gave them a queer figure. Naturally they are unable to deal with it.'

Now just between us, haven't you too been thinking: 'No wonder so many failed when he gave them a figure so unfamiliar!' But is it less familiar than the variations of the original figure which the teacher previously gave and which they solved? The teacher did give problems in which the figures varied greatly with regard to length of sides, size of angles, and size of areas. These were decided variations, and they did not appear at all difficult for the pupils. Did you notice, perchance, that my parallelogram is simply the teacher's original figure turned around? With regard to all the part-qualities it was not more but less different from the original figure than the teacher's variations. . . .

Now I shall tell what happened when I put the problem of the area of the *parallelogram* to subjects, especially children, after having briefly shown how the area of the rectangle is found, saying nothing further, giving no help, simply waiting for what they would say or do. There were grown ups of all types, students who showed by their reactions that they had entirely forgotten this theorem, and children who had never heard of geometry, even children as young as five.

There are different types of reactions.

First type. No reaction at all.

Or someone says, "Whew! mathematics!" and dismisses the problem with, "I don't like mathematics."

Some subjects simply wait politely for what is to come or ask, 'What else?'

Others say, 'I don't know; that is something I have not learned.' Or, 'I learned that in school but I have completely forgotten it,' and that is all. Some show indignation: 'How do you expect me to be able to do that?' To which I reply, 'Why not try it?'

Second type. Others search their memory intensively, some even frantically, to see if they can recall anything that might be of help. They search blindly for some scraps of knowledge that might apply.

Some ask, 'Could I ask my older brother? He surely knows.' Or: 'Could I look for it in a geometry book?' Which is certainly one way of solving problems.

Third type. Some start making speeches. They talk around the problem, telling of analogous situations. Or they classify it in some way, applying general terms, perform some subsumptions, or engage in aimless trials.

Fourth type. But in a number of cases one can observe real thinking at work — in drawings, in remarks, in thinking out loud.

'Here is this figure — how can I get at the size of the area? I see no possibility. The area just in this form?'

'Something has to be done. I have to change something, change it in a way that would lead me to see the area clearly. Something is wrong.' At this stage some children produce Figure 1. In such cases I add: 'It would be nice to be able to compare the size of the area of the parallelogram with the area of the rectangle.' The child is helpless, then starts anew.

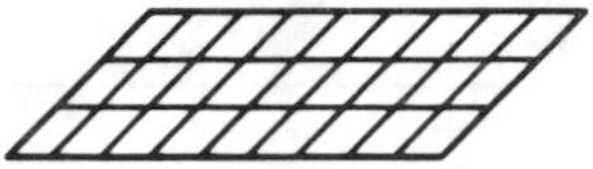

Figure 1

Figure 1

There were other cases in which the child said: 'I have to get rid of the trouble. This figure cannot be divided into little squares.'. . .

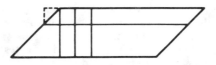

But there were cases in which the thinking went straight ahead. Some children reached the solution with little or no help in a genuine, sensible, direct way. Sometimes, after strained concentration, a face brightened at the critical moment. It is wonderful to observe the beautiful transformation from blindness to seeing the point!

First I shall report what happened with a 5½-year-old child to whom I gave no help at all for the parallelogram. Given the parallelogram problem, after she had been shown briefly how to get at the area of the rectangle, she said, 'I certainly don't know how to do *that.*' Then after a moment of silence: 'This is *no good here,*'pointing to the region at the left end; 'and *no good here,*' pointing to the region at the right.

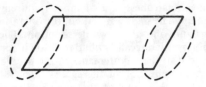

'It's troublesome, here and there.' Hesitatingly she said: 'I could make it right here... but...' Suddenly she cried out, 'May I have a scissors?' What is bad there is just what is needed here. It fits.' She took the scissors, cut vertically, and

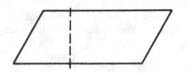

placed the left end at the right. Another child proceeded in a similar way to cut off the triangle.

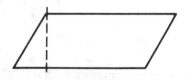

In several cases the procedure ran this way:

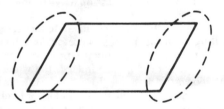

1. 'Disturbance'   'Disturbance also'
2. 'Too much here'   'Too much here'
3. ——————————   'No! This needs over here at the right just what is
                           too much at the left,'

and she put the left end 'in order.' Then, looking at the other end, she tried to do the same thing there, but changed suddenly from seeing it as 'too much' to seeing it as 'gap.'

There were other ways. A child to whom I had given the parallelogram, a long one cut out of paper, remarked in the beginning, 'The whole middle part is all right, but the ends —' She continued to look at the form, clearly interested in the ends, suddenly took the paper figure, and, with a smile, made it into a ring, bringing the two ends together. Asked what this meant, she answered, holding the two ends together with her little fingers: 'Why, I can cut it now, this way' and indicated a vertical somewhere in the middle, 'Then it is all right.'...

What are the operations, the steps in the procedure?

We saw that in such genuine, positive processes as those just described, there are operations (such as) regrouping with regard to the whole, reorganization, fitting; factors of inner relatedness and of inner requirements are discovered, realized, and followed up. The steps were taken, the operations were clearly done in view of the whole figure and of the whole situation. They arose by virtue of their part-function, not by blind recall or blind trial; their content, their direction, their application grew out of the requirements of the problem. Such a process is not just a sum of several steps, not an aggregate of several operations, but the growth of one line of thinking out of the gaps in the situation, out of the structural troubles and the desire to remedy them, to straighten out what is bad, to get at the good inner relatedness. It is not a process that moves from pieces to an aggregate, from below to above, but from above to below, from the nature of the structural trouble to the concrete steps.

It is also interesting to observe the behavior of children (even of very young children) in the following situations. Four solid figures of this kind are given:

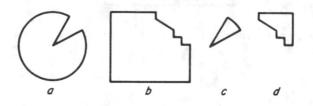

Children often show a strong trend to bring them together properly, to fit c into a, d into b. If the grownup tries to do it the other way, insists on placing d with a, and c with b, or puts c with a, and d with b but improperly, children are often not only puzzled, or amused, but interfere passionately, fitting the figures into their proper positions.

In all these cases we have structural changes, tendencies toward the better structure, toward fitting, with the disappearance of disturbances.

Such changes are often dramatic in productive processes, much more so than in this modest example of the parallelogram. Indeed, the whole process is often a kind of drama with powerful dramatic forces — with tension and dramatic structural changes in the transition from an incomplete or inadequate structure to a view of the complete, consistent structure, in the transition from not having understood structurally, from being troubled, to really grasping and realizing the requirements.

The most urgent need in the experimental investigation of the problems seems to be not so much to get the quantitative answer, 'How many children achieve a solution, how many fail, at what age?' etc., but to get at an understanding of what happens in good and in bad processes.

A physicist studying crystallization may try to find out in how many cases he finds pure crystals and in how many he does not — there are crippled crystals some corners of which are jagged, there are impure crystals, there are Siamese twin crystals improperly grown together, there are even crystals shaped by artificial polishing into perfect forms entirely incongruous with their nature. All such cases are of primary interest to the physicist, not as problems of statistics but for what they reveal of the inner nature of genuine crystallization.

It is also important to find out what are the conditions under which pure crystallization may take place, what conditions favor it, what factors endanger it.

And so in psychology.

* * * * * *

DO NOT LOOK AT THIS INVENTORY UNTIL YOU HAVE COMPLETED THE FIRST PART OF THE LEARNING EXPERIMENT

Short inventory of approaches to studying

Please answer every item quickly by giving your immediate response. Circle the appropriate code number to show your *general* approaches to studying.

4	(√√)	means Definitely agree
3	(√)	means Agree with reservations
1	(x)	means Disagree with reservations
0	(xx)	means Definitely disagree
2	(?)	is only to be used if the item doesn't apply to you or if you find it impossible to give a definite answer.

√√ √ x xx ?

1. I find it easy to organize my study time effectively.

   4 3 1 0 2 │A│

2. I try to relate ideas in one subject to those in others, whenever possible.

   4 3 1 0 2 │C│

3. Although I have a fairly good general idea of many things, my knowledge of the details is rather weak.

   4 3 1 0 2 │G│

4. I like to be told precisely what to do in essays or other set work.

   4 3 1 0 2 │B│

5. The best way for me to understand what technical terms mean is to remember the text-book definitions.

   4 3 1 0 2 │F│

6. It's important to me to do really well in the courses here.

   4 3. 1 0 2 │A│

7. I usually set out to understand thoroughly the meaning of what I am asked to read.

   4 3 1 0 2 │D│

8. When I'm reading I try to memorize
    important facts which may come in useful later.   4 3 1 0 2 | B |

9. When I'm doing a piece of work, I try to bear in
    mind exactly what that particular teacher/lecturer
    seems to want.   4 3 1 0 2 | A |

10. I am usually cautious in drawing conclusions
    unless they are well supported by evidence.   4 3 1 0 2 | E |

11. My main reason for being here is so that I can
    learn more about the subjects which really interest
    me.   4 3 1 0 2 | D |

12. In trying to understand new ideas, I often try to
    relate them to real life situations to which they
    might apply.   4 3 1 0 2 | C |

13. I suppose I am more interested in the
    qualifications I'll get than in the courses I'm
    taking.   4 3 1 0 2 | B |

14. I'm usually prompt at starting work in the
    evenings.   4 3 1 0 2 | A |

15. Although I generally remember facts and details,
    I find it difficult to fit them together into an
    overall picture.   4 3 1 0 2 | F |

16. I generally put a lot of effort into trying to
    understand things which initially seem difficult.   4 3 1 0 2 | D |

17. I often get criticized for introducing irrelevant
    ideas into essays or discussions.   4 3 1 0 2 | G |

18. Often I find I have to read things without having
    a chance to really understand them.   4 3 1 0 2 | B |

√√ √ x xx ?

19. If conditions aren't right for me to study, I
generally manage to do something to change
them.   4 3 1 0 2 A

20. Puzzles or problems fascinate me, particularly
where you have to work through the material to
reach a logical conclusion.   4 3 1 0 2 E

21. I often find myself questioning things that I hear
in lessons/lectures or read in books.   4 3 1 0 2 D

22. I find it helpful to 'map out' a new topic for
myself by seeing how the ideas fit together.   4 3 1 0 2 C

23. I tend to read very little beyond what's required
for completing assignments.   4 3 1 0 2 B

24. It is important to me to do things better than my
friends, if I possibly can.   4 3 1 0 2 A

25. Tutors/teachers seem to want me to be more
adventurous in making use of my own ideas.   4 3 1 0 2 F

26. I spend a good deal of my spare time in finding
out more about interesting topics which have been
discussed in classes.   4 3 1 0 2 D

27. I seem to be a bit too ready to jump to
conclusions without waiting for all the evidence.   4 3 1 0 2 G

28. I find academic topics so interesting, I should like
to continue with them after I finish this course.   4 3 1 0 2 D

√√ √ x xx ?

29. I think it is important to look at problems
rationally and logically without making intuitive
jumps.   4 3 1 0 2 | E |

30. I find I have to concentrate on memorising a
good deal of what we have to learn.   4 3 1 0 2 | B |

THE MARKING SCHEME FOR THIS INVENTORY WILL BE FOUND
IN APPENDIX A. IT WILL, HOWEVER, BE IMPOSSIBLE TO INTER-
PRET YOUR SCORES UNTIL AFTER YOU HAVE READ PART II OF
THIS BOOK.

DO NOT LOOK AT THIS QUESTIONNAIRE UNTIL YOU HAVE
FINISHED READING THE WERTHEIMER EXTRACT

Questionnaire on the Wertheimer article

Answer the first question before turning over to look at subsequent questions.

1. Write down what you have learned from the article. Imagine you were
    going to describe what the article is about to someone who had not read it.
    What would you say?

2. *Specific questions*

   (a) What is traditional logic mainly concerned with?

   (b) To what did Wertheimer compare the rules of formal logic?

   (c) What was John Stuart Mill's contribution to logic said to be?

   (d) How does associationism treat thinking?

   (e) On what grounds did Wertheimer consider each of these approaches to thinking to be inadequate?
   (i) logic   (ii) associationism.

   (f) What method did the teacher in Wertheimer's example use to teach childen how to find the area of a parallelogram?

   (g) Why did Wertheimer consider this method to be inadequate?

   (h) Wertheimer uses the analogy of a physicist's interest in the growth of crystals to illustrate the research approach he recommends for studying thinking. What is that approach and how does the analogy illustrate it?

3. Students tackle the task of reading articles or books in many different ways, and with different expectations of what is required of them and of what they should be getting out of their reading. How did *you* tackle this article? Was this approach typical of, or different from, what you would do in your normal studying?

KEEP YOUR ANSWERS TO REFER TO WHEN YOU READ PART II

APPENDIX B ILLUSTRATES THE QUALITATIVELY DIFFERENT CATEGORIES OF ANSWER GIVEN TO QUESTIONS 1 AND 3, AND THE ANSWERS TO QUESTION 2. AGAIN THE CATEGORIES WILL BE UNDERSTOOD ONLY AFTER READING PART II OF THE BOOK.

PART II

How Students Learn

CHAPTER 4

Approaches to Reading and Studying

The preceding chapter was included to show how ideas about study methods and thinking have been discussed by philosophers and early psychologists, predominantly using methods of introspection. Many of these ideas have been of seminal importance in affecting subsequent developments in psychology, but are rarely mentioned today. From time to time it will be helpful to refer back to these early ideas, but the next two sections of the book will concentrate on recent evidence on learning derived by the use of the empirical research methods described in Chapter 2.

Part II looks at how *students* learn and draws mainly on evidence from two American studies conducted in the 1950s and three on-going research programmes in Gothenburg, London, and Lancaster. Rather than presenting a full review of many pieces of research, the intention in this section is to look closely at this small group of related studies. Their findings form the basis for a model of learning in higher education, which in turn provides a framework within which to describe the more basic educational psychology presented in Part III. It will be important throughout Part II to relate the research findings on students to your own personal experience, and to look out for the principles of learning which might be expected to generalize to the teaching situations with which you are currently most concerned. What implications might these results have for *you?*

As might be expected by the discussion of research methodology in Chapter 2, the studies described here make use of contrasting approaches — case studies, surveys and realistic experiments. Impressionistic data from interviews are combined with findings from surveys of larger samples using more objective forms of measurement. The research on which the 'learning experiment' was based will be introduced later in this chapter. Our starting point is a consideration of what lecturers *expect* students to learn in higher education, and an examination of some evidence about the ways students *do* develop intellectually during their college years.

65

Lecturers' expectations

One of the studies at Lancaster was concerned with lecturers' aims and objectives and with students' experiences of higher education. Lecturers in various academic departments were asked questions about what they expected from 'good' students and what they saw as the characteristics of weaker students.* Although there were, of course, great differences in the specific comments of lecturers in contrasting departments, there was an important common thread running through most of the replies. While knowledge and technical skills were expected, students had to be able to use these effectively — to combine and interrelate ideas. Short extracts from the comments of three of the lecturers provide an impression of what, in one way or another, most lecturers were demanding.

An English lecturer, for example, said:

> 'I would be expecting a kind of alertness and openess — that may sound very general. Alert to what? Alert to all the signs of interest or significance in passages of literature. We try to develop their evaluative skills... to develop the sense of what is the first hand piece of writing and what is purely drivative.... The prime moral outcome of a literature course (should be the) ability to enter into different individual and social conditions... to be able to realise what it is like to be somebody else, so that we can properly interact with other people and not always expect them to be mutations of oneself or of one's own culture.'

A history lecturer saw the need for using evidence effectively, again combined with a form of social awareness.

> 'History, typically, does involve the assembly of evidence, coming to conclusions about certain problems... (you tend) to consider (an idea) from all angles with a critical eye. Basically if you're treating it non-academically you tend merely to accept it and then to file it,... (but) then there's going to be no progress or change. Things are not going to move if you merely accept. You've got to scrutinize what you're doing (to see) if the thing cannot be done better.'

In the science departments there was, of course, much more emphasis on knowledge of facts, but even so there was also a recognition that factual information, in itself, is a rapidly diminishing asset. 'Knowledge' has to be reinterpreted to include:

> 'techniques of analysis, rather than knowledge of facts; knowledge of techniques for finding facts, rather than the facts themselves.'

The unifying theme both in the interviews and in the general literature on the aims of university education is that of 'critical thinking', or as Ashby has described it — 'post-conventional thinking'.

---

*These interviews were carried out by Keith Percy and have been reported in more detail elsewhere (Entwistle and Percy, 1971; 1974).

'The student (moves) from the uncritical acceptance of orthodoxy to creative dissent over the values and standards of society.... (In higher education) there must be opportunities for the intellect to be stretched to its capacity, the critical faculty sharpened to the point where it can change ideas' (Ashby, 1973, pages 147-9).

What evidence is there that students *do* develop towards the intellectual goal described by lecturers? The first two studies, conducted in America, rely entirely on interview data and impressionistic analysis, but come independently to rather similar conclusions about the most characteristic form of intellectual development among the students they interviewed. It will also be interesting to see how this evidence tallies with the more recent studies which have examined how different types of student tackle their academic work.

The 'Reasonable Adventurer'

Roy Heath (1964, 1978) carried out interviews at Princeton University. He worked as an academic counsellor to a group of 36 male students who began their studying in 1954. He talked to them once every week throughout their time at university and gradually built up an impression of the students both in terms of their personality and their intellectual development. He noticed marked similarities and differences among the students which he described in terms of three personality types and an ideal of intellectual development.

Heath gave all four types descriptive labels and an identifying letter. The three personality types were described as 'non-committers' (X), 'hustlers' (Y), and 'plungers' (Z). These three types of student approached their work in contrasting ways which seemed to reflect underlying personality differences. However all these students progressed during their time at college towards a single intellectual goal or ideal type — the 'reasonable adventurer' (A). Thus Heath was able to describe a single dimension of intellectual development common to all the students in his sample, but characteristic differences in the paths along which they moved towards that single intellectual goal.

The starting-points were the extremes represented by the salient characteristics of the three personality types. Heath's own descriptions of these types cannot be bettered.

'The X is named the "Non-committer"... because of his marked tendency to avoid involvements. He apparently views a commitment as a possible entanglement which might reduce his freedom to get out of the way when trouble threatens. When storm clouds do break he'll hold on and hope for the best. In other words, he takes a passive role in a conflict situation.... .

Why is the X so prone to choose neutrality? This puzzled me for a long time. I finally discovered that some Xs have a secret, a very precious myth about themselves. As protection for the myth they want freedom to bide their time. The great ally of the X is time. One would have to be privy to an X's fantasies in order to realize that the myth is one of invincibility, of high-potentiality. He could do a lot of things, the myth says, if he really went all-out. He could make better grades, he could made that team, he could make that girl, etc.... (But) to go all-out presents a horrendous risk, namely the discovery that the myth has no basis in fact.... . Xs vary from some who consistently appear cautious and attentive, to others who appear bland, carefree, and deceivingly innocent. Underneath, however, they are much the same. They are all neutralists' (pages 14, 16, and 19).

Y is characteristically a hustler. He thrives on activity but it is purposeful activity. He seems to possess an inordinate need for achievement, for concrete success.... . He is a great competitor. In his relations with others he is often aggressive and insensitive to their feelings. This is unfortunate for he possesses a strong desire to be received favourably and affectionately.

Y is impatient with the *status quo*. He must keep moving beyond his present level. Wasting time is for him a cardinal sin, a lost opportunity... . In his philosophical outlook, Y is a 'hard guy'; life is a battle. People must look out for themselves, must solve their own problems. He prefers courses that emphasize logic and factual material over courses that require subjective judgement and aesthetic appreciation... .

The Y is a study in antithesis... a personality that is at war with itself. He is a strong-willed man coupled with equally strong inhibitions and control over his deeper impulses. He rarely allows his feelings direct expression. In short Y distrusts and rejects his inner-self; much of his overt behavior is seen as a counter offensive to nullify the alien instinctual drives, either aggressive or sexual in nature. It is a close battle fought out in the peripheries of consciousness. Attaining success or doing "good" becomes an imperative to offset the "weakness" or "evil" that he suspects is within' (pages 20, 22).

The Z is unusual. He is also the least common of the varieties along the dimension of temperament... In contrast to X, who maintains a remarkable stability of mood, Z is known for his variability of mood. Today he might feel on top of the world; ... tomorrow might find him bitter, sad, alone. His moods ebb and flow as the tides but not as predictably. Whether high or low, he seems at the utter mercy of his feelings. He responds as strongly to guilt as he does to his urges. He lacks the emotional shock absorbers of X... .

X is an under-reactor, Y counteracts his feelings, but Z is an over-reactor. He works and loves in spurts. This puzzles both his teachers and his lovers. He may beg permission to go ahead with a project, ... only to lose interest later, particularly if hard uninteresting work looms.... (Also Z) often has difficulty in communication. Since many of his expressions are direct outcroppings of an active inner-self, they are apt to be highly individualistic, even surrealistic. His thoughts zip from one idea to another without apparent connection... . Z characteristically neglects to clothe his ideas in a framework that would make his utterances comprehensible to others... . Consequently, Z is frequently misunderstood and occasionally viewed as a little odd' (pages 24-26, 68).

Finally Heath describes the 'reasonable adventurer' (A) towards which all the students moved during their time at Princeton. This description thus represents an ideal of development, rather than a personality type. Each of the three personality types moved along different developmental paths towards this intellectual goal. Students differed both in their starting points and in their proximity to the ideal by the end of the course (see Figures 4.1 and 4.2).

Again using extracts from Heath's own character sketch this ideal type emerges.

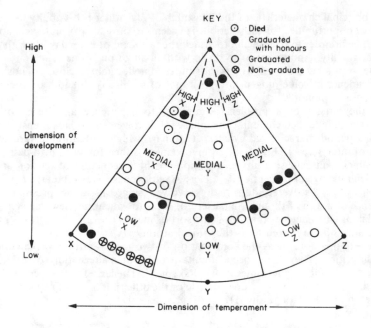

Figure 4.1 First year (freshman) positions and college outcomes (from Heath, 1964)

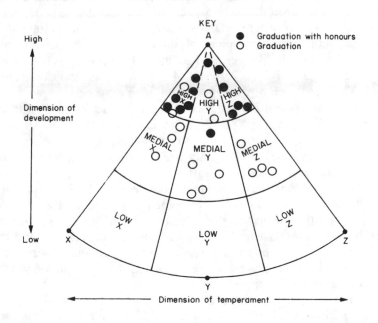

Figure 4.2 Final year positions and type of degree (from Heath, 1964)

'The principal characteristic of the Reasonable Adventurer is his ability to create his own opportunities for satisfaction. He seems to have his psychological house in sufficient order to release him to attack the problems of everyday life with zest and originality. And he seems to do so with an air of playfulness.

The A is characterized by six attributes: intellectuality, close friendships, independence in value judgements, tolerance of ambiguity, breadth of interests, and sense of humor.. . . .

In the pursuit of a problem A appears to experience an alternation of involvement and detachment. The phase of involvement is an intensive and exciting period characterized by curiosity, a narrowing of attention toward some point of interest.. . . This period of involvement is then followed by a period of detachment, an extensive phase, accompanied by a reduction of tension and a broadening range of perception.. . . Here A settles back to reflect on the meaning of what was discovered during the involved stage. Meaning presumes the existence of a web of thought, a pattern of ideas to which the 'new' element can be related. One imagines that this is the sort of mental operation that takes place in a stance often referred to as the critical attitude.. . . .

We see, therefore, in A the combination of two mental attitudes: the curious and the critical. They do not occur simultaneously but in alternation. A at times is a "believer" but at other times he is a "skeptic". The less effective personalities may show tendencies toward one attitude or the other but may not experience the full reach of either' (pages 30-31).

Heath explains little about the way in which he analysed his extensive interview data. He seems to have relied almost entirely on intuition and hunch to find the best ways of describing his data. There is also no attempt to work out relationships between different aspects of the students' experiences. The nearest Heath comes to such an analysis is to locate each student in relation to the temperamental and developmental dimensions of his scheme at the beginning and end of the project, and to show these positions in relation to degree performance. Figures 4.1 and 4.2 provide an indication of the relationship between each of the types and academic success.

Of the 36 students who entered, six dropped out and two died (all Xs), leaving 28 in the final year (11 Xs, 8 Ys, and 9 Zs). The descriptions of students in terms of allocation to one or other of the personality types were remarkably consistent throughout the project. Only *one* student was put into a different category, and that was a marginal shift from Y to Z. There were, however, substantial changes along the developmental dimension. In the freshman year 21 students were in the lowest developmental category. By the second (sophomore) year this group had dwindled to 8. In the junior year 5 students were left, but by the final, senior year no student was categorized at this lowest level. The highest developmental category began with only four students, doubled in size in the sophomore year, reached 9 in the junior year, and jumped to 16 in the final senior year.

Looking now at links with academic performance, Xs and Zs were almost equally successful in graduating with honours: Ys did far worse. But perhaps the closest link, as might be expected, is between A — the critical attitude — and degree performance. Of the 13 students graduating with honours, 12 were in the top section of the diagram closest to the A ideal type. Only four the 15 non-honours students were in this section.

It thus seems likely that Heath's description of the 'reasonable adventurer' is closely linked to what lecturers are looking for when they give high grades to their students. The small sample and the subjective analysis must, however, make that conclusion tentative for the time being.

Relativistic reasoning

The second American study provides a much more detailed analysis of the intellectual and ethical development of students, this time at Harvard and Ratcliffe colleges. This study was carried out by William Perry (1970) using a similar research methodology (open interviews) and discovering an equivalent dimension through which to describe the intellectual development of students.

Perry interviewed 67 students once in each of their four years at college. He deliberately avoided putting his own ideas into the students' mouths by starting each interview with a very open question.

'Why don't you start with whatever stands out for you about the year?'

The responses to this question led students into a description of the events of each year which had had personal significance for them. From reading and re-reading transcripts of these interviews, Perry gradually found a conceptual scheme which made sense of the individual comments. Through all of these there seemed to run a dimension which described the progress which the students were making towards 'contextual relativistic reasoning'. Eventually Perry was able to describe nine positions along this dimension of intellectual and ethical development and to have independent judges check his categorizations. He was also able to identify three conditions of 'delay, deflection, and regression' which affected students' progress. Perry's summary of these positions and conditions is presented below.

Main line of development

'*Position 1:* The student sees the world in polar terms of we-right-good *vs.* other-wrong-bad. Right Answers for everything exist in the Absolute, known to Authority whose role is to mediate (teach) them. Knowledge and goodness are perceived as quantitative accretions of discrete rightnesses to be collected by hard work and obedience (paradigm: a spelling test).

Position 2: The student perceives diversity of opinion, and uncertainty, and accounts for them as unwarranted confusion in poorly qualified Authorities or as mere exercises set by Authority 'so we can learn to find The Answer for ourselves'.

Position 3: The student accepts diversity and uncertainty as legitimate but still *temporary* in areas where Authority 'hasn't found the Answer yet.' He supposes Authority grades him in these areas on 'good expression' but remains puzzled as to standards.

Position 4: (a) The student perceives legitimate uncertainty (and therefore diversity of opinion) to be extensive and raises it to the status of an unstructured epistemological realm of its own in which 'anyone has a right to his own opinion', a realm which he sets over against Authority's realm where right-wrong still prevails, or (b) the student discovers qualitative contextual relativistic reasoning as a special case of 'what They want' within Authority's realm.

Position 5: The student perceives all knowledge and values (including authority's) as contextual and relativistic and subordinates dualistic right-wrong functions to the status of a special case, in context.

Position 6: The student apprehends the necessity of orienting himself in a relativistic world through some form of personal Commitment (as distinct from unquestioned or unconsidered commitment to simple belief in certainty).

Position 7: The student makes an initial Commitment in some area.

Position 8: The student experiences the implications of Commitment, and explores the subjective and stylistic issues of responsibility.

Position 9: The student experiences the affirmation of identity among multiple responsibilities and realizes Commitment as an ongoing, unfolding, activity through which he expresses his life style.

Conditions of delay, deflection, and regression

Temporizing: The student delays in some Position for a year, exploring its implications or explicitly hesitating to take the next step.

Escape: The student exploits the opportunity for detachment offered by the structures of Positions 4 and 5 to deny responsibility through passive or opportunistic alienation.

Retreat: The student entrenches in the 'dualistic, absolutistic structures of Positions 2 or 3.' (Perry, 1970, pages 9-10.)

To get a clearer idea of Perry's scheme, it will be helpful to look at some of the interview data. The developmental trend can be understood best by considering the pole positions, 1 and 9, and also what Perry refers to as the 'pivotal' Position 5 where relativistic reasoning is consciously recognized and incorporated into academic activities.

Very few students in Perry's sample arrived at college with views as naive as Position 1 — a belief in the existence of clear-cut, right and wrong answers to all problems. Most students looked back to an earlier time when they had thought in this way. But there were a few students who exhibited characteristics of this attitude in their earliest experiences at university, perhaps as a regression created by the awe in which university lecturers are held in the public imagination.

'When I went to my first lecture, what the man said was just like God's word, you know, I believed it because he was a professor... and this was a respected position' (Perry, 1970, page 61.)

A similar sense of awe was reported in one of the Lancaster interviews by a first-year student.

'University confronts the student with a rigid intellectual authority: a body of teachers with a far greater degree of knowledge and expertise challenges and intimidates.'

Given this starting point it cannot be surprising that students do not readily challenge the information and explanations given to them. Yet lecturers expect students to adopt a relativistic stance, to interpret evidence, to compare theories critically, and to reach their own balanced conclusion. At first many students are confused by these demands which they may see as arbitrary rules in an artificial, academic game. Students are particularly prone to react to the dim recognition of relativism by a belief that 'anyone's opinion is as good as anyone elses' — not realizing the way evidence can be used to narrow the boundaries of uncertainty. During this stage of intellectual development, students are perhaps most likely to espouse strong beliefs in one or other of the political philosophies which have been put forward as panaceas of all social ills. As students develop a greater sensitivity to the implications of relativism, the pivotal Position 5 is reached. The recognition of the reality of ultimate uncertainty, while intellectually liberating, can also provoke an emotional crisis in the lives of some students. As the safe, certain answers to fundamental philosophical questions crumble, feelings of panic are not uncommon. This is when the student is most likely to exhibit the characteristic interruptions in intellectual development, described by Perry as 'temporizing' (playing for time), 'escape' (avoiding the demand for commitment to a particular world view) and 'retreat' (seeking the safety of absolutist views again).

Although many students do face an 'identity crisis' in resolving the implications of relativism, most of them come to see its positive advantages and to recognize that the lecturers' demands for relativistic reasoning are a necessary part of the university's attempt to develop the abilities to think critically, analytically and 'post-conventionally'. As one of Perry's students at Position 5 commented:

> 'The more I work here, the more I feel that what I'm trying to do is to become what you might call a detached observer of... any situation.... One who can... detach himself emotionally... and look at the various sides of a problem in an objective, empirical type of way — look at the pros and cons of a situation and then try to... analyze and formulate a judgement... bringing into consideration... what the other person would feel and why he would feel so' (page 126).

Perry argues that students should be expected to progress beyond this *recognition* of relativism, towards a readiness to take up a *commitment* to a personal world view which retains tolerance for different value positions. It is important to distinguish this commitment to a particular view from the earlier dogmatic assertion of perhaps the same view. In the later stages of intellectual and ethical development the student accepts the provisional, tentative nature of most knowledge in the humanities, but bases his commitment on a careful evaluation of evidence in relation to his own experience. He recognizes that other, even opposite, views are possible and that his commitment represents a *personal* decision and no more.

One student who was considered to have reached this stage of maturity (Position 9), reviewed his own intellectual development in these words:

> 'I used to think that you could evaluate decisions in terms of a right and a wrong.... And I think that lately I've been somehow rejecting this..., that you can't make right and wrong decisions. You simply make decisions, and whichever way you go there's not going to be any violent repercussion.'

This student went on to describe the toleration he had acquired for other people's committed views.

> 'Once you find out where you stand,... then you just have to say, if you're confronted with a person who doesn't do things like *you* do, 'Well, *he* has decided to do things like this — I *wouldn't*. I don't think it's *right'*. And yet you have to come back and say 'But this is only *subjective* — this is only my way of looking at things. I can't say, in absolute terms, that this is immoral' (pages 172-173).

STOP and THINK

- Can you think of examples from your own academic specialism of competing theories which necessitate a relativistic view in reconciling them?

- Can you think, from your own experience, of important decisions you have had to take which have involved contradictory possibilities? How did you resolve these contradictions?

- Perry seems to imply that *all* knowledge is uncertain. Do you accept this? Can you think of examples where definite right answers may exist? Would you expect differences between academic disciplines?

- Perry brings together intellectual and moral development into a single dimension. Would it have been better to keep these two aspects separate? Why?

- To what extent does Heath's description of the 'reasonable adventurer' tally with Perry's student at Position 9?

- How strong is the evidence presented by Heath and Perry? What additional evidence, if any, would you want before accepting these descriptions of the intellectual development of students?

Although for certain purposes it may be useful to separate intellectual and either ethical or emotional aspects of thinking or behaviour, any such separation is in Bronowski's terms 'a convenient simplification' and also 'a distortion' of reality. Where Perry's scheme is perhaps at its weakest is in the apparent reliance on the comments of students studying the humanities or social sciences. If the student is brought face-to-face in his academic studies with the fundamental dilemmas of humanity, the link between intellectual development in his work and general ethical development as a person may be clear to see. But would a scientist face the same situation? Does he have to make a commitment to a particular view, at least as an undergraduate? Perry stresses the emotional conflict which stems from a recognition of relativism and the restructuring of previous ideas and experience which this necessitates. But would a physicist feel the same *emotional* conflict in having to restructure ideas about, say, magnetism. New evidence may necessitate restructuring ideas, but it would not challenge personal values in the same way as in the humanities. There may still be emotional crises for the scientist, but these are perhaps more likely to be created by the rapid growth in complexity and abstractness in their curricula.

There is a close parallel between Perry's description of students at Position 9 and the characteristics of Heath's 'reasonable adventurer'. But Perry does not demonstrate any connection between his scheme and the quality of academic work, nor does he identify different routes by which students may approach relativistic reasoning — except in terms of various forms of delay. On the other hand he does provide a much more detailed description of the general developmental process occurring during higher education.

As in Heath's description of contrasting types of student, Perry's scheme relies heavily on intuitive impressions from interview transcripts. It is difficult to demonstrate the validity of the findings, except by appeal to the reader's own experiences of higher education. Perhaps what is most lacking in Perry's research is any indication of the way in which a student's every-day activities lead to intellectual development. For example, do different approaches to studying have an effect on the student's understanding and intellectual development?

Reading academic articles

The Swedish research carried out by Ference Marton at Gothenburg has looked closely at one particular every-day activity of students — how they tackle the task of reading academic articles or texts. This is where the learning experiment at the end of Part I links with the research evidence. Again the evidence relies on students' introspection and the intuitive analysis of interview data, but here the interviews were part of an experimental design which systematically examined different aspects of the problem.

The starting point was to discover what students learned when they were asked to read articles which, although new to them, were drawn from one of their academic subjects. The intention of the research was to relate qualitative differences in what students had learned to their approach to the task given to them. In the first experiment some 30 first-year women students were seen individually. Each was asked to read in her own time a 1500 word article, making notes if need be, and to be ready to answer questions on it afterwards. The questions took the form of an interview and started with a general question.

'Well now, perhaps you can tell me about what you've been reading?'

Students were encouraged, through neutral 'prompts' and 'probes' to recount what they had remembered. They were then asked more specific questions about sections of the text, followed by another general question, again supplemented by additional queries, to discover how they had interpreted the instruction to read the article, what their intention was in approaching the task (what they expected to get from the article), and how the experimental situation had affected them (were they very anxious, for example). Finally questions were asked about their *normal* approach to studying.

The interviews were tape-recorded and transcribed. Analysis of the lengthy transcripts was difficult and time-consuming. The interviews were initially read through as a whole and then responses to separate questions were examined. To begin with there was no imposed theoretical framework: the research workers expected explanatory concepts to emerge from the data. They looked for ways in which students exhibited consistencies in their individual approaches and for important differences between students. Eventually it was possible to describe regularities both in the qualitatively different outcomes of learning (what students were able to recall about the articles) and in their approaches to learning.

Levels of understanding

The problem with categorizing the outcome of learning is that it necessarily depends on the particular article read. But as long as the article is appropriately difficult and presents a clear argument supported by evidence, it is possible to use a general classificatory scheme for describing differences in the levels of understanding reached by students in these experiments. It is usually possible to identify *four* types of response (Fransson, 1977; Säljö, 1975).

A. *Conclusion-orientated, detailed*

    The student summarizes the author's main argument, shows how evidence is used to support the argument, and explains the thoughts and reflections used to reach personal understanding of that argument.

B. *Conclusion-orientated, mentioning*

    Again there is an adequate summary of the main argument, but the use of evidence or personal experience to support that argument is not made clear.

C. *Description, detailed*

The student gives an adequate list of the main points presented in the article, but fails to show how these are developed into an argument.

D. *Description, mentioning*

A few isolated points are made, some relevant, others irrelevant. At the bottom end of this category an impression of confusion and misunderstanding is given by the student's comments.

Appendix B illustrates these levels of understanding in terms of the Wertheimer article used in the learning experiment.

Approaches to learning and studying

The transcripts also provided a clear-cut distinction between students in their approaches to learning. Marton has described these differences as deep-level compared with surface-level processing (Marton and Säljö, 1976a). Some students described a *deep approach* to learning. They started with the intention of understanding the meaning of the article, questioned the author's arguments, and related them both to previous knowledge and to personal experience, and tried to determine the extent to which the author's conclusions seemed to be justified by the evidence presented. Other students seemed to rely almost exclusively on a *surface approach*. Their intent was to memorize those parts of the article which they considered to be important in view of the types of questions they anticipated afterwards. Their focus of attention was thus limited to the specific facts or pieces of disconnected information which was rote learned. These students also tended to be conscious of the conditions of the learning experiment and to be anxious about them.

In later experiments in Gothenburg (Fransson, 1977) and in Lancaster (Entwistle and Robinson, 1976; Entwistle *et al,* 1979a) it has been necessary to subdivide each of these approaches into two, depending on the degree of activity, attention, and involvement shown by the student. The four categories can be described as deep active; deep passive; surface active; and surface passive. Typical of the *deep active* approach was the following comment of a Lancaster student.

'I read more slowly than usual, knowing I'd have to answer questions, but I didn't speculate on what sort of questions they'd be. I was looking for the argument and whatever points were used to illustrate it. I could not avoid relating the article to other things I'd read, past experience, and associations, etc. My feelings about the issues raised made me hope he would present a more convincing argument than he did, so that I could formulate and adapt my ideas more closely, according to the reaction I felt to his argument.'

Another student with a deep active approach said:

'Whilst reading the article, I took great care in trying to understand what the author was getting at, looking out for arguments, and facts which backed up the arguments.... . I found myself continually relating the article to personal experience, and thus facilitated any understanding of it.... . The fact of being asked questions on it afterwards made my attention more intense.'

In contrast the next extract shows an example of a *deep passive* approach.

'I read it in a casual interested manner, not being influenced by the fact that I was to be questioned, mainly because I didn't expect the questionnaire to ask for any details of the article. Consequently, I read with impartial interest — extracting the underlying meaning but letting facts and examples go unheeded.'

The *surface active* approach can be illustrated by two more students from Lancaster.

'In reading the article I was looking out mainly for facts and examples. I read the article more carefully than I usually would, taking notes, knowing that I was to answer questions about it. I thought the questions would be about the facts in the article.... . This did influence the way I read; I tried to memorize names and figures quoted, etc.'
'I tried hard to concentrate — too hard — therefore my attention seemed to be on "concentration" rather than on reading, thinking, interpreting and remembering, something I find happening all the time I'm reading text-books.'

An interesting point about these two students is that both of them recognized that their approach had been rather ineffective. Later on in the questionnaire the first of these students added, when asked to comment on the adequacy of his answers.

'I feel that some of my answers are vague and need more detail.... . I made the mistake of trying to retain everything, rather than just the important features.'

Finally, the *surface passive* approach was described by Fransson (1977) from his transcripts.

'*Interviewer:* If I have understood what you have said you were not thinking of what the text was about... , but of memorizing the details,
Student: Yes, I did.
Interviewer: Would you like to tell me something about how you read? Did you read it as you read a newspaper, as you read a good book, or as you read course material?
Student: In the beginning I read very carefully, but after that I hurried through it. I lost interest, I didn't think about what I was reading.' (page 249).

STOP and THINK

- Look back at your answers to Questions 1 and 3 of the questionnaire on Wertheimer's article. Did you reach a deep level of understanding? If not, was it because you adopted a surface approach to reading?

- Did Question 2 in the questionnaire make you think you should have read the article in a different way?

- If you adopted a surface approach, why do you think you tackled the article in this way? Is it the way you normally read? Or was it to do with the type of questions you expected, or the way the instructions were worded?

- What implication does the distinction between deep and surface approach have for studying as a whole? Would a student adopting a deep approach necessarily be more successful?

Marton was initially interested in the relationship between the approach to learning and qualitatively different levels of outcome. He classified the approaches used by students as deep or surface if they showed at least *one* clear indication of either of these approaches. Where the approach was unclear, a third category was used. The relationship Marton established can be seen in Table 4.1.

Table 4.1. Relationship between level of outcome and approach to learning (From Marton and Säljö, 1976a)

Level of Understanding	Approach to Learning		
	Deep	Not Clear	Surface
High	9	6	1
Low	0	1	13

A deep approach is thus, at least in this small sample, clearly related to a deep level of understanding. Marton also found that the deep approach was associated with better recall of detail, particularly after a five week interval. Svensson (1977) has argued that this relationship should be thought of not simply as statistically significant, but as to some extent inevitable. While it is possible for a student adopting a deep approach to fail to reach a deep level of understanding through lack of previous knowledge or lack of attention or effort, it is impossible for a student adopting a surface approach ever to reach a deep level of understanding, as long as he persists with that approach. If deep understanding depends on being able to relate evidence and conclusion, a student's approach must necessarily have included this activity if deep understanding has been reached.

Factors affecting the approach to studying

The next step in the Gothenburg studies was to examine the link between a student's approach to learning in the experiment and the normal approach to studying, based on the final question in the interview. Svensson (1977) was able to detect deep and surface approaches to normal studying and to compare these both with the experiment and with the examination performance of the students at the end of their first year. Table 4.2 shows that there were close relationships in both these ways. 23 out of 30 students were categorized as taking the same approach in the experiment and in normal studying. Of the students classified as being deep in both, 90 per cent had passed in all their examinations, while only 23 per cent of the doubly 'surface' students had this level of success.

Table 4.2. Relationship between approaches to learning and studying, and examination performance (From Svensson, 1977)

Cognitive approach		Examination performance		Total
Experiment	Normal studies	Passed all	Some failure	
Surface	Surface	3	10	13
Deep	Deep	9	1	10
Deep	Surface	4	2	6
Surface	Deep	1	0	1

Svensson went on to show that students adopting a deep approach also tended to spend longer in studying. Again this relationship is almost inevitable. Students who study their subjects deeply are likely to find the material more interesting and easier to understand. Long hours of work become no hardship then. Students who adopt a surface approach are concentrating on an inappropriate technique of learning — rote memorization. It takes a long time to cover books in this way, and it is a tedious and unrewarding activity. Thus, eventually, students who persist with the surface approach are likely to do less and less work and eventually fail their examinations. Svensson (1977) reported the results of one examination in which 9 out of the 11 students adopting a deep approach to normal studying, also did three or more hours' independent work a day. All 9 passed the examination. 19 of the students adopted a surface approach and 8 of them, even in the first year, admitted to working less than three hours a day. All 8 failed the examination.

In another study Säljö was interested in whether students' approaches to studying were affected by the type of questions they were given in tests (Marton and Säljö, 1976b). He used two comparable groups of students and three separate passages of prose. The students were asked to read each of these passages, and after each passage they were asked a series of questions. After each of the first two passages one group was given questions designed to encourage a deep approach — attention to the underlying meaning. The other group was given specific factual questions, intended to induce a surface approach (very like Question 2 in the learning experiment). After the third passage both groups of students were given the same set of questions containing both 'deep' and 'surface' questions. Säljö found that students in the 'surface' group who had initially adopted a deep approach tended to have shifted to a surface approach by the time they read the third passage. Although there was an effect on students in the 'deep' group, most of the students who had initially adopted a surface approach apparently found it difficult to move fully to a deep approach. Instead they adopted what Säljö called a 'deep technified' approach, which can be compared with the 'deep passive' approach mentioned earlier. These students were content with summarizing the author's argument without examining it actively or in detail. Säljö's conclusion that it is much easier to induce a surface approach than a deep one could be important. We shall refer back to it in subsequent chapters.

Another of Marton's colleagues examined the level of understanding of basic concepts reached by first-year students of economics. Dahlgren (1978, Dahlgren and Marton, 1978) paid particular attention to the naive concepts, such as that of 'price', which students had at the beginning of the course and to the technical meanings they should have understood by the end. The layman's idea of price, for example, can be expressed as what an article is worth — what its value is. This implies that 'price' is a fixed attribute. The economist's concept of price brings in the idea of supply and demand. The price of an article depends not just on the production costs and raw materials, but also on its popularity in relation to its availability. Dahlgren was able to show that although the results of a first-year examination implied that students should have developed an understanding of the technical meaning of such basic concepts, in fact:

'if a more thorough understanding is required in order to answer a question, the number of acceptable answers is very low. . . . In many cases. . . it appeared that only a minority of students had apprehended basic concepts in economics in the way intended by teachers and text-book authors. Complex problems seem to be solved by application of memorized algorithmic procedures. . . . In order to cope with overwhelming curricula, the students probably have to abandon their ambitions to understand what they read about and instead direct efforts towards passing the examinations. . . (which reflect) the view that knowledge is a quantity, and that the higher the level of the educational system, the more pieces of knowledge should be taught per time unit' (Dahlgren, 1978, pages 1, 11, 12).

Putting together Säljö's findings and Dahlgren's comments we see that the type of question given in a test can induce a surface approach to studying and that the factual overburdening of syllabuses and examinations may be responsible for the low level of understanding exhibited by students when prevented from reproducing answers by well-rehearsed methods.

In many of the reports produced by the Gothenburg research group there is a repeated emphasis on the importance of both *content* and *context* in affecting a student's approach to learning. Thus it is not possible to characterize a *student* as 'deep', only an *approach* to a particular academic task. The effect of content and context is shown elegantly in the last of these studies. Fransson (1977) examined how levels of interest and anxiety affected students' approaches to learning. Level of interest was controlled by selecting an article concerning examination procedures in the education department. One group of students were in that department; another group, from a different department, were expected to have much less interest in the article. Two situations, or contexts for learning, were created. In one condition students were told that after reading the article, one student would be chosen to explain out loud what he had learnt. The explanation would be tape-recorded for subsequent detailed analysis. A large tape-recorder placed in a prominent position reinforced what was intended to be an anxiety-provoking situation. In the contrasting situation, attempts were made to create a relaxed friendly atmosphere.

It was clear from the results that both interest and anxiety did affect the students' approaches to learning, but not in a simple way. It was not so much that anxiety-provoking *situations* induced a surface approach to learning, but that students who *felt* the situation to be threatening, whether that was intended or not, were more likely to adopt a surface approach. This mechanical, rote learning approach was also related to lack of interest in the text and attempts to gear learning to anticipated questions. Thus where a student feels threatened, or under pressure to respond to examination demands on syllabuses which have little personal relevance, it is less likely that a deep approach will be adopted.

STOP and THINK

● To what extent do stressful conditions affect your own approach to learning?

● Would you say that the last examinations you took tended to make you adopt a surface approach to the course and to revising for the examinations?

● Would you consider the tendency to adopt a deep approach to studying to be a relatively consistent characteristic of a student? Or would the approach vary greatly from topic to topic and from course to course?

● Can you think of any other aspects of the learning situation or characteristics of the student which might affect the intention to adopt a deep approach?

● Does the intention to extract meaning from an article necessarily lead to a deep level of understanding?

● Could a deep approach sometimes involve rote learning? Could a surface approach lead to a deep level of understanding?

● Compare Marton's ideas on reading with those of Watts (pages 33-34).

In evaluating the Gothenburg studies again we must consider how clear-cut the findings are. The research approach is imaginative and combines the use of qualitative analyses of students' introspections with the systematic approach used in experimental methods of research. The studies have relied on small samples and the methods of analysis are subjective and time-consuming. The samples have also mainly been of first-year students drawn from departments in the social sciences. However, the fact that the same important explanatory concepts have been derived independently from the same data, and also repeatedly from different small samples, is reassuring. On the other hand all the studies have been carried out by the same research group with shared views about students' learning. There is, for example, a strong belief that the approach to learning should be explained in terms of the content and context of learning, not by reference to the characteristics of the learner. Thus consistent approaches to learning are not expected. Yet Svensson's study showed how closely linked was the approach to learning in the experiment and the general approach to studying. This implies a certain amount of consistency, at least among first-year undergraduates. Fransson's study also points up the importance of paying more attention to the students' characteristics. His results made much more sense when he analysed his data in terms of the individual's perception of the situation, rather than by reference to the situation itself.

What other characteristics of the student might affect the approach to learning? In Chapter 1 we identified intelligence, motivation and personality as important characteristics related to learning. To these should also be added prior knowledge. The processes of thinking which Marton uses to define the deep approach include the analytic skills which Dewey described, the cross-referencing of James, and the imaginative reconstruction of Wertheimer. In short, the deep approach demands an appropriate level of intelligence as a prerequisite. It presumably also requires sufficient prior knowledge and interpretative skill to make sense of the author's arguments and evidence. Fransson's study showed the effect of interest on the approach to learning. It is thus reasonable to expect the student's general level of motivation (his will to succeed, perhaps) to affect how he tackles academic tasks and learning experiments.

How might personality affect the approach to learning? We have already seen that anxiety inhibits a deep approach. It seems possible that other facets of personality might affect the way an individual tries to understand academic topics. Marton's description of the deep approach implies that there is one route towards understanding, yet we have already seen, in Heath's study, the possibility that students may develop intellectually towards the same goal along different paths.

In Chapters 6 and 7 we shall examine psychological evidence about the thought processes which may be involved in the deep and surface approaches to learning. From these discussions it will be argued that a deep approach to learning may involve rote learning on occasions, but memorization alone cannot lead to deep level understanding.

In the next chapter the two British studies on higher education will be described. These introduce the ideas of learning style and study strategies. But as a postscript to these very recent research findings it is salutory to recognize that the underlying ideas are by no means new. Both Watts and Dewey made comments which anticipated aspects of the findings and their educational implications. Watts contrasted readers who by study, meditation, and labour of the mind 'penetrate deeper into the themes of knowledge' with those whose 'eye slides over the pages, or the words slide over their ears, and vanish like a rhapsody of evening tales, or the shadow of a cloud flying over a green field in a summer's day.'

Dewey also contrasted depth with superficiality and linked this with implications for teaching

'The depth to which a sense of the problem, of the difficulty, sinks, determines the quality of thinking which follows; and any habit of teaching which encourages the pupil for the sake of... a display of memorized information to glide over the thin ice of genuine problems reverses the true method of mind training....

'In some lessons... the pupils are immersed in details, their minds are loaded with disconnected items... (and encouraged) to hurry on to a vague notion of the whole of which the fragmentary facts are portions, without any attempt to become conscious of *how* they are bound together as parts of this whole' (Dewey, 1910, pages 97, 37).

These early ideas may have some similarities with those gleaned from the Gothenburg research, but that is no criticism. The notion of deep and surface approaches to reading may not be entirely new, but the concepts have been worked out more precisely and supported with evidence which can be corroborated. In psychology, many of the useful 'new' theories are reworkings of earlier ideas. As Brown (1965) commented on a similarly persistent idea

'So good an idea is never invented. The antecedents of the authors we have discussed have also their antecedents, and in the end, we find, the idea seems always to have existed. What has changed is the precision of its statement and the implications which are developed' (page 604).

Summary

Studies by Heath and Perry suggest an important dimension of intellectual development among university students which is close to the idea of critical, or post-conventional, thinking described by lecturers as an all-important aim of higher education. Perry brings together intellectual and ethical development into the single developmental scheme which shows how students gradually begin to use contextual relativistic reasoning in their academic work, and then see the relevance of this way of thinking in their everyday life. Perry also points out the emotional conflicts which may be created by the recognition of a permeating uncertainty in explanations of human values and actions.

Heath's ideal type — the reasonable adventurer — has most of the qualities ascribed by Perry to the highest position in his scheme. But Heath also describes three contrasting personality types — non-committers, hustlers, and plungers. These students appear to move towards the same developmental ideal during their time at university, but they approach that goal along different paths. Heath's description of the ideal in relation to the contrasting starting-points suggests that students have to learn to become more aware of their own strengths and limitations, and to balance or integrate the different facets of their personality in a way which brings personal satisfaction and social acceptability.

While the American research concentrated on the general intellectual and personality development of students, the series of studies carried out by Marton and his colleagues in Sweden examined a specific academic task — reading an academic article or text-book. This research group has established that approaches to learning are closely linked to levels of understanding. The early studies used the simple distinction between deep and surface approaches to learning, but later work has used four categories.

Approach to learning	Level of understanding
Deep active	Understands author's meaning and shows how argument is supported by evidence
Deep passive	Mentions the main argument, but does not relate evidence to conclusion
Surface active	Describes the main points made without integrating them into an argument
Surface passive	Mentions a few isolated points or examples

The studies carried out at Gothenburg have shown.

1. The approach to normal studying is similar to the approach used in the experiment and that students using a deep approach work longer hours and are more successful than those adopting a surface approach.

2. Using different types of questions in a test can affect the approach to learning. Surface questions induce surface approaches, but deep questions lead to no more than a deep passive approach among students who previously adopted a surface approach.

3. Students taking economics showed less understanding of basic concepts than implied by the examination results. Overloading the factual content of syllabuses may prevent students using deep approaches to learning.

4. Anxiety and over-awareness of task demands (or examination requirements) are likely to push students towards surface approaches. Interest and relevance in subject content encourage a deep approach.

CHAPTER 5

Contrasting Styles of Learning

In Britain Gordon Pask in London and the author, while at Lancaster, have supervised extensive programmes of research concerned with how students learn. Pask and his colleagues have concentrated on experimental procedures often monitored by a computer, supplemented by the use of psychological tests and inventories. The Lancaster research groups started with an emphasis on large scale surveys, but greater use has subsequently been made of in-depth interviews.

Approaches to learning

The Lancaster research began in 1968 with attempts to identify lecturers' aims and objectives in higher education and to use measures of motivation and personality to predict students' degree results. The interviews with lecturers were mentioned in the previous chapter, while the prediction of academic achievement will be discussed in a later section. The most recent work (Entwistle *et al.*, 1979a) has been concerned with developing Marton's ideas on approaches to learning and relating these to the earlier work at Lancaster and to Pask's research.

As Marton had used only small groups of students and had not included scientists in his samples, the research group at Lancaster has been trying to develop a questionnaire variant of Marton's learning experiment which could be used with larger samples of students in different areas of study. Again the aim was to discover how the students read academic articles.

Three substantial articles (3200-4800 words) were chosen, all written for the 'intelligent layman' and making no specific demands on previous knowledge. Each article contained a clear argument supported by evidence. As in Marton's experiments students were asked to read an article in the normal way they would prepare for, say, a tutorial where they knew they would be asked questions. Following the procedure for the learning experiment on the Wertheimer extract at the end of Part I, students were then given an unrelated task which was designed to prevent memorization being transferred directly to answering questions. The questionnaire contained a general question about the meaning of the article, detailed specific questions, and a question about approach to learning. Finally there was a question about how familiar the students were with the ideas in the article. This rating was used as a crude index of previous knowledge.

This type of questionnaire data is inevitably weaker than that collected in interviews where there are opportunities to prompt or probe the student's understanding and memory. But it was still expected that similar patterns of relationship between approach and outcome would emerge. Level of general understanding was coded in terms of three overall impression ratings of the students answers to the first question (integration or imposing personal meaning, knowledge of main aspects covered, and understanding of the argument). The answers to the specific questions produced two scores in terms of essential points and incidental facts. The approach to learning was again assessed by overall impression ratings of three aspects of the deep approach (looking for meaning, using previous experience, and relating facts to conclusion) and of the surface approach (looking for facts, unease about the situation and likely outcome of learning, and efforts to memorize). (Further details of this study can be found in Entwistle *et al*, 1979a).

The clearest pattern of results came from the responses of 96 science students. Similar, but less clear-cut findings were reported from two other groups of students. The analysis involved looking at the interrelationships between every index of both approach and outcome. To try to identify underlying *patterns* of relationship, factor analysis was used. This technique brings together groups of variables which interrelate most closely. Each group is replaced by a *factor* which summarizes what is common to the contributory variables.

Table 5.1 shows the results of this analysis. The individual indices are listed and each column of figures describes a separate factor. Each figure represents a factor loading (rather like a correlation coefficient), which indicates how large a contribution that variable has made to the factor. Thus the meaning of each factor can be built up from the variables having the largest loadings on that factor. Factor I has its highest loading (.73) on knowledge of essential points, closely followed by all three ratings of the level of understanding. The positive but lower loadings on 'looking for meaning' and 'using previous experience' show that Factor I is made up of components of both deep outcome and deep approach. Factor II has its highest loadings on knowledge of essential points, relating facts to conclusion, and previous knowledge (familiarity). Factor III brings together two aspects of the surface approach (memorization and looking for information) and shows that high ratings on these are associated with low ratings (negative factor loadings) on both the first two indices of a deep approach and all the indices of a deep level of outcome.

These results provide useful support for Marton's main findings. Factors I and III show that levels of understanding are related to approaches. There may, however, be an important distinction between Factor I and II, perhaps

Table 5.1. Factor analysis of questionnaire responses in Lancaster learning experiment (adapted from Entwistle *et al.*, 1979a)

General dimension	Specific index	Factor loadings		
		I	II	III
Level of understanding	Integration (personal meaning)	61		−43
	Knowledge of main points	52		−54
	General understanding	64		−43
Knowledge of details	Essential points	73	48	
	Incidental facts	43		
Previous knowledge	Familiarity with content area		32	
Deep approach	Looking for meaning	26		−56
	Using previous experience	37	30	−51
	Relating facts and conclusion		40	
Surface approach	Looking for facts		48	
	Unease about situation	−32		
	Efforts to memorize			68

Decimal points omitted
Loadings of less than |0.25| have been omitted.

suggesting the need for considering *three* types of deep approach. The deep passive approach is similar to Factor I — understanding is sought without paying sufficient attention to detailed evidence. Factor II may represent either an excessive reliance on previous knowledge or an orientation towards the facts and logical arguments to the exclusion of the author's overall message. This orientation towards the essential points still involves an attempt to understand, in contrast to Factor III which is clearly the unsuccessful reliance on memorization in trying to remember the main points. What was previously described as a 'deep active' approach did not come out as a distinct factor but appears to represent the successful marrying of the two other deep approaches (Factors I and II). Pask's research would, as we shall see, lead us to expect these two different approaches *and* their combination into the most effective approach of all.

Holist and serialist strategies

Pask and his colleagues have carried out several series of experiments in trying to discover important differences between students in their learning strategies. Marton deliberately left his instruction about reading the article vague. The students had to decide for themselves whether reading for understanding or rote memorization would be the best way of answering the subsequent questions about the article. Through this ambiguity it was possible to demonstrate the contrasting approaches to learning that students considered appropriate for this academic task. In most of Pask's experiments, however, the students are *required* to reach a deep level of understanding, and Pask is interested in the strategies they use in trying to carry out this instruction.

In the first series of experiments reported by Pask (Pask and Scott, 1972) he asked students to try to establish for themselves the principles of classification underlying the division of two imaginary species of Martian animals — the Clobbits and the Gandlemullers — into a series of sub-species. In the first experiment, information about Clobbits was provided in the form of 50 cards. These were placed face down in ten columns (each column representing a separate subspecies). The five rows contained separate categories of information about the ten subspecies (e.g. habitat, physical characteristics, drawings of animals, etc.) Students could also write their own information cards if they found this helpful.

Students were asked to turn over the cards to obtain the information they wanted. They were told to turn the cards over one at a time and to give a reason for the particular card they had chosen. Each reason amounted to a hypothesis about the nature of the classification system which the information on the card was expected to test. A record was kept of the order in which the cards were used and also of the hypothesis given at each step. Finally students were required to 'teach-back' to the experimenter what they had learned about these Martian animals.

Pask discovered interesting differences both in the types of hypothesis used by students and in the ways in which they explained the classification schemes. Some students concentrated on a step-by-step strategy in which they used simple hypotheses about, say, a single property of the animals

'Do Gandlemullers have sprongs?'

This strategy was described as *serialist,* indicating the linear progression from one hypothesis to the next. Other students used more complex hypotheses which combined several properties simultaneously.

'Are there more kinds of Gandlers with mounds (dorsal or cranial) than Plongers?'

This strategy was described as *holist,* indicating a more global approach to problem solving. Pask also identified an additional type of holist, *the redundant holist,* who depended on individualistic ways of discriminating between the sub-species.

'The ones that were discovered first are gentle; the other kinds, the aggressive beasts were found later, well they are the ones with less mounds.'

The important aspect of the redundant holist is that imaginary descriptive terms are used. In the above example, there was nothing in the information given to the student to suggest either an order of discovery or 'temperamental' differences between the sub-species. What seems to happen is that the redundant holist personalizes learning. The order of discovery is probably the order in which he turned up the cards, while an impression of gentleness or aggressiveness was perhaps created by the drawings. In the end the redundant holists understood the principles of classification just as well as the holists or serialists, but they relied on personal (redundant) 'props' to aid that understanding.

When students were asked to 'teach-back' what they had learned, very similar differences were found between the two main types. The serialists described the principles of classification in a straightforward logical manner keeping to the bare essentials. For example,

'Zoologists have classified the Gandlemuller on the basis of physical characteristics. The three main types are Gandlers, Plongers, and Gandleplongers. Gandlers have no sprongs. Plongers have two sprongs. Gandleplongers have one sprong. There are four subspecies of Gandler: M1, M2, B1, and B2. The M's have one body, the B's have two bodies. The M1 and B1 have a single cranial mound. The M2 and B2 have a double cranial mound... etc.'

In contrast a redundant holist set about the description in a very different way.

'I want to tell you about a funny Martian animal which has been recently discovered and classified by scientists conducting surveys. They are funny sluglike things with various protuberances. These animals are called Gandlemullers, because they churn about in the swamps near the Equator and Gandle is the Martian for swampmud, hence the swampmudmiller (Müller is German for miller). These things churn through the mud eating it by some curious process which means they eat and excrete at the same time.'

Only after a great deal of redundant elaboration does this holist describe the essential properties of the various sub-species, and even then they are presented in an idiosyncratic order. It is perhaps unfair to describe the holist as illogical; it may be that the order follows a different set of rules. There may well be understandable principles in his ordering of the information, if so, they seem to be more like those used by novelists or journalists than by scientists. The holist starts with what seems to be the most interesting or striking point and includes a good deal of human or personal interest. The holist thrives on anecdote, illustration, and analogy, while the serialist uses these sparingly, if at all.

In later series of experiments Pask and his colleagues have been able to extend the descriptions of holists and serialists. For example, holists tend to look further ahead when asked to work their way through a hierarchy of sub-topics towards an understanding of the topic as a whole (Pask, 1976b). They also have a wide focus of attention, bringing together several sub-topics, right from the start (Robertson, 1977). Where students are given a choice between a series of abstract topics and an exactly parallel series of topics which are drawn from the 'real world', serialists work their way step-by-step´through *either* the abstract topics *or* the real world topics, bringing them together only when forced to do so to achieve overall understanding of the main topic. The holists in contrast move from real world to abstract and back again, examining the analogies between the two sets of topics as well. In the end both groups of students can reach the same level of understanding, but their ways of reaching that understanding are very different. The serialists apparently put much more emphasis on the separate topics and the logical sequences connecting them, forming an overall picture of what is being learned only rather late in the process. The holists try to build up that overall picture, as a guide to learning, right from the start and see where the details fit into that picture much later on.

STOP and THINK

- Can you see any links between Pask's descriptions of holists and serialists and (a) Heath's 'plungers' and 'non-committers'; or (b) the two different deep approaches suggested by the factor analysis on page 89.

- Pask insisted, in these early experiments, that all the students reached a deep level of understanding. If he hadn't, what sort of mistakes do you think holists and serialists would make?

- If students differ in the extent to which they look for logical structure·or a wide range of illustrations and practical examples, what implications can you see for teaching?

Pathologies of learning

Pask (1976a) has developed what he calls a conversational theory of learning which describes how a student works his way towards a full understanding of a topic by questioning, or trying out his ideas on, either a teacher or an 'alter-ego', another part of the mind which monitors and interacts with the learning process. Pask argues that a full understanding occurs only when the student can explain the topic by reconstructing it, and can also demonstrate that understanding by applying the principles learned to an entirely new situation. The theory also indicates that appropriate analogies are as important a part of understanding and 'teach-back', as the recognition of the logical steps and processes through which an understanding of the topic is built up. Pask argues that the two major pathologies commonly found in learning are the failure to examine the logical structure or the evidence in sufficient detail, and the failure to make use of appropriate analogies. The link between the holist and serialist strategies and learning pathologies, at least within Pask's theory, should now become clear.

The holist strategy involves looking at the whole area being learned, taking a broad perspective, seeking interconnection with other topics and making use of personal and idiosyncratic analogies. The examination of the logical structure and of the supportive evidence comes later when understanding is demanded, but left to himself the holist is likely to put off what he may see as the more boring parts of learning. This description could have a familiar ring to it; remember Heath's descriptions of the 'plunger' (Z).

'His thoughts zip from one idea to another without apparent connection;... characteristically (he) fails to clothe his ideas in a framework that would make sense to others... He may beg permission to go ahead with a project, ... only to lose interest later, particularly if hard uninteresting work looms....'

Pask describes as *globetrotting* the tendency of the holist to make inappropriate or vacuous analogies. This pathology might also take the form of an over-readiness to generalize from insufficient evidence to form hasty, personal judgements.

The serialist falls into the opposite trap. He fails to make use of valid and important analogies and may not build up for himself any overall map to see how the various elements of the topic interrelate and how the topic fits into the subject area in general. Pask calls this pathology *improvidence*.

Styles of learning

The strategies of learning described so far might be no more than reactions to a single task (the Clobbits) or to a particular piece of apparatus which controls learning in a somewhat atypical way. Pask accepts that his early experiments did artificially accentuate differences between students, but he argues that the holist and serialist strategies are manifestations of important underlying differences in the way people think and tackle problems. He argues that some students are disposed to act 'like holists' whenever they are given that opportunity, whereas others behave 'like serialists'. The *general tendency* to adopt a particular strategy is referred to as a *learning style*. The 'holist like' style is called *comprehension learning* which involves 'building descriptions of what is known'. The 'serialist like' style is called *operation learning,* which is 'the facet of the learning process concerned with mastering procedural details'. Pask (personal communication) has likened these two aspects of thinking to the way an architect designs a building. He has to build up the overall plan (description building) and also to work out the detailed processes, and the logistics of those processes, (operation and procedure building) whereby the plan can be converted into an actual building. Any weakness either in the plan, or in the description of the operations and procedures which will satisfy the implicit demands of that plan, will prevent the building being satisfactorily completed (understanding being reached).

Students who show sufficient consistent bias in their learning strategies to be described as 'comprehension learners' or 'operation learners' are likely to show equally consistent pathologies of learning. But there are other students who are readily able to adapt their learning strategy to the requirements of the particular task, emphasizing either comprehension learning or operation learning as appropriate, and using both in tandem wherever possible. Pask describes these students as having a 'versatile' style of learning.

> 'A student who is *versatile* is not prone to vacuous globetrotting; he does indeed build up descriptions of what may be known by a rich use of analogical reasoning, but subjects the hypotheses to test and operationally verifies the validity of an analogy and the limits of its applicability' (Pask *et al.*, 1977, page 68).

STOP and THINK

● Look back at Heath's types — X, Y, Z and A. Does the versatile student fit any of these?

● Look back at the discussion of Table 5.1. Is there a particular approach to learning which fits Pask's description of a versatile style?

● There is a danger in making these comparisons. Can you see it?

Pask's description seems to echo Heath's ideal type — the reasonable adventurer (A). It is worth repeating part of his character sketch of such students.

> 'We see... in A the combination of two mental attitudes: the curious and the critical. They do not occur simultaneously but in alternation. A at times is a 'believer' but at other times he is a 'skeptic'. The less effective personalities may show tendencies toward one attitude or the other but may not experience the full reach of either.'

The factor analysis of the Lancaster data tentatively identified Factor I as understanding 'sought without paying sufficient attention to detail', Factor II as possibly showing 'an orientation towards the facts and details to the exclusion of the author's overall message', and the 'deep active' approach as possibly the successful marrying of Factor I and Factor II.

The most obvious danger in making these comparisons is that we are arguing only by verbal similarity of description. To be sure of these connections we should have to interview students and categorize them in terms of Heath's types, ask the same students to do the learning experiment and use Marton's criteria to indicate deep and surface approaches. Only by showing empirical evidence of relationships could we avoid the danger of 'globe-trotting' into seeing tempting, but only superficially similar, links between concepts. Another danger is that the research reported here is not carried out in isolation. Thus, for example, the interpretation of the factors in the Lancaster study could have been influenced, consciously or unconsciously, by Pask's ideas about learning styles. Of course, factor analysis cannot create connections which do not occur in the data, but the research worker can put more or less stress on a particular aspect of his findings.

Matching styles of learning and teaching

Perhaps one of the most important of Pask's experiments was his investigation of the effects of matching and mismatching learning materials with students' learning strategies. On the basis of the Clobbit experiment students were identified as having adopted holist or serialist strategies. Pask then asked the students to work through a set of programmed learning materials and take a test to discover how much they had learned. There were two versions of this material. One version was designed to suit the comprehension learner, being rich in analogy and illustration. The other was presented in a logical, step-by-step sequence without 'enrichment'. Students were assigned either to a matched or a mismatched condition (holist with holist material; holist with serialist material; etc.). The results were dramatic, although based on small samples; there was little overlap in the scores of the matched and mismatched groups. The students in the matched conditions were able to answer most of the questions about what they had learned, whereas the other students generally fell below half marks.

The implication for education is presumably that teachers need to provide opportunities for students to learn in a way which suits their preferred style of learning. If teachers adopt too extreme a method of teaching, perhaps reflecting their own learning style, one group of students will find the approach alien to their way of learning. But do teachers adopt extreme approaches which might lead to severe mismatching? In Pask's experiment the learning materials were deliberately designed to create an extreme contrast in presentation. There is no direct evidence of the extent to which teachers adopt teaching styles akin to comprehension or operation learning, but later on we shall come to evidence drawn from primary education that contrasting teaching methods are differentially effective for pupils with different personality characteristics. Here we have to rely on personal experience in higher education. Some lecturers have a strong belief in the efficacy of small-group discussion classes; others are equally convinced of the superiority of lectures. And even among lecturers there seem to be distinct styles of lecturing which recognizably exhibit aspects of globetrotting or improvidence. In the absence of research evidence, we shall have to rely on anecdote to indicate the differences in presentation which might be analogous to Pask's styles. Here is a novelist's description of two contrasting chemistry lecturers:

'He began lecturing in the dry and level way he reserved for these occasions. "Today we begin with the consideration of several important groups characterized by the presence of the molecules of a carbon and oxygen connected by a double bond. This is called a carbonyl group". He drew the carbonyl group on the board. His voice sounded unshaken in his own ears, normal, unaffected by events (a student's death). For once he was thankful for his own peculiar lecturing style which deliberately suppressed the intrusion of his own personality... .

'It was the antithesis, for instance, of the style affected by Merrill Foster, the other organic chemist in the department... . Foster lectured in a bright and deliberately colloquial manner which pleased some students but also weakened discipline. Foster referred to the useless material prepared by side reactions in the course or synthesis as "junk" or "crud". He never *added* pyridine; he always gave a reaction a "squirt of pyridine"' (Asimov, 1968, pages 44-46).

As this particular novelist has been a university lecturer, these descriptions are presumably 'drawn from life'. As evidence for the existence of lecturing styles which parallel learning styles it is, of course, very weak. But combined with Pask's teach-back protocols from students, and evidence on personality and cognitive style which will be introduced in Chapter 10, it seems probable that there is sufficient variation in the way lecturers choose to teach, to create problems for students with mismatching learning styles.

If there are parallels in teaching to the characteristic pathologies of learning, there should also be versatile teachers, reasonable adventurers who can communicate their curiosity and criticism to students. Pask also has ideas on the way knowledge can be structured to facilitate the learning of *all* students, but discussion of these aspects of his work will be delayed until the concluding section of the book (Part IV).

Personality, motivation, and degree results

Heath relied on intuition to identify three distinctive personality types — the non-committer, the hustler and the plunger. As we have seen, there seem to be some conceptual parallels between his description of the plunger and Pask's 'redundant holist'. It could be that the 'serialist' is emotionally irresponsive, but there is no clear match with either the non-committer or the hustler. In any case, Pask's research is not the ideal source of parallels: he was not concerned with descriptions of personality. A more fruitful source of corroborative evidence will be found in the early phases of the research at Lancaster — the attempts to predict degree results from characteristics of students measured during their first year at university. The main research question being posed at that time was: What factors are associated with high or low levels of academic performance? Do students in different subject areas exhibit different personality characteristics?

To investigate these questions a large scale follow-up survey was conducted. Information was collected over a 3-4 year period on 1,087 students from seven universities. Six distinct subject areas and ten specialist disciplines were represented in the sample. The information collected included academic record at school, a test of academic aptitude, scales of personality and social attitudes, a questionnaire to measure values, an inventory covering motivation and study methods, and a self-rating scale. (Detailed descriptions can be found in Entwistle and Wilson, 1977, chapters 8-11.)

The analyses of these data were designed to identify factors associated with academic success. Simple correlations with degree performance showed no close relationships, except between 'A' level grades and degree performance in the science faculties. In other faculties the measures of motivation and study habits were as good predictors as 'A' level grades — but both sets of correlations were rather low. Using factor analysis three main factors emerged. One, as might be expected, contrasted arts and science specialisms. Of the other two, one contrasted motivation and ambition at one pole with neuroticism and radicalism at the other, while the second factor contrasted hard-work and good 'A' level grades with extraversion and being active in societies. Figure 5.1 shows how two groups of variables distinguished on the one hand between good degree results and poor results, and on the other hand between arts and science orientations.

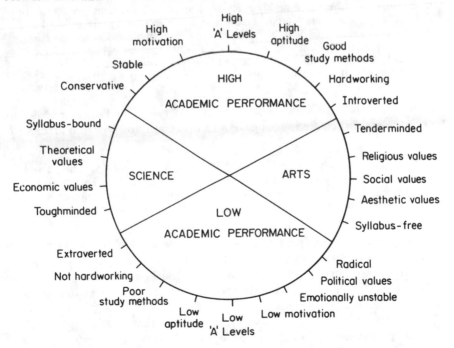

Figure 5.1 Relationship between students' characteristics, faculty membership, and level of academic performance (Adapted from Entwistle and Wilson, 1977, page 148)

There was one interesting variation in this overall pattern. Although motivation and ambition were associated with emotional stability (low neuroticism) for men, motivation was linked with high neuroticism among the women. This was the first hint that we should distinguish between at least two different kinds of motivation.

One of the disadvantages of using factor analysis is that it creates the impression that there is only one path towards academic excellence. It identifies a set of variables which help to predict success, but does not indicate whether certain combinations of these variables might be particularly efficacious. Another way of examining the data (cluster analysis) provided evidence for the existence of different 'types' of successful student — groups of students who had very similar profiles of scores. Cluster analysis thus provides an objective analytic procedure to detect the sort of personality types that Heath reported from his intuitive analysis of interview data. Some of the clusters could also be recognized when interviewing students at Lancaster. Combining the two types of analysis strengthens the likelihood that important, meaningful descriptions of students have been obtained. In the cluster analyses three distinct groups of students who had above-average degree results were identified.

'Cluster 1 contained students with high 'A' level grades who were satisfied with their courses... they were highly motivated and had good study methods. In personality they were emotionally stable and had high scores on theoretical and economic values, linked with a tendency towards tough-minded conservatism. This combination of characteristics suggests a rather cold and ruthless individual, governed by rationality and spurred on by competition to repeated demonstrations of intellectual mastery' (Entwistle and Wilson, 1977, page 129).

These students were also encountered in interviews at Lancaster,* where their confident, articulate replies gave an impression not far from arrogance.

'I *enjoy* doing exams. I think it is the *challenge*. You've got 3 or 4 hours and, somehow or other, you've got to get out of yourself enough of a pattern to knit something up, to knit 3 or 4 garments out of a tangle of wool. It's fun, when you *know* enough to *make* it fun' (Entwistle *et al*, 1974, pages 387-8).

There is clear evidence from both the cluster analysis and the interviews that this group has a type of motivation which we might call 'hope for success'. Their surface confidence and determination is markedly similar to the group Heath called the 'hustlers', but the Lancaster students were much more successful than those in Heath's study.

The second group of students, although still reaching a high level of academic performance, had almost an opposite type of personality.

---

*These interviews were conducted by Jennifer Thompson.

'The main defining features of (this group) were high scores on neuroticism and syllabus-boundness, and rather low scores on both extraversion and motivation. Their self-ratings were uniformly negative. They saw themselves as neither likeable nor self-confident. They had no active social life and had few aesthetic interests.... It is tempting to see these students as motivated mainly by "fear of failure" ' (Entwistle and Wilson, 1977, page 130).

In the interviews these students seemed to have unrealistically pessimistic views of their own ability: they seemed to be haunted by the inevitability of failure. Assessment requirements and the 'demands' of lecturers to prepare work for tutorials loomed large in their perceptions of university. When pressed they would admit that their course work grades were good, but they insisted that when it came to the final examinations they would do badly.

'As soon as I look at the paper, I panic and think I can't do anything. Eventually, I get my nerve back and regain control. Occasionally, though, perhaps two or three times throughout the exam, I go all hot, and think I've got it all wrong. And one bad question *really* mucks me up' (Entwistle *et al.*, 1974, page 390).

These students were certainly dominated by course requirements (syllabus-bound) and worked long hours. However, on the inventory they had rather low scores on both motivation and study methods. In retrospect it became clear that the inventory measured only 'hope for success' and conventionally 'good' study methods. These students were driven by anxiety rather than self-confidence, and had unconventional, though effective, approaches to studying.

The final group of successful students were less distinctive, and did not stand out in the interviews. These students were found mainly in arts and social science faculties. They had high verbal aptitude scores combined with high motivation, good study methods and long hours of study. In contrast to the anxious students, this group were syllabus-free and had high aesthetic values and radical attitudes. Many of these students also came from 'professional' home backgrounds.

The student types identified in the Lancaster study contained a similar variety of groups of students with average and below average degree results. But when an overall summary was attempted, four main types were selected — stable and motivated; anxious, fear of failure; extraverted, syllabus-free; and idle and unmotivated. There is by no means an exact correspondence between these types and those identified by Heath. But remember there were no girls in his sample, the college was highly prestigious, and the study was conducted in the 1950s. Exact correspondence could not be expected. Nevertheless there is some apparent overlap between the stable, motivated, hope for success group and Heath's hustlers, and between the extraverted, syllabus-free cluster and the plungers. Although the similarities are not altogether convincing, both studies do reinforce the important point that students of different personality types may pursue the same academic goals in very different ways.

Psychological evidence introduced in Part III will provide a clearer indication of which aspects of personality are most likely to affect students' approaches to learning. For the moment it is sufficient to highlight the explanatory value of holist and serialist styles of learning, and to point up the distinction between 'hope for success' and 'fear of failure' as contrasting modes of motivation.

Dimensions of study strategy

The work at Lancaster made clear that our initial attempts to describe motivation and study methods did not allow for the variety of approaches used by students. A new inventory has since been developed which distinguishes different forms of motivation and incorporates the newer dimensions of study strategy. It includes the important concepts described by Marton and Pask and also draws on the work of an Australian, John Biggs, who has also been seeking to identify dimensions which describe aspects of study strategy (Biggs, 1976, 1978, 1979).

The Lancaster inventory was initially developed without reference to Bigg's work, but in its later stages it incorporated modified versions of some of his items and scales. The Lancaster inventory is still in the process of further development, but a recent version contained the fifteen sub-scales shown in Table 5.2.

Using a sample of 767 first year (second term) students from nine departments in three British universities, factor analysis revealed three main dimensions of study strategies. The factor loadings, shown in Table 5.3, indicate that Factor I links the deep approach to intrinsic motivation, and also to comprehension learning and syllabus-freedom (the negative loading on

Table 5.3 Factor loadings of study strategy scales (From Entwistle *et al.*, 1979b)

	I	II	III	IV
Deep approach	62		33	
Comprehension learning	73			
Intrinsic motivation	54		47	
Internality	61			
Openness	50			
Surface approach		67		
Operation learning		67		
Extrinsic motivation		61		
Fear of failure		36		−32
Syllabus-boundness	−41	50		
Strategic approach		41		
Organized study methods			64	
Achievement motivation		36	45	
Disillusioned attitudes			−55	
Sociability				58

Table 5.2. Sub-scales in the Lancaster Inventory of Study Strategies

Scale	Description	Origin
Organized study methods	Consistent work, well-organized and regular	Lancaster 1[a]
Achievement motivation	Competitive approach equivalent to the 'hope for success' found in cluster analyses and interviews	Lancaster 1
Fear of failure	Motivation fed by anxiety, as found in cluster analyses and interviews	Lancaster 1
Disillusioned attitudes to study	Showing little involvement in work; cynical and disenchanted with their university experience	Lancaster 1
Syllabus-boundness	Relies on clear instructions, structure and defined syllabus to guide studying	Parlett (1970) as modified in Lancaster 1
Sociability	Involvement in social life at university — interest in people	Lancaster 1
Deep approach	Looks for meaning; interacts actively; links with real life	Marton
Surface approach	Relies on rote learning; conscious of exam demands	Marton
Comprehension learning	Uses analogies in building up descriptions of topics, emphasizing the outlines of ideas and inter-connections	Pask
Operation learning	Relies on step-by-step, logical approach emphasizing factual details	Pask
Strategic approach	Tries to obtain cues from lecturers or previous papers about likely examination questions; tries to impress staff — likes to be noticed	Miller and Parlett (1974) modified by Ramsden (1979)
Intrinsic motivation	Interested in learning for its own sake	Biggs
Extrinsic motivation	Sees university as a way of obtaining necessary qualifications	Biggs
Internality	Uses internal standards of truth	Biggs
Openness	Sees university as place where values are questioned	Biggs

[a] The first Lancaster inventory of motivation and study methods.

syllabus-boundness). Factor II brings together the surface approach with extrinsic motivation, syllabus-boundness, the strategic approach, and to a lesser extent fear of failure and achievement motivation. Factor II also has a high loading on operation learning. Factor III has its highest loadings on organized study methods and positive attitudes to studying (negative loading on disillusioned attitudes), but it also contains elements of achievement motivation (hope for success), intrinsic motivation and, to a lesser extent, deep approach.

These three factors are closely similar to results reported by Biggs (1978, 1979). There seem to be three main orientations towards studying, three intentions which are related to underlying motives and which affect the strategies adopted. Biggs (1978, page 276) suggested a framework for understanding the various dimensions of study processes which, in an adapted form, is shown below.

Orientation	Value	Motive	Strategy
Personal meaning (Factor I)	Personal development as overall goal of education	Intrinsic — interest in what is being learned	Work satisfying only if personal meaning established by relating new information to existing knowledge
Reproducing (Factor II)	Vocational preparation as main purpose of university	Extrinsic — need for qualifications or fear of failure	Limit activities to those demanded (syllabus-bound) Learn by rote
Achieving (Factor III)	University as a game providing competition and opportunities to show excellence	Achievement — need for success	Structuring, organizing work, meets deadlines, plays the game (to win)

The results from the Lancaster factor analysis fit closely into this framework, making the evidence for this description of study processes very strong. Biggs interpreted his factors without having heard of Marton's work in Sweden. Also his analysis differed from that at Lancaster in using an inventory developed from his own previous work and in having samples drawn from Australian universities. The agreement between analysis in three different countries is remarkably close. Certainly the distinction between deep and surface processes can be considered to be firmly established as a useful way of describing approaches to studying.

Perhaps the main difference between the Lancaster results and those from Sweden and Australia is the attempt to include stylistic differences in the dimensions of studying. This factor analysis did not, in fact, produce a separate factor of comprehension versus operation styles of learning.

Comprehension learning went with the deep approach, and operation with the surface approach. Yet conceptually there do seem to be differences and the most recent results from Lancaster support this separation. We shall come back to this distinction between approach and style shortly.

STOP and THINK

● Look back at the inventory which you completed as part of the learning experiment and score it using the instructions in Appendix A.

● Try to relate the scales there to the dimensions of studying described above. Look back at the individual items in the inventory to see how they build up the meaning of each of the scales.

● To what extent do your scores, in relation to the norms provided, make sense to you in terms of your own experience? Do they seem to be a fair description of your approaches to studying — or have important aspects been missed out?

The meaning of the scales in the short inventory used in the learning experiment is shown below

A Achieving orientation — contains items relating to organized study methods and competitiveness

B Reproducing orientation — relates to syllabus-boundness, attempts to memorize the extrinsic motivation

C Comprehension learning — attempts to relate ideas to real life, to map-out subject areas.

D Meaning orientation — looking for meaning, motivated by interest in topics and courses

E Operation learning — cautious in using evidence, interest in logical problems and rationality

F Improvidence — emphasis on facts and details, difficulty in building up overall picture

G Globetrotting — rather superficial approach, individualistic methods of organising knowledge, tendency to jump prematurely to conclusions or to seek generalizations without sufficient evidence.

The main limitation in this way of describing studying is that it concentrates exclusively on the characteristics of the individual. By relying on general questions about typical approaches to studying, it overlooks the importance of the content and context of learning. The approach adopted by a student depends not just on his own attitudes, habits, abilities and personality, but also on the demands made by the staff or the institution. Students are rarely free to learn what they like, when they like, or how they like. Course syllabuses, teaching, and assessment all place constraints on the students, constraints which may differ from department to department, course to course, and even assignment to assignment. We must thus try to broaden our view of studying to incorporate aspects of the social setting in which learning takes place. Research on the context of learning has to rely even more on qualitative analyses of students' own descriptions of their experiences.

The context of learning

Interviews have recently been carried out by Paul Ramsden (1979) at Lancaster which have systematically explored students' perceptions of the departments in which they work. Analysis of students' comments enabled a questionnaire to be developed which provides descriptions of departments in terms of the students' experiences. Sub-scales in this questionnaire measure relationship with students, commitment to teaching, formal teaching methods, vocational relevance, workload, clear goals and standards, freedom in learning, and social climate. Even on the relatively small number of departments covered so far it is clear that there are large differences between departments on many of these scales. Some of the differences may be obvious, reflecting well-known contrasts between arts and science departments. But other differences are more interesting: departments from the same faculty can be seen in very different ways by their students. And in the interviews some of the students make clear that their approaches to learning are very much affected by their perceptions of their departments. Methods of assessment perhaps have the greatest effect on students' study strategies, as Säljö's work predicts. For example a student in a department which used periodic short-answer tests as part of the assessment procedure commented

'I hate to say it, but what you've got to do is have a list of the "facts"; you write down ten important points and memorize those, then you'll do all right in the test... if you can give a bit of factual information — so and so did that, and concluded that —for two sides of writing, then you'll get a good mark'.

Also important to most students are the attitudes and enthusiasms of the staff.

'I find that the courses I do most work on are the courses where I get on with the tutors best and enjoy the seminars, because... a tutor can put you off the subject.. some of them don't like students, so they're not interested in what students say.... .

If the (tutors) have enthusiasm, then they really fire their own students with the subject, and the students really pick it up.... . I'm really good at and enjoy (one particular course), but that's only because a particular tutor I've had has been so enthusiastic that he's given me an enthusiasm for it.... .'

The student's comments also reinforced Marton's argument that we should not expect students consistently to adopt either deep or surface approaches towards their academic work. For example, one student who had described a deep approach to writing essays in one subject, contrasted her approach to another subject which she found confusing. In that subject

> 'When it comes to writing essays, because I'm not very interested in it, I tend to rush through the books I'm reading for the essays, so I don't really understand it when I've finished reading. And because there's such a lot of information I think you can either oversimplify or get into too much detail. I think I tend to oversimplify.'

This student appears to be recognizing from her own experience the pathologies of globetrotting and improvidence, besides emphasizing the importance of interest in affecting her approach to learning. In many of the interviews both interest and previous knowledge were clearly factors which affected their study strategies. If anything, interest was seen as more important by arts students, while previous knowledge was mentioned more frequently by scientists.

Other evidence of variability in students' approaches to contrasting academic tasks comes from a recent study by Laurillard (1979). Of 31 students in one of her experiments using Marton's approach, 19 used different strategies on different occasions while 12 used deep approaches every time. Laurillard also examined the consistency with which students could be classified as comprehension or operation learners on contrasting tasks. Again her conclusion was that students do vary their strategies considerably from task to task. This leads her to query the usefulness of descriptions of learning which assume the existence of consistent individual characteristics among students. However, as we shall see later, it is possible to accept that there can be both consistency and variability in students' approaches to learning. The tendency to adopt a certain approach, or to prefer a certain style of learning, may be a useful way of describing differences between students. But a more complete explanation would also involve a recognition of the way an individual student's strategy may vary from task to task. Knowing something about that student's interests and previous knowledge, and about the varying demands of different courses, both approaches to and outcomes of learning should become more predictable. The possibility of such prediction leads us towards a model of learning which may help us to understand not only the way students learn at university, but also provide insights into how pupils learn in school.

Summary

Research at Lancaster has provided additional evidence that deep and surface approaches to learning can be identified and that these relate to the level of understanding reached by students when reading an article. Factor analysis also indicated different ways of attempting a deep approach — one which relied more on facts and previous knowledge and another which concentrated on building up personal meaning.

Pask has argued for the existence of distinct styles of learning — comprehension learning and operation learning — which in their extreme forms are shown as holist and serialist strategies both in trying to understand and in 'teaching back' what has been learned. The *holist* tends to make more elaborate hypotheses, look further ahead, build up a picture of the whole task, look for links with other topics, and, in extreme cases, rely heavily on personal analogies and idiosyncratic descriptions. This style of learning has apparent similarities with Heath's 'plunger'. The *serialist* prefers a narrower focus in learning, concentrating on simple hypotheses and step-by-step learning, paying attention to details and processes, but neglecting the broader perspective and links with other topics. He is unlikely to make much use of personal experience in learning academic topics.

Pask argues that thorough understanding normally involves both description building and operation building — a use of the overall picture and a careful examination of details. And this coincides with Marton's description of deep level processing. Some students have a *versatile* learning style. They can use holist or serialist strategies as appropriate and in an effective sequence — a description which echoes Heath's 'reasonable adventurer' who alternates between curiosity and critical thinking.

Although students' strategies will vary to some extent from task to task, Pask argues that these are influenced by their underlying, and relatively stable, learning styles. These distinct styles also lead to characteristic pathologies of learning. An overemphasis on comprehension learning leads to *globetrotting* in which little attention is given to evidence or supportive detail and the student becomes over-ready to generalize or reach unsubstantiated conclusions. In contrast an overemphasis on operation learning leads to *improvidence* where the student fails to build up adequate links between neighbouring areas of knowledge and so has a narrow limited view of the topic learned. Similar pathologies can be anticipated in teaching or presenting information and Pask has demonstrated that students mismatched with learning materials incorporating the organizational principles of the opposite learning style reach rather low levels of understanding.

Earlier research at Lancaster had related personality, study methods and motivation to both subject area and degree results. The research identified different 'types' of students, thus paralleling by statistical analysis the intuitive analysis of Heath. The four main types were described as stable and motivated (hope for success or hustler?); anxious (fear of failure); extraverted, syllabus-free (plunger?); and idle and unmotivated (drop-out).

Work at Lancaster has also involved the development of a study strategies' inventory which has confirmed three main dimensions related to studying — orientations towards meaning, reproducing, and achieving. Each of these dimensions has a component of study strategy and differs in terms of the characteristic form of motivation associated with it.

Finally very recent work by Ramsden on the effects of different contexts of learning shows how students adapt their learning strategies to the perceived demands of lecturers and departments. In interviews, students emphasized the importance of assessment procedures and the friendliness and enthusiasm of staff in affecting their readiness to adopt a deep approach to a course. Scientists also emphasized the importance of previous knowledge in influencing their strategy, while arts students were likely to mention interest as the more important factor.

BRIDGE

Models of Student Learning

Part II has looked mainly at recent educational research on how students learn. The studies have remained close to the real experiences of students in higher education. Part III provides an outline of mainstream and educational psychology within a conventional framework of topics — memory, intellectual abilities, development, motivation, personality and cognitive styles. But these topics can also be understood, at least in part, within models of learning which summarize the work on students. This bridge passage thus looks at three models of student learning which have developed out of this research. These models then provide ways of re-examining the traditional topics in educational psychology to give greater overall coherence to this subject area.

It should be stressed straight away that none of these models presents a complete picture of student learning. One reason for using three models is that each provides a different perspective or focus on the experiences of students. It is impossible to provide a single model which can cover both many perspectives and different depths of focus. The three models bring out some of the many facets of the real situation from which they have been abstracted, but much is still left out.

The academic achievement game

Research by Becker *et al.* (1968) in the United States describes students' behaviour in higher education in terms of a series of coping ploys for 'Making the Grade'. The early research findings from Lancaster were combined with results from a study in Aberdeen (Wilson, 1969) to produce a model of student learning in the form of a board game called *The Academic Achievement Game* or TAAG (Entwistle and Wilson, 1977).

The game was designed to incorporate three main principles emerging from the combined research. First, that academic performance can, to some extent, be predicted on the basis of 'entry conditions', such as ability level, 'A' level grades, and prior training in study skills. Second, that it is possible to distinguish at least four 'types' of student who approach studying in characteristically different ways which again affect subsequent academic performance. And finally, that students during their studies are likely to encounter a wide variety of unpredictable events which again may affect their academic progress, and to which students of different personality may react differently.

The outline of the game can be seen in Figure B1. The board presents three 'tracks' representing arts, science, and social science. Students begin the game by allocating themselves to one of the tracks and to four starting conditions — ability level (three sets of dice have different numbers on the faces to ensure fast, medium, and slow progress round the board); 'A' level grades (up to two free throws to start the game); and school preparation for university (one free throw). Finally students are required to choose their personality type (indicated by plastic counters of different colours) — stable and motivated; anxious, fear of failure; extraverted, syllabus-free; or idle and unmotivated. (These are the 'types' identified in the cluster analysis described on page 99).

The game is then begun with students progressing around the tracks by throwing the dice. The tracks contain a series of coloured squares labelled B (Bonus), H (Hazard), and * (Chance). These squares represent events and students experiencing these (landing on these squares) move forward (bonus), move back (hazard), miss throws (chance). The particular event to occur is decided by the student selecting a card from the appropriate packs of cards provided. Each card names an event and allocates different levels of penalty or reward for each personality type, as in Table B.1.

The values ascribed to the different events are partly based on interviews with students, but still depend on a good deal of guesswork.

The outcome is decided when the first of the players reaches the graduation square. The other degree awards are then indicated by the positions on the board reached by that time.

The game was created for two purposes. First to use with first-year students as a simulation exercise. Students who play this game begin to understand the way in which their experiences may affect their academic performance. But the game was also intended as a way of summarizing the research findings. Unfortunately the research had not gone far enough to be used to suggest the most likely events to create bonuses and penalties. The game did, however, have the great advantage of being dynamic — allowing fortunes to change over time. Moreover it showed that the outcome of learning is partly predictable in terms of student characteristics on entry, but also that it is affected by subsequent experiences. Finally the game drew attention to the way in which students of different personality are likely to react differently to those experiences.

Study orientations and outcomes

At the time TAAG was developed, there was little known about the processes students used in studying. As a result of the work described in Chapters 4 and

Table B.1. Events, penalties, and bonuses

Card	Event	Student type			
		Stable and Mot (Orange)	Fear of Fail (Black)	Extrav S-free (Green)	Idle and Unmot (Brown)
Bonus	You have an inspiring teacher	+5	+3	+1	0
Bonus	You find you have covered much of the syllabus at school	+1	+5	0	0
Bonus	Your tutorial group is stimulating and constructive	+5	+3	+5	+1
Bonus	You get better marks than you expected for your essay	0	+3	+1	0
Bonus	Your flat mates are conscientious workers	+1	+1	+3	+3
Hazard	Lectures are boring	−2	0	−2	−4
Hazard	You get a lower essay mark than you expect	+2	−2	−2	0
Hazard	The course is badly organized	0	−4	−2	−2
Hazard	Your tutor is very sarcastic	−2	−6	−2	0
Hazard	You fall in love	0	+4	−4	−6

Card	Event	Throws missed			
Chance	You are wrongly arrested at a demonstration	1	2	1	1
Chance	Your lecture notes are stolen	2	4	1	1
Chance	You decide on a career	If 'brown' change to 'orange'. If 'green' or 'black' take one extra throw.			
Chance	You find student politics more interesting than academic study	If 'orange' change to 'green'. If 'brown' take one extra throw.			
Chance	You become pregnant (females only!)	If 'black' or 'brown' retire from the game. If 'orange' or 'green' miss three throws.			

(The full range of events will be found in Entwistle and Wilson, 1977, pages 153-155).

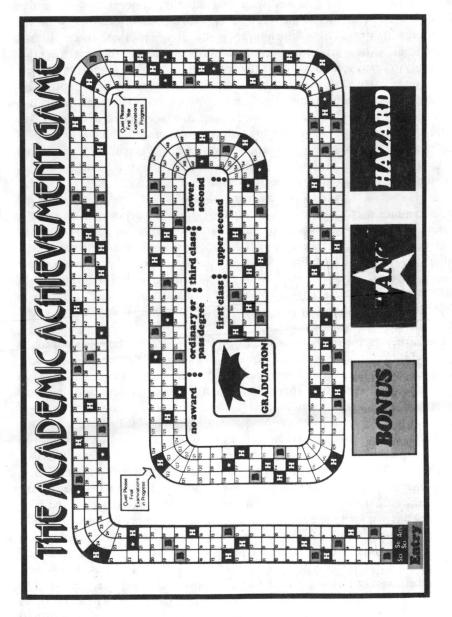

Figure B.1 The Academic Achievement Game

5, it should now be possible to provide a model which brings together the findings on approaches and styles.

It seems clear that, in normal studying, students approach learning with very different intentions, indeed with contradictory conceptions of learning (Säljö, 1979). The factor analyses of the inventories, together with the qualitative analyses of Gothenburg, make it clear that three distinct orientations exist. Students may look predominantly towards personal meaning, towards reproducing, or towards achieving high grades. And these orientations carry with them characteristically different types of motivation and are associated with contrasting learning processes. Of course, individual students may have high scores on more than one dimension. They may, for instance, show a clear orientation towards personal meaning, but also towards achieving high grades. An orientation towards achievement may necessitate looking for meaning on some occasions and relying on reproducing on others, depending on the demands made by lecturers.

Pask's work suggests a further complication. Students seeking understanding may adopt different learning strategies dependent on stylistic preferences. Some students may build up understanding mainly through discrete steps, looking in detail at facts and rather narrow links between topics. Others may prefer to look first for the way individual topics fit into a broader conceptual map within the subject area. The redundant holists are likely to make wide use of anecdote, analogy, and illustration in building up understanding and they may rely on idiosyncratic, personal ways of tying new ideas into previous experience.

The earlier factor analyses showed no clear separation between approach and style. Yet there is a conceptual distinction, though a fine one. Comprehension learning and operation learning can be seen as essential to full understanding. The deep approach demands the overview and personal integration of the holist combined with the caution and attention to detail of the serialist. In short the deep approach can be equated with Pask's versatile style of learning. Students seeking understanding may, however, place too much emphasis on one or other style and so exhibit the characteristic pathologies. The holist may fail to pay sufficient heed to the detail or evidence, while the serialist may fail to see important interconnections between ideas. The holist strategy may well lead to a level of understanding associated with the deep passive approach, while the serialist strategy may be mistaken for a surface approach. However, the serialist strategy involves building up meaning from the component facts, while the surface approach is characterised by a reliance on memorization. It is easy to see why there is an empirical link between operation learning and the surface approach. If the serialist fails to establish links between the parts, understanding of the whole becomes impossible. Then the student is forced to rely on memorization and reproducing the parts as a substitute for understanding. Where the meaning is grasped, the facts are tied into previous frameworks of knowledge, making retention and subsequent recall much easier (as we shall see in Part III).

Orientation and intention	Motivation (personality type)	Approach or style	Process — Stage I	Process — Stage II	Outcome
Personal meaning	Intrinsic (Autonomous and syllabus-free)	Deep approach/versatile	All four processes below used appropriately to reach understanding		Deep level of understanding
		Comprehension learning	Building overall description of content area	Reorganizing incoming information to relate to previous knowledge or experience and establishing personal meaning	Incomplete understanding attributable to globetrotting
	Extrinsic and fear of failure (Anxious and syllabus-bound)	Operation learning	Detailed attention to evidence and steps in the argument	Relating evidence to conclusion and maintaining a critical, objective stance	Incomplete understanding attributable to improvidence
Reproducing		Surface approach	Memorization	Overlearning	Surface level of understanding
Achieving high grades	Hope for success (Stable, self-confident, and ruthless)	Organized/achievement orientated	Any combination of the six above processes considered appropriate to perceived task requirements and criteria of assessment		High grades with or without understanding

Figure B.2. A model of study orientations and outcomes (from Entwistle et al., 1979b)

Now we are in a position to fit the research evidence into a simplifying framework. Figure B2 summarizes the above distinctions between orientation, approach and style in relation to the anticipated consequences of these study processes — different levels of understanding. The three orientations and their characteristic motivations should now be familiar. The central portion of this framework postulates four processes in learning — two being aspects of comprehension learning (mapping and restructuring) and two linked with operation learning (attention to detail and relating evidence to conclusion). Logically, in each case, one necessarily precedes the other, thus stages I and II have been separated. These four processes are all necessary in understanding meanings. The surface approach depends on memorization and overlearning, while the achieving orientation may require all six of these processes to guarantee high grades. The final column suggests the levels of outcome likely to be associated with the different approaches and styles.

A model of teaching and learning

The framework shown in Figure B2 focuses narrowly on certain aspects of the teaching-learning situation in higher education. It indicates only links between intention, approach, style, and outcome. To provide a more complete picture we should have to include a developmental progression (Perry and Heath) and build in the probable effects of differing teaching styles and departmental ethos. Figure B3 is an attempt to widen the focus, so as to include at least the possible effects of the teacher on the learning process.

This model is much more speculative. In the absence of research evidence it has to rely on personal experience and logic to complete an otherwise incomplete picture. Figure B3 lists on the left-hand side certain characteristics of both student and teacher which may affect the learning outcome. The student and teacher characteristics are seen as relatively stable, but definitely modifiable, depending on subsequent experiences as well as on past experiences.

Figure B3 should be read as a flow-diagram. Starting on the left, moving to the right, and returning through a feed-back loop to the beginning. Student and teacher experiences follow separate, but interacting, loops. Thus looking first at student characteristics, these predispose the student to perceive the task presented by the teacher in particular ways. But the perceptions will, naturally, also depend on the task itself. It will probably be perceived in terms of what is thought to be required by the teacher, its interest and relevance, its importance to the student or course requirements, its difficulty, and how potentially threatening it seems to self-esteem. These perceptions, together with the continuing effects of previous knowledge, motivation, anxiety, and so on will affect the approach, process and outcome of learning. It is probable, as we shall see later, that personality is related to the particular learning style adopted. The likely outcome may be recognized by the student early enough to modify his perceptions of the task and hence his learning strategies. The outer

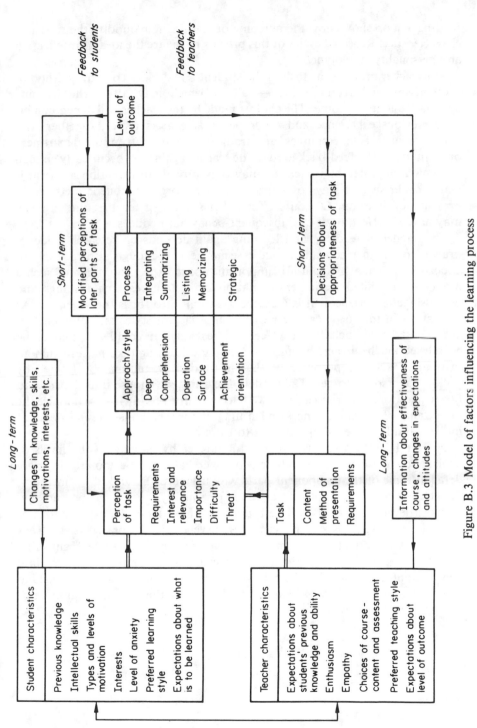

Figure B.3 Model of factors influencing the learning process

feed-back loop shows how the outcome of learning may modify the student's characteristics. Repeated cycles of this process introduce the idea of intellectual and personality development.

The teacher presents the task to the student. He decides content, method of presentation and requirements — all of which may affect the learning approach and its outcome. The choices made by the teacher will depend on his own previous experience and other personal characteristics, together with course requirements, resources, and tradition stemming from the department or institution. The feed-back loop to the teacher again may occur early enough to allow a modified approach, or may only provide information afterwards which could suggest ways of improving course organization or methods of presentation later on. Of course, for either student or teacher, the outcome may have no effect at all on subsequent behaviour or ideas.

This model of teaching and learning again depends on research evidence drawn from higher education, but it seems general enough also to apply to education in schools. Again it is important not to expect too much of such a model — a limited static representation of certain research findings and professional experiences. It is a device to simplify, to focus the attention. As we have seen the focus can be narrow (approaches, styles and outcome) or made broader to include the effects of teaching. It could, of course, be broadened much further, because teaching and learning take place within an institution, and the purposes of that institution are ultimately decided by political and social forces. The model of learning we choose thus depends on how narrow or how broad a focus we select. With a broad view we may see the importance of social influences on learning, but we shall miss the fine detail of individual differences in approaches to learning.

In Part III we narrow the focus still further by moving to the levels of explanation preferred by psychologists. We shall thus be looking in more detail at some of the component parts within Figures B2 and B3 — memory, intellectual abilities, motivation, and personality. Even in psychology, different levels of analysis will be found. We move from the explanations of educational psychologists in terms of psychological constructs such as intelligence or motivation, to a much finer grain analysis where the focus shifts to physiological or neurological processes — glandular or cerebral concomitants of an individual's behaviour. However, as Part III is intended to provide an outline of *educational* psychology, only the occasional glimpse of this narrowest view will be provided.

PART III

Topics in Educational Psychology

CHAPTER 6

Memory: Structure and Processes

The models of the learning process developed in Part II depend almost entirely on evidence from educational research on students' learning. They seem to provide a useful way of looking at the complex forms of learning which take place in education. However this research on students has drawn explicitly and implicitly on a variety of important psychological concepts whose meaning cannot be fully understood without examining the way in which they are used in the psychological literature. The following chapters examine these concepts in some detail, and consider evidence derived from studies on children. The intention is to fill in frameworks provided by the models and so build up a more complete picture of educational psychology out of which implications for teaching and learning can be explored in Part IV.

Which important concepts have been used so far? In Chapter 4 both Heath and Perry described a dimension of intellectual development during the college years. To understand their ideas better we need to look at theories which describe the intellectual development of children and adolescents. These theories, which are introduced in Chapter 8, will also indicate to what extent our models of learning are likely to apply at earlier stages of intellectual development. Part II also suggested how different forms of motivation and personality were associated with contrasting approaches to, or styles of, learning. Thus Chapter 9 examines research on personality and motivation, particularly that concerned with their effects on attainment or behaviour in school. Pask's work on learning styles has its roots both in theories of learning and in the psychological literature on cognitive styles. Clear parallels with Pask's concepts and his findings are discussed in Chapter 10.

The starting point of this outline of educational psychology is the approach to learning. The distinction between deep and surface approaches was clear-cut in the research on students. It appeared to be a fundamental distinction. If so, we should expect to find a similar distinction within the psychological literature. There are two areas of psychology which have looked at intellectual processes in rather different ways. Chapter 7 covers the survey research on individual differences in intellectual abilities which has grown out of the attempt to define 'intelligence'. This chapter concentrates on the experimental

119

research tradition. Initially this research attempted to outline general laws of learning based on conditioning, but here we restrict the outline to the more recent work on the cognitive processes associated with memory and thinking processes.

It is clear from Marton's research that the term 'memorization' is in a sense, misleading. It implies that there is *one* way to remember. Yet the deep approach, which makes little use of memorization as a learning strategy, usually leads to effective recall of both facts and ideas. Understanding and reproducing are *both* ways of transferring material to the memory. This chapter examines the psychological evidence for the existence of distinct memory processes, even distinct types of memory, which might be seen to parallel the different approaches to reading and studying.

As research on the human memory is progressing rapidly at the moment, any attempt to provide an outline of this work is extremely difficult. A variety of models of the memory and ways of thinking are being introduced and tested in experiments, and most descriptions still have to be considered as tentative. To simplify the presentation in an extremely complex area, one particular model of the memory is described in some detail, to be followed by a brief indication of an alternative approach.

How do we remember?

William James provided an early attempt at explaining how we remember. He used the idea of linkages between thoughts and speculated that such linkages were laid down in the brain. But we remember so many different types of things — events, faces, names, numbers, formulae, emotions, theories, and so on, that even by introspection we could be fairly sure that any single process would be unlikely to explain all these different instances.

The difficulty facing the experimenters and theorists can be seen by asking a number of specific questions. How do you hold an unfamiliar telephone number in your mind long enough to dial it? How do you remember events from childhood? How do you remember a familiar tune, or the meaning of 'antidote', or a mathematical proof? What about Julius Caesar's birthday? How did you know that it was not even worth searching your memory for that fact? When you forget something you feel you should remember, how do you know that the information is there, somewhere, even if you cannot find it at that moment? Why does such information often subsequently 'pop up' when we have given up the search?

Cognitive psychologists are still trying to find fully satisfactory answers to such questions. As already indicated, the models that are being proposed have still to be viewed as provisional, although they seem to have much greater explanatory power than earlier attempts which relied exclusively on either introspection or stimulus-response psychology. It would be inappropriate here to go into great detail about the experimental evidence on which the recent ideas on perception and memory are based, as it is readily available in existing

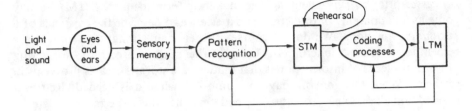

Figure 6.1 A simple information processing model

psychology texts (e.g. Baddeley, 1976; Klatzky, 1975; Cofer, 1975; Herriot, 1973).

'Information processing' models of memory have developed out of work on selective attention carried out by Donald Broadbent (1958), among others. They take perceptions as being incoming information which has to be processed. The simplest of these models — the 'duplex' model — shows distinct stages occurring in sequence, as in Figure 6.1. Even in this diagram, however, there are 'feed-back loops' which interrupt the sequence of processing. If the model is expected to explain all that we already know about the attributes of memory, complex interrelationships and parallel processes have to be incorporated into a more elaborate model which will be presented later.

Taking this simple description first, there is general agreement that incoming signals of light and sound produce relatively complete representations of our focus of attention in *sensory registers*. Our eyes produce an *iconic* image which lasts some three or four seconds (Gilmartin *et al.,* 1975). At this stage the images may not yet have been interpreted, but processing then begins. Comparisons with familiar patterns of light or sound held in the memory enable provisional interpretations to be made. The recognized patterns are passed into a *short-term memory* (STM) which holds a limited amount of information in terms of symbols, words, or ideas for a short while — initially not more than about 20 seconds (Peterson and Peterson, 1959). The contents of the STM may be retained by rehearsal, that is by sub-vocal repetition, unless additional incoming perceptions displace them. The STM is also the working memory in which problems are solved by relating several pieces of information simultaneously, but its limited size is restricting. Miller (1956) has suggested that there is a 'magical' number of 7 ± 2 which represents the maximum number of units or 'chunks' of information which can be held in the STM. Broadbent (1975) has recently challenged this interpretation and suggested that information is more often grouped in *three* chunks, rather than seven. However, as these chunks may themselves be complex ideas, the size restriction is not easy to define for anything except single units of information, such as number digits, nor is the restriction as severe as it might otherwise appear. The material in the STM may undergo a further series of *coding processes* prior to permanent storage in a long-term memory (LTM). It may come as an apparent contradiction of experience to describe the existence of a *permanent* memory. We do, of course, forget many things, but others are remembered almost indefinitely. One of the main reasons for forgetting important pieces of information is that inadequate storage creates problems in retrieval. What has gone in may not come out when it is needed! Retrieval depends on the coding processes which determine where the material will be stored, and hence where subsequently it will be expected to be found.

The long-term memory has been compared to a library, to sets of pigeon holes and to a filing system (Broadbent, 1966), where concepts, ideas and records of past events are stored. Information from the STM is compared with existing material in the LTM and stored in an appropriate place.

This simple model has its success, mainly in relation to simple learning tasks, but to understand, for example, different approaches to reading, a fuller and more complicated model must be described in detail.

Short-term memory

The idea of a short-term memory provides an acceptable explanation of our attempts to hold a telephone number in our mind. Most of us are probably well aware of the rehearsal strategy necessary to prevent the number from fading. Any interruption between using the directory and dialling is usually fatal — the information is pushed out of STM by competing new perceptions. A three-digit town code combined with a five-digit individual number stretches the STM to its limits, but by repeated rehearsal some meaningless strings of numbers or letters can be transferred to LTM. If the repetitions recur frequently, such *overlearning* allows initially meaningless strings of numbers or words to be stored indefinitely. Servicemen, even if they only did National Service, generally remember their service number. Mine comes back in three groups 27-67-425, which is in line with Broadbent's comments on using groups of three. Looking further back my memory contains assorted fragments of what seem to have been rote-learned material in school. For example, a certain string of Latin words is, for some reason, very easy to recall.

> Odi profanum, vulgus et arceo,
> Favete linguis, carmina non prius...

Working out the meaning of this fragment of a Horace ode is now rather difficult, but the memory of the words must be associative. It is an example of a simple form of learning, called *verbal-chaining* (Gagné, 1970), in which strong stimulus-response bonds have been established. Although the activity of rehearsal is associated with the STM, at some stage the rote-learned chains of associations have to be stored in the long term memory, if the information is likely to be needed again.

Episodic LTM

The ability to remember depends on retrieval, and retrieval depends on systematic organisation. If the long-term memory contains concepts, ideas and records of past events, how are these organized? Tulving (1972) has suggested that two types of long-term memory should be distinguished — our memory for events and our memory for words and meanings. For the moment, this over-simple, but useful, distinction will be accepted. Past events or episodes may be considered to be stored in an *episodic* memory, while words and meanings are held in *semantic* memory. But even if the separate *terms* are helpful, the interconnections between these memories must be recognized. Some episodes involve memories about what people said; they contain words. It is perhaps useful to imagine that the episodic memory enables us to remember if an event has happened, and if so when and under what circumstances. It contains strings of associations — particularly visual images and sounds, organized in part as sequences over time, with recent events more accessible than earlier ones. But recall is also dependent on the importance of the events, on the effects of repetition and on cross-linkages with the semantic memory.

The effects of rote memorization are presumably to strengthen the associative links between the component parts and to impress on the whole learning episode a 'feeling tone' indicating that it will be needed later. It may be that William James was describing the workings of the episodic memory rather well when he talked about associates (events) which act as hooks with which to pull up chains of linked associations. The beginning of a chain will presumably have to be more memorable than the subsequent parts of the chain to start the process of recall, and there will also have to be more *conscious* links between separated, but related, episodes. An example of such an effect would be our ability to anticipate the first chord of the next track of a favourite record immediately after we have heard the final chord of the previous track. Introspection helps to provide the 'flavour' of the episodic memory, but evidence for its separate identity derives from experimental studies.

Klatzky (1975) sees the distinction between episodic and semantic memories as important in interpreting the results of traditional experimental learning tasks, such as the recall of word lists.

> 'Undoubtedly such lists of words are held in episodic memory. For example, if I give you a twenty-word list containing the word FROG, I am not actually teaching you the word "frog". The word will be stored in your semantic memory before, during, and after you learn the list. But I am teaching you that "frog" is currently in your list — a fact that depends on this time and this situation. That fact will be stored in episodic memory. What this means is that traditional psychology experiments are studying episodic memory, not semantic memory' (page 133).

There must also be the possibility that, after initial pattern recognition, perceptions will be able to enter the episodic LTM directly, without processing in the short-term memory. But the very act of 'recognition' implies the interaction between LTM and incoming perceptions. Thus even a simple perception involves active reconstruction using the memory. Much of this information processing must occur at a sub-conscious, automatic level through the interactions indicated in the simple model (Figure 6.1).

Take an example of the process of recognition — a close-up photograph of part of a familiar object (Figure 6.2). What is it? We need to interpret initially puzzling patterns in terms of familiar, recognizable patterns. We may have to review and mentally compare memories of a variety of familiar objects before accepting a particular interpretation. Once that interpretation is accepted, it is difficult to understand how we failed to recognize it immediately. And if the picture can be interpreted in more than one way, it is difficult to switch from the initial recognition to a different one. For example, Figure 6.3 is a drawing of a young woman with a feather in her hat. Or is it? It could also be a stooped old woman. Both interpretations are possible: they are also distinct.

What is held in the LTM to allow automatic processing of easily recognized perceptions? Neisser (1976), and Norman and Bobrow (1975), have explained what is observed by suggesting the existence of *schemata* which have a crucial function in bringing about recognition or interpretation.

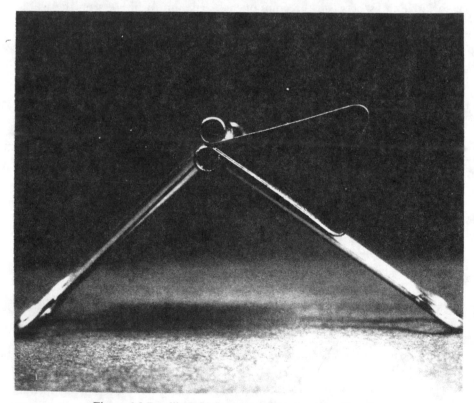

Figure 6.2 Familiar object viewed from an unusual angle

Figure 6.3 Portrait of a woman (Taken from J.R. Averill, Patterns of Psychological Thought, Wiley, New York, 1976, page 6)

'We believe that the aim of cognitive processes is to form a meaningful interpretation of the world. That is, the sensory information available to a person at any moment may be gathered together and interpreted in terms of a coherent framework. We assume that past experience has created a vast repertoire of structural frames or schemata that can be used to characterize the propositional knowledge of any experience. The problem of the perceptual processes is to determine the appropriate schemata and to match the present occurrences with the frame provided for them. If there are too many discrepancies, either a new schema must be selected or the current one must be reorganized' (Norman and Bobrow, 1975, page 119).

Neisser (1976) stresses that perception, though generally automatic, is an *active* process in which incoming perceptions are matched to schemata. If the initial perceptions are not immediately identified, additional information is sought. Searching may not always solve the problem of interpretation. Failure to match incoming perceptions with what was expected to be the correct schema could cause anxiety and intense mental activity, through a form of 'cognitive dissonance' (Festinger, 1957), until a new, satisfactory schema has been produced.

Although schemata have been used so far to explain processes of perception there must also be a store of schemata, or components of schemata, related to the interpretation of events and semantic information. The recognition of words and meaning in the semantic LTM will depend on a similar process in which incoming information is interpreted in terms of expectation and previous experience.

Semantic LTM

One of the main problems in trying to understand LTM is to identify the organising principles by which meaningful information is stored. The problem has been compared to filing letters or memoranda, or classifying research articles for future reference. Under which headings should they be stored? Author's name suggests an alphabetic classification system, but more often than not it is the *content* which is important. It follows that there must be cross-classification, to allow important aspects of the content to be identified when required. How are the 'important' aspects to be decided? Importance may be indicated through perceived incoming structure or emphasis, or by reference to well-used schemata — the person's own interests. We shall come back to this later.

Information reaching STM has to be correctly coded prior to storage in LTM. Again it may be helpful to envisage interaction processes through schemata. Incoming information must be coded by active comparisons with stored frameworks to produce meaning. Such frameworks might be words, concepts, ideas, attitudes or values, and many schemata may be in use simultaneously in coding the incoming information fully and appropriately. Recall will depend on an accurate interpretation of the important features of what is held in STM and the number of cross-references which can be made between schemata. To carry out effective coding it will be essential to have a large number and variety of conceptual schemata which are distinct and clearly defined, and which also have well-established cross-linkages.

The way in which some of these schemata may initially be established in the semantic STM will be described in Chapter 8. Here it is sufficient to indicate that this semantic memory contains

'all the information we need in order to use language. It includes not only words and the symbols for them, their meaning and other referents (what they represent), but also the rules of English grammar, chemical formulas, rules for adding and multiplying, knowledge that autumn follows summer — facts that do not depend on a particular time or place, but are just facts' (Klatzky, 1975, page 132).

But how are semantic schemata organized in LTM? What determines relatively permanent cross-linkages between schemata? Lindsay and Norman (1972) see these linkages as depending on the properties which define the schemata and which enable them to be related to more general classes or to other similar instances, and to be distinguished from other schemata. Take a schema which is a concept, like 'dog'. What cross-linkages would there be? The links become part of a definition. 'Dog' belongs to a more general *class* — 'animal'. It has the *properties* of four legs, a distinctively shaped head, a hairy body and a tail. The concept has a certain similarity to other *examples* of animals — cats, horses, foxes — and also connections with concepts which describe many different varieties of dog — alsation, labrador, corgi, poodle. This example emphasizes the *formal* definition of this concept; it ignores the *personal* linkages to past experiences of dogs and other pets. It is important to recognize that each individual has a unique conceptual structure of system of schemata. While people may agree about the formal definition of 'dog', their understanding of abstract concepts, such as 'education', 'theory', or 'justice', are unlikely to be identical. A concept is built up from the individual's own experience of instances of that concept, but the integral components of, say, 'justice' are not obvious from examples of it, and each individual will thus have his own way of understanding it. With people from the same culture there is usually enough overlap in meaning to allow communication of the idea, but also sufficient differences in personal interpretation to be a source of disagreement.

Finally it is worth considering a recent theory about the way cross-linkages are established between concepts which postulates the existence of different types of coding process. Das and his colleagues (Das, Kirby, and Jarman, 1975; 1979) have suggested two distinctive principles by which linkages are established. These they term *simultaneous* and *successive* processing. In simultaneous processing a hierarchy of connections is established to create a synthesis of several items. The way these linkages are established makes 'all portions of the synthesis... accessible without dependence on their position within the synthesis.' In other words the items can be reviewed simultaneously, providing a global view of that group of items, *or* in sequence with links only to the item on each side in the temporal sequence, which makes 'access to any element... dependent on the preceding events' (Kirby and Das, 1978). Although there is still little independent evidence to confirm the importance of this distinction, it is interesting to note the apparent parallel with the styles of learning adopted in comprehension (simultaneous) and operation (successive) learning (see Das *et al.*, 1979, pages 141-142).

Neurological evidence for the existence of STM and LTM

There is by now substantial psychological evidence for the existence of different memory processes. There is also confirmation from an entirely independent area of research. Neurological studies into changes which occur in the neurones (nerve cells) of the cerebral cortex have identified quite separate processes associated with short-term and long-term memories. Eccles (Popper and Eccles, 1977), in a summary of this work, describes a short-term memory which involves continued rehearsal of the material being retained. The neural events associated with STM appear to be the maintenance of particular connected circuits of neurones through which a minute electric current flows while the rehearsal period continues. This process ends as soon as attention is diverted: no change has occurred in the structure of the brain. In contrast LTM appears to involve structural changes in the connection (synapses) between neurones. The synapses are either strengthened or extra branches grow to make additional connections with neigbouring neurones.

While this level of analysis is far removed from the main concern of educational psychology, it does strengthen models of the memory which envisage two or three distinctive memory processes. The duplex theory of memory postulates the existence of STM and LTM. But how do we use these memories when we need to retrieve a piece of information? And what happens when we forget? The next part of the chapter explores some important memory processes before considering an alternate model of the memory which emphasizes process rather than structure.

Strategies for remembering

Besides storing events, concepts and properties, LTM must also contain rules for search strategies to be used with both STM problems and LTM retrieval. Dewey described clearly the type of logical analysis of problems, and search for corroborative evidence, which is part of scientific thinking and seems to be involved in a deep approach to studying. Such complex strategies develop out of simpler ones and seem to be built out of strings of associated rules, in a way similar to the links between schemata. At the root of many of the strategies will be comparisons of properties against existing schemata, looking for similarities and detecting significant differences. Similarity will lead to association, and difference to discrimination: these strategies in processing perceptions begin very early in life, probably soon after birth.

Certain strategies for retrieving information from LTM are well-known. Most rely on cues to identify promising associations, and many make use of the strength of imagery in the episodic memory. It is often much easier to remember where and when we obtained a piece of information, or roughly what it 'looked' like, than what the information actually was. The implication is that semantic material often has linkages in episodic memory, and remembering events may bring back the associated ideas. The separation into episodic and semantic components may be a helpful way of trying to describe

LTM, but the strong links which undoubtedly exist between them make the distinction rather artificial (Baddeley, 1976). Many systems of mnemonics depend either on the over-learning of rhymes or names, or on linking information to visual images. Luria (1975) describes the incredible, but pathological, *Mind of a Mnemonist*. This man, in one experiment, was asked to memorize many lines of nonsense syllables such as

va   sa   na   va   na   ma

Not only was be able to recall the list perfectly afterwards but he also remembered it when, without warning, he was asked to recall it eight years later. He tackled the task by visualizing a street scene and linking the nonsense syllables to similar real words which became part of the scene. Luria describes how the man recalled the above syllables.

'Aha! Here on the corner of Kolkhoznaya Square and Sretenka is the department store where the watchman turns out to be my friend, the pale milkmaid Vasilisa (VASA). She's gesturing with her left hand to indicate that the store is closed... (the Yiddish NAVA), a gesture that's intended for... the wet nurse NAMA, who has turned up there wanting to go to the store' (Luria, 1975, page 47).

This passage illustrates the way in which episodic and semantic memories can work together in efficient retrieval, where the material is otherwise difficult to learn. But an effective method of remembering meaningful material would still, within the information processing model, be similar to the one William James described. In other words information will be more likely to be retrieved if it has been associated with a large number of schemata in both episodic and semantic memories. Thus, in reading an academic article, for example, the 'deep' activity of considering how any new idea is related to a whole variety of existing ones, and to previous experience, will extend the utility of that idea (the possibility of making valid connections with other ideas) and the probability of it being recalled by a variety of different cues.

This model of LTM hints at the possible effects of other aspects of different search processes. Three important characteristics will be *speed, breadth,* and *location* of search. The initial perception of the task conditions and requirements will affect the strategies used. If the conditions are stressful and time is limited, the search is likely to be fast and narrow — and restricted to areas immediately associated with the task content. Anxiety, as Fransson found, is likely to induce a surface approach to learning, an over-hasty attempt to memorize facts or to pick up the obvious links with incoming information. Interest, on the other hand, is likely to slow down the process, to encourage a more leisurely, exploratory search which may throw up unusual combinations of ideas from different locations in LTM.

Although search processes will depend, in part, on the task set, people may also develop characteristic preferences for certain initial approaches to problems. These characteristic search strategies may be another way of describing Pask's learning styles or the cognitive styles which will be introduced later.

STOP and THINK

● How would you now explain each of the examples of remembering given on page 120, in terms of strategies within the information processing model?

● How would you explain forgetting?

The problem about telephone numbers has already been explained in terms of rehearsal and STM, but what strategy would be used to recall events in childhood. Presumably there is some initial monitoring of the question. How likely is it that I should remember the event? How important is it that I do remember? This monitoring controls both the effort and the strategy. If the memory is not impossibly remote or trivial, presumably we would use episodic memory to track events down in terms of time, geographical location, and circumstances. To remember tunes we may need the beginning or a well-known phrase to pull out the associated strings of sounds. The meaning of 'antidote' involves semantic LTM and associated examples and properties. Perhaps we might start with general location (medicines), then associations (poison), then examples (snake bites), and then begin to construct a definition. 'An antidote is...' (can be liquid, or solid presumably)... 'a substance used to counteract the harmful effects of poison or drugs'. We then analyse the accuracy and completeness of the reconstructed definition, perhaps checking its etymological roots — something which is 'given against'.

The mathematical proof might come by association, otherwise its components would have to be assembled and reconstructed as with a verbal definition. Julius Caesar's birthday would probably be rejected at the initial review procedure — 'the question could be answered, but not by me'. These examples indicate that, besides the storage banks of LTM there must also be a function of the brain which serves not only as an 'index', checking the contents prior to searches of the stored data, but also having an active role in controlling and organizing systematic search procedures. Here we come up against a major philosophical problem concerned with the nature of consciousness. Is this to be described solely in terms of the activities of various parts of the brain, or is there also a separate entity, the conscious mind or inner self, which is responsible for coordinating and integrating the whole range of neural activities of the physical brain?

Eccles (Popper and Eccles, 1977) is clear about his own preference. He postulates the existence of a self-conscious mind which is seen as superordinate to brain activity

'...There is the self or the ego that is the basis of our personal identity and continuity that each of us experiences...; there is a *unitary character* about the experiences of the self-conscious mind.... It is proposed that the self-conscious mind is actively engaged in searching for brain events which are of present interest, the operation of attention, but it also is the integrating agent, building the unity of conscious experience from all the diversity of the brain events' (pages 360-1, 373).

Eccles looks for an analogy for this operation, starting from the popular idea of conscious attention as a searchlight, but rejects it.

'Perhaps a better analogy would be some multiple scanning and probing device that reads out from and selects from immense and diverse patterns of activity in the cerebral cortex and integrates these selected components... The self-conscious mind can bring about activities in the brain which are effective in the retrieval of information from the data banks.... The retrieved information is read out... and checked against the expected result by what we might call the recognition memory function of the self-conscious mind. By virtue of this memory recognition, the self-conscious mind may discover that the retrieval from the data bank is erroneous and institute a further search through the data banks of the brain in the attempt to secure a memory that is recognized as being correct' (pages 363, 378).

It should be stressed that this comment represents the personal view of this eminent neuro-biologist. Others would see no necessity to introduce a superordinate entity controlling the search processes.

Reasons for forgetting

When our search process does fail, what happens then? It is often more difficult, for example, to match the correct term to a description than to give a definition of a word like 'antidote'. What would you call a 'solid body of men' or a 'formation of soldiers'? This type of question often creates the 'tip of the tongue' phenomenon. We know the answer but cannot recall it. If the initial semantic search for meaning fails, try to produce cues from the episodic memory. Is it a long or short word? What does it sound like? What letter does it begin with? Look again for semantic associates. What words *do* I remember which describe 'bodies of men' or armies? After considerable effort the search is abandoned. No more thought is given to it, yet suddenly, perhaps half an hour later, 'phalanx' may appear — not with a question mark, but with a feeling of certainty. The search had been continued at a subconscious level, while our conscious attention had been busy with other matters. It appears that if the problem has been given enough importance, and if considerable initial effort has been put into the conscious search, a review procedure of associated schemata continues. Not only does the subconscious search carry on, but it is capable of breaking through into consciousness when the solution is found.

At other times, of course, our memory fails altogether. A great deal of research effort has gone into explaining certain aspects of forgetting. In laboratory conditions, what happens immediately before or after learning affects recall. These effects are called *proactive* and *retroactive interference*. If, say, a passage of prose has to be read and remembered, and a very similar prose passage has been read immediately before, proactive interference occurs and less is remembered of the 'target' passage. If similar material is learned afterwards, retroactive inhibition causes interference with recall of the 'target' passage. In the literature (see, for example, Howe and Colley, 1976) this effect has been demonstrated clearly, but only when the similarity between the passages has been artificially accentuated, so that the content is almost identical and hence necessarily confusing. Under more realistic conditions, although there may still be interference effects, these are less easy to demonstrate.

Forgetting will occur if meaningless material is not overlearned, and if meaningful material is not properly coded into LTM. Coding depends on speed of presentation, and volume of material; information will not be effectively coded if it comes too fast or in too great a quantity for the limited STM to analyse. Forgetting will also occur if attention falters, and this effect begins to create problems for the information processing model. Why does attention falter? The explanation, in everyday terms, would be that the material was boring, or even too interesting. Boredom and interest lead to different channels of thought being explored. When reading, or when listening to a lecture, it is often difficult to maintain attention strictly to the content: constantly, the attention has to be dragged back to the main task.

Forgetting will also occur if the learning is not invested with sufficient importance. In stimulus-response theory, learning depends on positive or negative reinforcement — reward or the absence of it. Within our model of learning, rewards would affect the degree of importance given to learning, and hence the level of attention and investment of effort. The 'strength' of a particular event or idea coded in the memory must depend on the amount of effort put into either overlearning or analysis. But the amount of effort will depend on how the task is viewed (interesting, important) and how we are feeling (tired, ill). The model would also have to cope with interference from emotional events recorded in the unconscious levels of the memory to account for 'Freudian slips' and certain persistent blockages of painful or embarrassing memories. Figure 6.4 is an attempt to incorporate the various aspects of memory structure and processes which have been discussed so far. It is inevitably complex, as it is summarizing several aspects of memory processes. The static box-like nature of this model should be recognized as no more than a convenient way of summarizing the processes which have been identified. The processes are inevitably interacting and dynamic in reality. Some critics of this two-box or duplex model have, however, suggested that its mechanical representation of memory is dangerously misleading. The use of such mechanical analogies can lead to mistaken beliefs about the way memory operates. And the evidence derived from experimental psychology can be interpreted in a different way which emphasizes level of processing rather than types of memory.

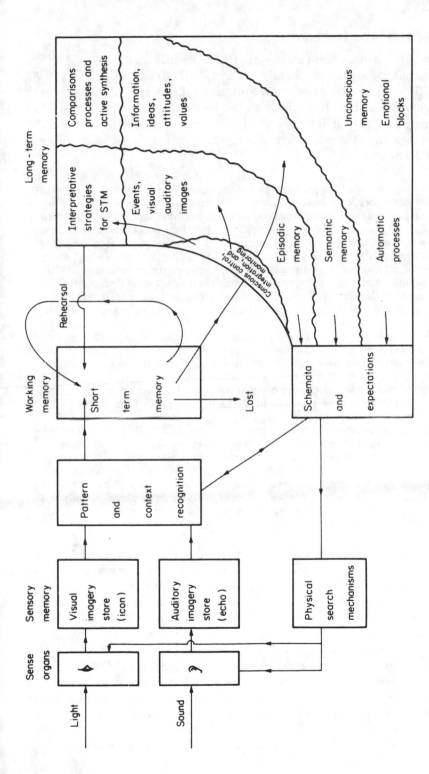

Figure 6.4 A composite information processing model of memory

Levels of processing in the memory

A strenuous opponent of the duplex model has been Fergus Craik of Toronto who, with his colleagues (Craik and Lockhart, 1972; Craik and Tulving, 1975), has put forward an alternative framework using the idea of different levels of processing. Craik starts from the accepted view that perception involves 'the rapid analysis of stimuli at a number of levels or stages' and then extends this idea to cover the distinctions between episodes and semantic memories and between STM and LTM.

> 'Preliminary stages (in perception) are concerned with the analysis of such physical or sensory features as lines, angles, brightness, pitch, and loudness, while later stages are more concerned with matching the input against stored abstractions from past learning; that is, later stages are concerned with pattern recognition and the extraction of meaning. This conception of a series or hierarchy of processing stages is often referred to as 'depth of processing' where greater 'depth' implies a greater degree of semantic or cognitive analysis. After the stimulus has been recognized, it may undergo further processing by enrichment or elaboration. For example, after a word is recognized, it may trigger associations, images or stories on the basis of... past experience with the word....
>
> It is perfectly possible to draw a box around early analyses and call it sensory memory and a box around intermediate analyses called short-term memory, but that procedure both oversimplifies matters and evades the more significant issues....
>
> Thus we prefer to think of memory tied to levels of perceptual processing,... as a continuum from the transient products of sensory analyses to the highly durable products of semantic-associative operations. However, superimposed on this basic memory system there is a second way in which stimuli can be retained — by recirculating information at one level of processing... . This type of processing merely prolongs an item's high accessibility without leading to formation of a more permanent memory trace.... This Type I processing, that is, repetition of analyses which have already been carried out, may be contrasted with Type II processing which involves deeper analysis of the stimulus. Only this second type of rehearsal should lead to improved memory performance' (Craik and Lockhart, 1972, pages 675-676).

In this initial statement of their model, it is apparently suggested that repetitions of Type I processing will not strengthen the memory trace. But in a later paper (Craik and Tulving, 1975) it is recognized that both *spread* and depth of encoding will improve retention. By 'spread' is meant 'extensive processing of the same general type' (Lockhart and Craik, 1978). Thus within this model it is still possible to recognize two distinctive ways of committing material to memory which parallel the descriptions within the duplex model. One approach involves rehearsal and overlearning in STM followed by transfer to episodic LTM, which can also be described as involving the repeated use of a single, shallow level of processing. The other approach involves the active encoding of material within semantic LTM with an emphasis on linkages with other meaningful material, or the use of Type II deep level processing. Relating back to our model of learning with the central concepts of deep and surface approaches to learning, it does seem that whichever of these two models of memory is used there is strong support for the idea that there are two distinctive ways of processing information. Furthermore, in a very recent paper Michael Eysenck (1978) has emphasized that the ability to recall material from memory depends not just on the spread and level of processing, but also on deliberate choices of strategy which control the subsequent search processes in LTM.

The central part of our model can now be accepted with rather greater confidence. The learning process in which material is to be committed to memory for subsequent use can now be seen to involve an initial deliberate choice of strategy and the outcome will depend on an appropriate match, at each stage, between the actual task requirements and the approaches, learning processes, and recall strategies used by the student.

Rote and meaningful learning sets

The evidence presented in this chapter has been drawn mainly from cognitive psychology and the level of analysis is remote from events in the classroom. Ausubel (Ausubel, Novak, and Hanesian, 1978) has developed what he terms an 'assimilation theory' of meaningful learning which describes memory processes at a less basic level. Ausubel uses the terms 'meaningful' and 'rote' to distinguish between materials which can be meaningfully linked with pre-existing concepts and knowledge and those, such as foreign language vocabulary, scientific terms, and names for unfamiliar objects, which cannot be linked to pre-existing knowledge. He argues that these materials should be learned in qualitatively different ways because

> 'potentially meaningful learning tasks are, by definition, relatable and anchorable to relevant established ideas in cognitive structure... Rotely learned materials, on the other hand, are discrete and relatively isolated entities that are relatable to cognitive structure only in an arbitrary, verbatim fashion.... They are learned and retained in conformity with the laws of association' (page 144).

Ausubel is thus stressing that meaningless materials can only be remembered by the process of establishing associations between their component parts by repetition. However meaningful materials can be learned by rote. Ausubel complains that, in school,

> 'potentially meaningful subject matter is frequently presented in such a way that (the pupils) can only learn it rotely' (page 118).

He goes on to argue that in approaching learning, children exhibit characteristic learning sets — dispositions either to look for meaning or to learn by rote. And Ausubel again rather sadly comments about conditions in schools which lead children to adopt a rote approach to learning.

'One reason why pupils commonly develop a rote learning set in relation to potentially meaningful subject matter is because they learn from sad experience that substantively correct answers lacking in verbatim correspondence to what they have been taught receive no credit whatsoever from certain teachers. Another reason is that because of a generally high level of anxiety or because of chronic failure experience in a given subject (reflective, in turn, of low aptitude or poor teaching), they lack confidence in their ability to learn meaningfully, and hence perceive no alternative to panic apart from rote learning.... . Moreover, pupils may develop a rote learning set if they are under excessive pressure to exhibit glibness, or to conceal, rather than admit and gradually remedy, original lack of genuine understanding. Under these circumstances it seems easier and more important to create a spurious impression of facile comprehension, by rotely memorizing a few key terms or sentences, than to try to understand what they mean. Teachers frequently forget that pupils become very adept at using abstract terms with apparent appropriateness — when they have to — even though their understanding of the underlying concepts is virtually non-existent' (page 43).

In Ausubel's theory of assimilation, meaningful learning occurs only if the material is presented in a way which is itself potentially meaningful, and if the pupil adopts a meaningful learning set and has the necessary anchoring ideas to establish links with the new material. Other aspects of Ausubel's theory will be considered in Chapter 10.

Again the parallels between this view of learning and the model developed out of Marton's ideas on approach to learning are clear. And Ausubel presents in his book a wealth of supportive evidence drawn mainly from studies with school children. Bringing together the evidence of different memory processes from the psychological literature and an independent analysis which emphasizes the distinction between deep (meaningful) and surface (rote) approaches to learning, the central portion of our model begins to be fairly well established. In the next chapter we turn to intellectual development and another research tradition which has provided evidence on different learning processes.

Summary

There is now substantial evidence, both psychological and neurological, for the existence of two apparently distinct memory processes. The predominant psychological model describes three types of memory. There is said to be a *sensory* memory which holds for a fraction of a second a complete image of whatever aspect of the environment happens to be our focus of attention. Patterns in these incoming light and sound signals are interpreted through comparisons with pre-existing schemata. Information then passes to a *short-term* memory which is limited in capacity and duration. STM is also the working memory. Information can be held there only by repeated rehearsal, but it can also be coded and fed into a *long-term* memory which appears to be built up by modifying neural interconnections in the brain. For some purposes it is useful to distinguish two aspects of LTM, the *episodic* which stores events and the *semantic* which is concerned with symbols and their meaning. Effective storing of memories in semantic LTM depends on appropriate 'cataloguing' and 'cross-referencing' or, in Ausubel's terms, relating and anchoring new materials to relevant established ideas in cognitive structure. Rote learning can be described, in contrast, as the repetitive overlearning of materials which are treated as meaningless and are presumably stored ultimately in episodic LTM. Ausubel draws attention to contrasting learning sets which predispose pupils to adopt meaningful or rote learning, thus paralleling Marton's ideas of a deep and surface approach to learning.

Recall of learned material can also be described in terms of the spread and depth of processing used in learning. Spread refers to the repeated use of a single level of processing, while depth describes the extent to which semantic and cognitive analysis has been undertaken. It also depends on conditions before, during, and after, learning, other learning immediately before or afterwards (proactive and retroactive inhibition), and the choice of strategy for recall. It is sometimes helpful to use cues in episodic memory (mnemonics) to aid recall from semantic LTM.

Establishing the existence of distinct memory processes in research at three levels — educational psychology (assimilation theory), psychology (duplex and level of processing models) and neurology — provides important supportive evidence for the central part of the model developed mainly at the level of educational research.

CHAPTER 7

Intellectual Abilities: Rote Learning, Reasoning, and Imaginative Thinking

The models of learning presented in Part II identified 'intellectual skills' as one of the characteristics which would affect students' approaches to learning. In this chapter we examine ideas on how best to classify those intellectual skills which might be relevant to the academic tasks facing pupils or students. But is it even necessary to talk about *separate* skills? Surely many of the differences in the speed and efficiency of pupils' learning can be explained by the single term 'intelligence'. Although this term has been vigorously attacked by some educational theorists, it is still perhaps the most commonly used in everyday life to describe individual differences.

STOP and THINK

● What does the term 'intelligence' mean to you?

● Does it imply a single quality or a summary of several different ones?

● How would you decide whether someone was 'intelligent' or not?

Use your own experience to think these questions through carefully before reading on. They raise important issues.

In the previous chapter we considered evidence for the existence of the two modes of thinking described by James and Dewey as associative and analytic. Within the information processing model, the distinction did make sense in terms of the extent to which learning relied on STM and episodic LTM (associative) or on STM and mainly semantic LTM (analytic). This chapter examines whether a similar distinction is found in the evidence drawn from surveys which have used tests of cognitive abilities. An important question will be whether there is a hierarchy of abilities in which certain skills are found in everyone, but the skills involving abstract thought are fully developed only in some people.

The attempt to develop a classification of mental skills has a long history, and has been approached from many different standpoints. Philosophers through the ages have tried to analyse human thought into different categories, as a way of understanding the distinctively human characteristic of self-conscious reasoning. One such attempt was made by the Scottish philosopher Thomas Reid (1785) in his *Essays on the Intellectual Powers of Man*. Like many previous philosophers he distinguished first between the 'powers of understanding and those of the will'.

'Under the will we comprehend our active powers, and all that lead to action, or influence the mind to act; such as appetites, passions, affections. The understanding comprehends our contemplative processes; by which we perceive objects; by which we conceive or remember them; by which we analyse or compound them; and by which we judge or reason concerning them.

Although this general division may be of use in order to our proceeding more methodically in our subject, we are not to understand it as if, in these operations which are ascribed to the understanding, there were no exertion of will or activity... ; for I conceive there is no operation of the understanding wherein the mind is not active in some degree... (and) there can be no act of will which is not accompanied with some act of understanding' (pages 65-6).

Reid eventually produced a list of the intellectual powers he considered to be distinct, namely perception, memory, conception, abstraction ('resolving and analysing complex objects and compounding those that are more simple'), judgement and reasoning. He added to those cognitive activities, the powers of taste ('discerning and relishing the beauties of nature and whatever is excellent in the fine arts'), moral perception and consciousness.

A more recent taxonomy developed by Bloom and his colleagues (Bloom *et al.,* 1956; Krathwohl *et al.,* 1964) has been widely used for helping teachers to think more clearly about what they are trying to teach or examine. This modern classification system again has two main divisions or 'domains', the cognitive and the affective, although a 'psycho-motor domain' has also been described. The cognitive domain is divided into six components — knowledge, comprehension, application, analysis, synthesis, and evaluation, while the affective domain contains five categories — receiving (being aware), responding (showing interest), valuing (being actively involved), organization (developing critical capacities) and characterization (effectiveness in the activity).

The cognitive domain, in particular, has been widely used in discussing educational objectives and the hierarchical progression, from knowledge and memorization to the higher-order analytic skills, has proved a useful distinction. Another taxonomy has been developed by Gagné (1970) out of the stimulus-response tradition of learning experiments. His classification is in terms of increasingly complex behaviour. The first three types of learning are simple stimulus response connections affecting behaviour, but the remaining five are related to thinking — verbal association, discrimination learning, concept learning, rule learning and problem solving. Bloom's taxonomy is of educational objectives; Gagné's 'conditions of learning' categorize the experimental tasks which psychologists have investigated. Both imply an underlying hierarchy of cognitive skills not dissimilar from that derived from introspection by Thomas Reid. But is there more direct empirical evidence of the existence of separate intellectual skills, and is it still possible to argue for a general intellectual ability or 'intelligence'?

Development of 'intelligence' tests

Spearman (1904, 1923) was one of the most influential British psychologists to consider the nature of intelligence, using both philosophical and statistical methods. On theoretical grounds he argued that intelligence involved three distinct components — the apprehension of experience, the eduction of relations and the eduction of correlates. 'Apprehension' was described as a lower level ability to recognize the quantitative and qualitative attributes of objects and ideas. 'Eduction' means a 'drawing out' and Spearman considered that there were two higher level abilities. One of these involved seeing the relationships between two or more objects or ideas (the eduction of relations) while the other demanded the ability to deduce a property or object which matched another object and a defined relationship (the eduction of correlates). An example of this last process would be to ask what is the opposite (relation) of 'fast' (property). By educing a correlate, an appropriate answer would be 'slow'. These ideas were published at a time of intense activity in developing measures of intelligence and reasoning tests, and appear to have influenced the type of items included in these tests.

Binet (1916) accepted the ideas of Spencer and Galton that there was an innate, general, cognitive ability and conceptualized it in a way similar to Spearman as 'the capacity to judge well, to reason well, and to comprehend well.' But Binet was given an important practical problem to solve. The introduction of universal education into France in 1881 had created an administrative difficulty. All children, except the feeble-minded, were required to attend school. The problem for Binet, and his assistant Simon, was to find a practical method of deciding which children could not benefit from education — to identify the ineducable (Tyler, 1976). Their approach was to determine what mental tasks normal children could complete at different ages. They developed a whole range of tasks, between five and eight for each year, which were typical of the attainments of children between ages 3 and 15. At age six, for example, the tasks in Burt's British version included knowing the number of fingers on both hands, counting 13 pennies, copying a diamond shape, naming all the days of the week, reconstructing an oblong card which had been cut into pieces, defining common objects (horse, chair, table) by their use, and repeating from memory five digits and sixteen syllables (Burt, 1921). Many similar tasks are still found in modern versions of *individual* intelligence tests — such as the Stanford-Binet, the Wechsler, and the British Ability Scales (Elliott *et al.*, 1977).

Binet and Simon were not, themselves, concerned with creating a *scale* of intelligence, but their tasks soon began to be used in this way. It was possible to assign a child to a *mental age,* based on that age level where *all* the tasks were completed satisfactorily plus an allowance for each subsequent task also completed. For example, a child of age six who completed all the tasks at age six, and four of the eight tasks at age seven, could be said to have a mental age of 6½. From this it was a short step to the idea of a scale of intelligence calculated as an *intelligence quotient.*

$$IQ = \frac{\text{Mental age}}{\text{Chronological age}} \times 100$$

The child in the above example could then be said to have an IQ of (6.5/6) × 100 = 109. This calculation immediately gives a spurious impression of exact measurement, which the originators of the test had never intended. Simon, even in 1959, 'continued to think of the use of the IQ as a betrayal (trahison) of the scale's objective' (quoted by Tyler, 1976). Once intelligence has been converted from a series of correctly performed tasks, into a number, a person can be labelled, without recognizing that the label may also be a *libel*. Test scores, however they are measured, retain the assumptions about the nature of intelligence built into the test, and carry with them a substantial error of measurement. As mentioned in Chapter 2, tests are expected to be *valid* — to measure what they are said to measure — and to be *reliable* — to give the same result consistently if they are used on a subsequent occasion (unless there is good reason to assume the person's ability has changed).

In practice even the best psychometric tests rarely have a reliability coefficient (correlation between test and retest scores) in excess of 0.92. Such a reliability would mean that there is a high degree of certainty (95 in 100) that the child mentioned earlier as having an IQ of 109, actually has an IQ in the range 101 to 117 — but even that range is only acceptable if the test really measures that elusive quality of 'intelligence'. Vernon (1970) warns that

'far too many psychologists and sociologists assume that test scores and the psychological or lay term, "intelligence", are interchangeable. But tests are merely a (particular) sample of cognitive abilities' (page 107).

That sample of abilities, with the best tests, may imply a reasonable definition of intelligence, but other good tests would produce a rather different IQ score.

Reasoning tests and standardized attainment tests

In the early days this reservation was not commonly expressed. The usefulness of the notion of an IQ for categorizing army recruits or allocating children to grammar school led to a boom in the 'psychometrics industry'. But the original way of calculating IQ and the Binet method of testing children individually first had to be modified. Mental age does not keep pace with chronological age, and thus the original division $\left(\frac{MA}{CA}\right)$ created anomalies (Thomson, 1924). An alternative approach was to assume that intelligence, like the height of adult males, was distributed along the 'normal' curve (see Figure 7.1), which can be described in terms of a precise mathematical formula. This curve has important properties. It is symmetrical about its central peak *(mean)* and its shape can be described by its *standard deviation* (SD). A small standard deviation indicates a steep slope and a narrow range of scores, while a large SD describes a flatter curve with a wide spread (see Figure 7.1).

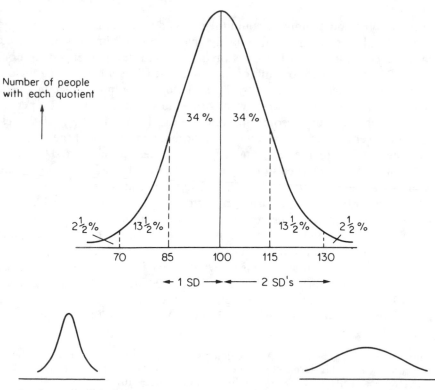

Figure 7.1 A normal distribution of intelligence quotients

Intelligence quotients are now described in terms of *standard scores* with a mean of 100 (SD 15). (These arbitrary values were chosen to make the new method of assigning IQ comparable with the old). Another property of a 'normal' distribution of test scores is that about 68 per cent of children will have scores within one standard deviation either side of the mean (85-115), with 16 per cent above 115 and the same proportion below 85. Some 95 per cent of children lie within two standard deviations of the mean (70-130). Thus children with IQ's of more than 130 are exceptionally bright, while those of less than 70 would be considered to be mentally retarded or backward — always remembering the warning about a possible lack of validity and the inevitability of measurement error.

The other problem in making cognitive tests more widely available was that Binet's method depended on a professional psychologist testing every child individually. It was essential to develop paper-and-pencil group tests. At this time Ballard (1923) had been advocating the use of objective tests, as a way of improving the reliability of examinations. By asking pupils to choose the right answer from a series of plausible alternatives, errors due to differences between markers could be eliminated. Thus *group tests* of verbal reasoning were developed which used a *multiple-choice* format, and contained items based partly on Binet's ideas and partly on theoretical analyses of the skills making up intelligence. Items typical of those used in a verbal reasoning test are shown in Figure 7.2. The items cover classification, detecting similarities and differences, recognizing analogies and completing numerical series.

While these verbal reasoning tests do emphasize reasoning rather than knowledge, content-free reasoning is impossible. Prior knowledge, particularly of the exact meaning of words, is essential before high scores on these tests are possible. In an attempt to overcome this problem, 'culture-fair' non-verbal reasoning tests have been developed in which logical relationships are described in terms of pictures or patterns (see Figure 7.3). Scores on these tests are less affected by home background and previous schooling, but they are still not entirely 'culture fair'. They still have inbuilt assumptions about the relative importance of different types of reasoning, which are not valid, for example, in primitive cultures (Neisser, 1976). It is difficult to appreciate the problems faced by children from primitive tribes, or even from some 'educationally disadvantaged' subcultures of industrial societies. There are many ways of thinking that we take for granted, but which are alien to them. In formal education there are many implicit expectations.

'In school, a problem should be tackled in the same way no matter which teacher assigns it to you... ; numerical problems are worked out regardless of whether apples or bombs are to be added... ; geography is to be mastered whether or not one has any interest in travelling. The school child learns to use one particular skill to solve many different puzzles... simply because they share an abstract structure. He also learns to work on problems as they are presented, whether he cares about the solutions or not' (Neisser, 1976, page 136).

Underline in the brackets the one word or phrase which correctly completes each of these sentences.

1. Every island has (*cliffs / mountains / a shore / natives / a boat*).

2. Every book has (*a shelf / pictures / a book-mark / an index / pages / a story*).

In each of the following questions the three words in capital letters are alike in some way. In the brackets there is ONE word which is like these three words in the same way but different from all the others. Underline this one word.

Example:

PLUM, PEAR, ORANGE (*lettuce / wheat / grass / apple / onion*)

'plum' and 'pear' and 'orange' are fruits: 'apple' is the only fruit mentioned in the brackets and so we have underlined 'apple'. Now do these.

3. CRADLE, BED, HAMMOCK (*cushion / bedroom / blanket / sleep / cot*).

4. HUG, CRUSH, EMBRACE (*carve / squeeze / crowd / jostle / crouch*).

Look at this example:

Kitten is to Cat as (*calf / puppy / lamb*) is to (*horse / lion / dog*).

'puppy' and 'dog' are underlined because just as a kitten is a young cat so a puppy is a young dog.

Now do these. In each question underline TWO words, one in each set of brackets.

5. WHEN is to TIME as (*now / where / there*) is to (*then / place / watch*).

6. SPECK is to DUST as (*spot / grain / small*) is to (*dusty / large / sand*).

Read this carefully:

In a certain town there is a castle, a cathedral, a library, a palace, a post office and a theatre. They are numbered, on a tourist map, 1, 2, 3, 4, 5, and 6, but not in that order.

Use the following clues to find the number given to each building.

The *cathedral,* the *library* and the *palace* all have even numbers. The number of the *cathedral* is greater than that of the *palace* and the sum of the numbers of these two buildings is equal to the number of the *library*.

The number of the *post office* is less than that of the *palace*; the number of the *castle* is greater than that of the *cathedral*.

Write in the table, under the name of each building, the number it is given on the map.

7. Cathedral	8. Library	9. Palace	10. Castle	11. Post Office	12. Theatre

Figure 7.2. Items from a verbal reasoning test

Analogies

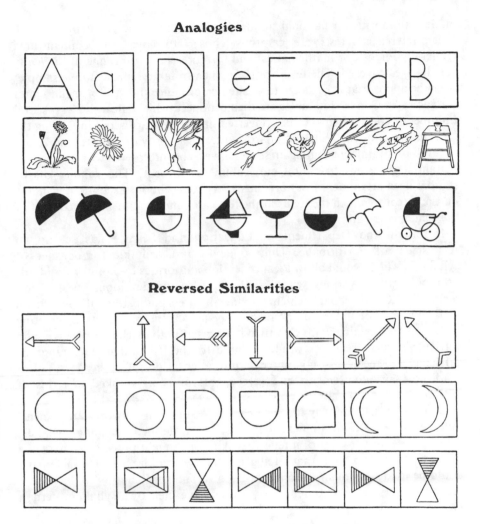

Reversed Similarities

Figure 7.3 Items from a non-verbal reasoning test

Another criticism of reasoning tests is that they give an unfair advantage to a child who answers quickly. A slow rate of response prevents the possibility of a high score. As a result *power* tests were developed. In such tests there is no time limit but the items show a sharp increase in difficulty level towards the end. Few children can answer all the items correctly, but all have the chance to do so, in contrast to the more usual timed, or *speed,* test. In practice, there is a high correlation between scores on these two types of test, but the power tests do identify some bright children who might otherwise be overlooked.

Besides the reasoning tests, measures of specific abilities (e.g. spatial, mechanical, clerical, musical) and standardized attainment tests have also been developed. The value of standardized tests is that they allow comparisons to be made with 'norms' or national standards of performance. The items for such 'norm-referenced' tests are carefully chosen to cover the content area (generally English or mathematics) and to represent a full range of difficulty for the ages covered. The tests are then given to large representative samples over the appropriate age-range to create performance 'norms' or mean scores for each age. Conversion tables are then produced which allow the 'raw score' (number of correct items) to be converted into a standard score indicating the 'attainment quotient'. Such standardized tests can provide a useful indication of levels of attainment, but again scores have to be interpreted with caution. In Britain there is no 'common curriculum' at present. The validity of the standardized attainment test may thus vary from school to school, depending on the extent to which the items in the tests are sampling the *actual* content of the school curriculum.

In Britain the Department of Education and Science has set up an Assessment of Performance Unit to devise tests suitable for a range of syllabuses which would allow local education authorities to monitor standards of attainment in various school subjects. Also the development of a new technique (Rasch scaling) which provides a direct indication of the general difficulty level of individual items has opened up the possibility of creating item banks containing items classified in terms of both teaching objectives and difficulty levels. Teachers would be able to specify content and range of difficulty and receive, by computer output, a 'criterion-referenced' test tailor-made to their requirements and yet capable of being marked in terms of national standards.

In a common-sense way it seems easy to distinguish between 'attainment' and 'intelligence'. Attainment depends on a defined teaching syllabus, intelligence refers to a set of intellectual skills or thought processes. There was also a tendency to assume that intelligence, being the more basic characteristic, could be used to explain different levels of attainment. But as we have seen reasoning tests are not content free — they have their own syllabus. Vernon (1970) argues that

> 'intelligence scores are achievement measures just as much as are reading or arithmetic scores, and they equally require to be "explained". The former does not cause the latter... (But they do) sample the more general conceptual and reasoning skills which a child has built up largely outside school, and which he should therefore be able to apply to the acquisition of more specialized skills in school' (page 106).

In the end Vernon seems almost to be contradicting himself, but it is still important to recognize that reasoning skills and attainment scores *both* require explanation.

General intelligence or specific abilities?

The overlap between all these different cognitive measures does, however, provide another way of examining the problem raised earlier, of whether it is possible to argue for a *general* intellectual ability — intelligence — or whether it is only possible to describe a series of separate specific abilities. Spearman (1904, 1927), arguing now from a statistical standpoint, was one of the first to see that intelligence, 'consists in just that constituent — whatever it may be — which is common to all the abilities', or that intelligence is 'what the intelligence tests test' (Boring, 1923).

This is not as meaningless a statement as it seems. At the logical level it appears to be circular, but the original choice of the items to be included in these tests did involve at least implicit definitions of intelligence. What intelligence tests have in common does at least represent a consensus of what psychometricians understand by intelligence. The development of the statistical technique of correlation enabled Spearman (1904) to demonstrate that there was in fact a great deal in common between all the tests and he argued strongly for the existence of a general intellectual ability (g). The introduction of factor analysis enabled the elements (factors) which tests had in common to be identified with more certainty, but it did not end the arguments about whether intelligence or specific abilities provided the best explanation. Most British psychologists supported Spearman's view of one over-riding factor of general intelligence, but the American psychologists were more impressed by the differences between tests than by their similarities. Thurstone (1938) considered that he had good evidence for the existence of some seven distinct 'primary mental abilities' — perceptual speed, memory, verbal meaning, spatial ability, numerical ability, inductive reasoning and verbal fluency.

The difference between the British and American psychologists was partly one of statistical method and partly one of the samples used. The Americans initially used students and allowed their factors to be interrelated while the British extracted distinct, unrelated factors from samples of schoolchildren. Thomson (1951) was one of the few Britons to accept the sense in allowing factors to be inter-related.

'(So far) we have kept our factors orthogonal; that is independent, uncorrelated with each other. It is natural to desire them to be different qualities and convenient statistically. In describing a man, or an occupation, it would seem both confusing and uneconomical to use factors which, as it were, overlapped. Yet in situations where more familiar entities are dealt with, we do not hesitate to use correlated measures in describing a man. For instance, we give a son's height and weight, although these are correlated qualities' (quoted by Butcher, 1968, pages 54-5).

More recent American research has, on the whole, continued the search for correlated specific abilities. Guilford (1967), for example, has argued that it should be possible to produce tests measuring as many as 30 distinct abilities, exhibited with four distinct types of content — 120 tests in all. Guilford's 'Structure of Intellect' model is shown in Figure 7.4. Although the model provoked much interest, the possibility of describing so many distinct abilities has not been widely accepted. As Vernon (1970) commented somewhat tartly:

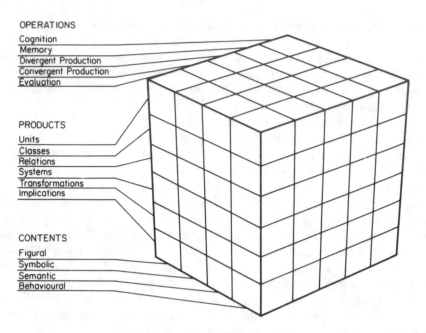

OPERATIONS
Cognition
Memory
Divergent Production
Convergent Production
Evaluation

PRODUCTS
Units
Classes
Relations
Systems
Transformations
Implications

CONTENTS
Figural
Symbolic
Semantic
Behavioural

Figure 7.4 Guilford's scheme of ability factors (from Butcher, 1968)

'While there have been many replications of the half-dozen or so factors that Thurstone originally described, in varied populations, few of Guilford's list have been reidentified by factorists outside the University of California' (page 103).

A hierarchy of mental abilities

Even some American psychologists have become alarmed by the rash of tests of narrowly defined specific abilities. McNemar (1964) wrote an article called 'Lost: our intelligence? Why?' in which he commented on the long history of the idea of intelligence and the way many psychologists had recently splintered it into non-existence. He concluded that:

'the concept of general intelligence, despite being maligned by a few, regarded as a second-order function by some, and discarded or ignored by others, still has a rightful place in the science of psychology and in the practical affairs of man' (page 881).

More recently Cooley and Lohnes (1976) have presented a new classification of cognitive tests which contains only six well-replicated dimensions. They support McNemar's defence of *general intelligence* as a valid and useful conception, as such a factor emerges from almost any group of cognitive tests in a very similar form. They also suggest that there are two major 'knowledge' traits — *English* (or mother-tongue language skills) and *mathematics* (including science), and conclude that these three dimensions provide an accurate indication of a student's general level of academic achievement. However, this interpretation is open to challenge. No doubt these knowledge traits are commonly found in factor analyses, but how fundamental are they? To what extent do these findings reflect a greater consensus between test constructors and teachers on what counts as 'attainment' just in these particular subjects?

The other three dimensions described by Cooley and Lohnes relate to performance on more specific, and simpler, tasks. They are visual reasoning or spatial ability, perceptual speed and accuracy, and memory. This list of abilities is closely similar to Thurstone's original ideas, with the important difference that it incorporates Spearman's factor of general intelligence. It also indicates that there may indeed be a *hierarchy* of intellectual abilities, perhaps arranged as follows

General intelligence

First Language   Mathematics

Memory   Perceptual Skills   Spatial Ability

Burt (1940) and Vernon (1950) argued explicitly for a hierarchy of abilities of which general intelligence (g) was the broadest. Below this were major group factors which Vernon identified as a verbal/educational factor (v : ed) associated with attainment in most subject areas, and a spatial/mechanical factor (k : m) the spatial part of which, Macfarlane-Smith (1964) argues, underlies attainment in advanced mathematics and science. At a lower level Vernon described minor group factors and then a wide range of factors specific to particular tests (see Figure 7.5).

Such a hierarchy helps us to understand the sense in which it is valid to argue for the idea of general intelligence, and yet also accept several contributory, specific abilities. But this hierarchy still does not fit the idea of distinct associative and analytic skills, which was found in the research on memory

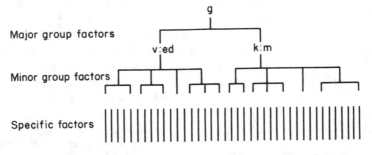

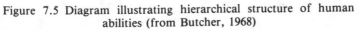

Figure 7.5 Diagram illustrating hierarchical structure of human abilities (from Butcher, 1968)

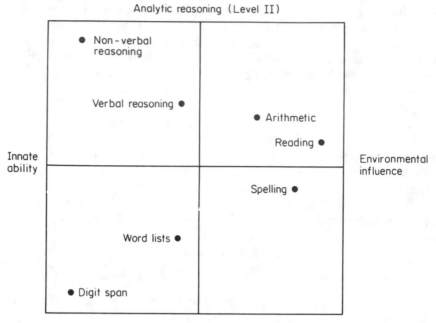

Analytic reasoning (Level II)

- Non-verbal reasoning

Verbal reasoning •

• Arithmetic

Reading •

Innate
ability

Environmental
influence

Spelling •

Word lists •

• Digit span

Associative learning (Level I)

Figure 7.6 Notional classification of tests (Adapted from Jensen, 1970)

processes. One reason for this is the existence of separate traditions of psychometric surveys and experimental studies of learning. The factor analysts have rarely included in their batteries, tests designed solely to measure simple associative tasks, such as the learning and recalling lists of word-lists. When such tasks *are* included, there does appear to be a different type of hierarchy, one which has been described by Jensen (1970). He classifies cognitive skills both in terms of their dependence on environmental and educational experience and by distinguishing associative, what he calls Level I, processes from the Level II processes involved in analytic reasoning. Figure 7.6 shows how certain tests can notionally be positioned within a grid made up of axes of experience and type of learning.

Jensen (1970) places a great deal of emphasis on social class differences in the distribution of scores on associative learning and analytical reasoning. He argues that less able children from the lower social classes may still learn quickly and effectively on associative tasks. The educational implications he has drawn from this suggestion have aroused fierce controversy.

'Present day schooling is highly geared to conceptual modes of learning, and this is suitable for children of average and superior Level II ability. But many children whose weakness is in conceptual ability are frustrated by schooling and therefore learn far less than would seem to be warranted by their good Level I learning ability. A certain important avenue of exploration is the extent to which school subjects can be taught by techniques which depend mostly upon Level I ability and very little upon Level II. After all, much of the work of the world depends largely on Level I ability and it seems reasonable to believe that many persons can acquire basic scholastic and occupational skills and become employable and productive members of society by making the most of their Level I ability' (page 186).

Attacks on Jensen's ideas are not directed at the more effective use of associative learning, but at the apparent implication that children from poor homes should be singled out for a 'second class' education. Jensen's argument depends on the extent to which analytic skills can be taught. If they are largely innate, then his reasoning must stand. But as we shall see in the next chapter, there is an equally strong viewpoint that early environment has a substantial effect on the development of reasoning. In that case there would be different educational implications, and these will be discussed in the final section of the book.

In the meantime, Jensen's argument for the existence of a hierarchy of mental skills needs closer examination. Is there any relationship between Level I and Level II abilities?

'Level II processes are viewed as functionally dependent upon Level I processes. This hypothesis was formulated as a part of the theory to account for some of our early observations that some children with quite low IQ's (i.e. 50 to 75) had quite average or even superior scores on Level I-type tests (simple S-R trial-and-error learning, serial, and paired associate rote learning, and digit span), while the reverse relationship did not appear to exist: children who were very poor on the Level I tests never had high IQ's. It also seems to make sense psychologically to suppose that basic learning and short-term memory processes are involved in performance on a complex Level II task, such as (a non-verbal reasoning test), although the complex inductive reasoning strategies called for by (such a test) would not be called upon for success in Level I tests... Therefore it was hypothesized that Level II performance depends upon Level I but not vice-versa. In other words, Level I is seen as "necessary but not sufficient" for the manifestation of Level II ability' (pages 158-9).

Even this aspect of Jensen's theory has been criticized, but mainly because there is still insufficient empirical evidence to accept his hypothesis as proved. Townsend and Keeling (1976) point that

'While the associative and conceptual abilities are not precisely defined, while the validity of (the) best available measures of these abilities is not known, and while there is no account of the way these abilities relate to what goes on in the classroom, specific tests of the theory are difficult to make' (page 317).

Although the educational implications of Jensen's two-level theory are still not widely accepted, the distinction between associative thinking and analytic reasoning is still useful in systematizing the range of skills related to intelligence.

Measuring imaginative thinking

Jensen's two levels are represented in the most recent individual test of intellectual abilities. The British Ability Scales (Elliott *et al.*, 1977) contain 24 tests covering the range of skills summarized below.

Spatial imagery

Perceptual matching

Speed (of information processing)

Short-term memory

Reasoning

Retrieval and application of knowledge

Jensen's Level I abilities are represented by the tests of short-term memory, while a series of visual and verbal reasoning scales relate to Level II abilities. The final category is reminiscent of the highest level of Bloom's taxonomy. Besides tests of reading and numerical skills, it contains a sub-test of 'verbal fluency'. This scale involves producing imaginative alternatives — a different type of thinking, akin to the 'productive thinking' described by Wertheimer. This intellectual skill is an aspect of what, in everyday language, would be called 'creativity'.

STOP and THINK

● What does the term 'creativity' mean to you?

● How would you decide whether someone was 'creative' or not?

● How would you distinguish 'creativity' from 'intelligence'?

In 1950 Guilford reminded psychologists that most intellectual tests were 'closed' — high scores depended upon a series of predetermined correct answers which demanded *convergent thinking*. He argued that equal attention should be given to 'open' tests of *divergent thinking*. Since then an enormous research effort has been put into measuring divergent thinking and investigating the factors associated with it. There is now a wide range of tests which tap divergent thinking. As with reasoning tests it is important to provide opportunities to think with different types of symbol — verbal, numerical and spatial, or visual. Essentially divergent tests aim to provide a 'fertile' stimulus to imaginative thought. Scores depend both on the number of responses produced and on their novelty. Two commonly used verbal tests of divergent thinking are called 'Uses of Objects' and 'Word Association'. The 'Uses of Objects' test asks for as many different uses as possible for such everyday objects as a barrel or a paperclip. The 'Word Association' test presents words like 'bolt', and asks for as many meanings as possible. Getzels and Jackson (1962) used both these popular tests; they also included 'incomplete fables' (children were asked to provide a humorous and a sad ending, as well as a moral for the story), 'numerical problems' (make up problems from given information) and a 'hidden shapes' test (identify a simple geometrical figure within a complex one).

Hudson (1966) drew attention to the wide differences in performance on the Uses of Objects Test, even of sixth-formers who were all highly intelligent. The inability of some pupils to think of more than the most obvious uses led Hudson to designate them as 'convergers', while the superabundance of uses produced by other boys indicated that they could be called 'divergers'. The label given depends on which test score was higher — the verbal reasoning test or the open-ended test. Hudson illustrates how wide the differences can be by quoting two extreme responses. The boys had been asked to list as many uses as they could think of for a barrel. Both boys were highly intelligent, but one was a mathematician and the other was an arts specialist.

'Converger — Keeping wine in, playing football.

Diverger — For storing old clothes, shoes, tools, paper, etc. For pickling onions in. For growing a yew-tree in. For inverting and sitting on. As a table. As firewood chopped up. As a drain or sump for rainwater. As a sand pit. At a party for games. For making cider or beer in. As a play-pen for a small child. As a rabbit hutch, inverted with a door out of the side. On top of a pole as a dove-cote. Let into a wall as a night exit for a dog or a cat. As the base for a large lamp. As a vase for golden rod and michaelmas daisies, as an ornament, especially if it is small one. With holes cut in the top and sides, either for growing wallflowers and strawberries in, or for stacking pots and kitchen utensils. As a proper garbage can or wastepaper basket. As a ladder to reach the top shelves of a high bookcase. As a casing for a home-made bomb. Sawn in half, as a doll's crib. As a drum. As a large bird's nest' (Hudson, 1966, page 90-91).

Hudson found that a majority of convergers studied science, while divergers mainly specialized in the arts. He also suggested that these interests, and the cognitive abilities associated with them, have their roots in child-rearing practices. The type of responses made by convergers led Hudson to the conclusion that these pupils were emotionally inhibited and he speculated that this inability to express emotion overtly stems from cool, overdemanding mothers.

Wallach and Kogan (1965) carried out an extensive study of the *Modes of Thinking in Young Children,* aged 10-11 years. They criticized previous attempts at measuring divergent thinking, because the tests were given under timed, competitive conditions. Their view was that children's abilities to think

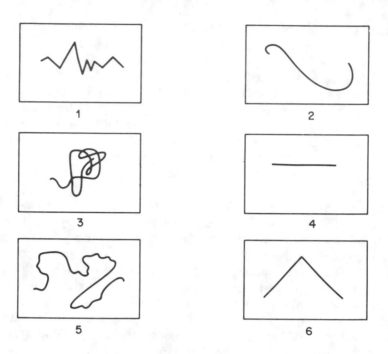

Figure 7.7 Some of the stimulus materials for the line meanings
procedure (from Wallach and Kogan, 1965)

imaginately have to be evoked by a relaxed, game-like approach. A stressful, examination atmosphere is likely to inhibit 'creative' responses. Besides tests of verbal fluency, Wallach and Kogan included two interesting tests using visual stimuli — one with patterns and one with lines (see Figure 7.7). With each drawing, children were asked to describe 'all the things it makes you think of'. From ten scores derived from verbal and visual divergent responses, a combined 'creativity' score was produced; a battery of reasoning and attainment tests was used to define 'intelligence'. With the game-like test conditions, Wallach and Kogan found little relationship between 'creativity' and 'intelligence' ($r = 0.09$), while under timed conditions, Getzels and Jackson (1962) reported correlations from 0.13 to 0.42 between their tests and 'intelligence'. There is thus no clear agreement about the extent to which tests measuring 'creativity' and 'intelligence' can be separated. Research findings depend both on the conditions for testing and on the types of test used to define these two terms.

Divergent thinking and creativity

So far we have seen that divergent thinking has been measured by various open-ended tests. But how does divergent thinking itself differ from convergent thinking? Is it possible to describe that difference in terms of the information processing model described in the previous chapter?

Consider first how problems are solved. Dewey described the stages he expected to be involved: defining the difficulty, locating possible solutions, considering the implications and seeking corroborative evidence. de Bono (1971) has argued that many problems require much more than logical, analytic thinking, which he likens to digging deeper and deeper holes often in quite the wrong place. He suggests that 'lateral thinking' is more likely to be effective — a series of shallow, exploratory holes prior to 'deep drilling'. Lateral thinking seems to be closely allied to divergent thinking, and de Bono sees it as being necessarily leisurely, often having a dream-like quality where the emotions, as well as the intellect, are given free rein. Crutchfield (1962) suggests that

> 'one source of original ideas lies in the ready accessibility to the thinker of many rich and subtle (emotional) attributes of the percepts and concepts in his mental world and to the metaphorical and analogical penumbras extending out from their more explicit, literal or purely logical features. For it is partly through a sensitivity to such (emotional) and metaphorical qualities that new and 'fitting' combinational possibilities among the elements of a problem may unexpectedly emerge' (page 124).

These strategies of thinking can be readily described in the terminology of the information processing model. Divergent thinking is a search strategy which has a broad focus and allows connections between schemata to be made, even when the justifications for the associations are not obvious. The wide sweep of relevant schemata encompasses both semantic and episodic elements within the LTM. In terms of the description given in the previous chapter the search is likely to be relaxed, slow, broad, and not limited to a specific location in the information store. On the other hand convergent thinking will tend to be narrowly focussed, intense, fast and limited to specific locations. Within this model, there would be no necessity to conceptualize 'intelligence' and 'creativity' as separate abilities: they would simply be different ways of using the same store of information and the same range of possible processes. But it would still be necessary to recognize individual differences in the predominant use of particular search strategies and in the way information was stored. The ability to think divergently would demand elaborate cross-classification to facilitate interconnections between schemata. It might also demand less stringent criteria for including a piece of information or an event within a particular category during the coding process. As we shall see in Chapter 10, 'category breadth' is a dimension of individual differences which has been used to describe aspects of both divergent thinking and cognitive style.

Leisurely review of possible connections between schemata is likely to facilitate unusual combinations of ideas. Koestler (1964) sees creativity as depending on what he calls *bisociation* — the bringing together of two domains of thought which were previously separate, and the recognition of unusual, but valid, connections between them. Imaginative thinking is important in problem solving in various ways. First it allows the problem to be reformulated, avoiding an exclusive focus on the most obvious interpretation. Then the review of possible solutions depends on a leisurely approach and a wide focus of attention which includes both likely and unlikely combinations of ideas. But the final stages of problem solving demand a return to tight, narrowly focussed logical thinking. The implications of possible solutions must be considered carefully, and corroborative evidence sought. It is thus important to recognize that divergent thinking *in itself* cannot guarantee either creativity or imaginative problem solving. It is from the appropriate combination of 'free-floating' imagination and rigorous, disciplined logical analysis that the most effective creative work will result. In music and art, mastery of technique blends with aesthetic imagination; in literature, rules of grammar and knowledge of words provide the raw materials from which imaginative ideas can be communicated.

Some recent Norwegian research in Bergen has been assessing the contribution of reasoning skills and divergent thinking to the solution of both practical and semantic problems. Raaheim (1974) argues that intelligence is 'a means whereby a person is able to deal with his partly unfamiliar present in terms of his better known past' and that problem solving shows 'intelligence at work'. In one study Raaheim and Kaufmann (1974) gave 15-16 year old pupils five problem situations in which tools had to be used in an unusual way to reach a solution. For example, pupils were asked how they might save a kitten stranded on a branch of a large tree. The kitten was on a branch too high to reach by jumping and the trunk gave no footholds. The solution depended on the appropriate use of several tools: a strong drill, a hammer, a pair of pliers, and a plane. The kitten could be reached using an improvised ladder. Holes had to be drilled in the tree, and the pliers, the hammer and the drill itself had to be fixed into the holes to provide the necessary footholds.

The five tasks were arranged in order of difficulty and, for the boys, there was a clear relationship between verbal reasoning scores and the ability to solve problems. Girls found the tasks difficult: presumably because they lacked the necessary prior experience of working with such tools to be able to explore their potentialities in problem solving. The solution to practical problems appears to depend on relevant previous experience, the activity level and interest in the task, besides the appropriate use of intellectual skills (Raaheim, 1974).

In a more recent study, Raaheim (1976) has confirmed that divergent thinking in itself is not enough to solve even semantic problems. Students were asked to work out the rationale which had led an imaginary family to prefer one of three objects (Bengtsson and Raaheim, 1976). By providing successive instances of the family's preferences, students could deduce the basis of the choice. The solution thus depends on being able to categorize the objects flexibly. In the second part of the test students were asked to work out in how many different ways the objects actually could differ, and correlations of 0.35 were found between number of categorizations and correct solutions. In the final part of the test, students were asked to reconsider their solutions to the first part. But even when students had produced a categorization which would have solved the problem, this was *used* to reach that solution in only one out of every four instances recorded. Raaheim (1976) concludes:

'This is, as far as I can see, a clear enough demonstration that divergent production is not automatically accompanied by problem solving ability' (page 7).

Translating this argument into an educational context we should expect to find that both convergent and divergent abilities were involved in producing a creative piece of work. There is now substantial evidence to support this conclusion. For example, as part of a study at Lancaster (Entwistle and Bennett, 1973) the beginning of a story, entitled 'If I were invisible', was read out to 11-year-old children, who were then asked to continue the story with their own ideas. The stories were marked for fluency and quality, and scores were compared with conventional attainment in English, with verbal reasoning, and with semantic divergent thinking.

The number of words written in the story (fluency) correlated 0.4 with all three test scores, while the impressionistic mark for quality correlated more highly with the convergent dimensions (0.7) than with the tests of semantic divergence (0.6). But again the conclusion must be that knowledge, reasoning, and divergent thinking are used in combination in creative production, as in problem solving.

Creativity and teaching methods

Wallach and Kogan (1965), in the study mentioned earlier, were interested in the classroom behaviour of children showing different levels of scores on their tests of divergent and convergent thinking. They formed four groups and reported marked differences in behaviour. For example, those children with high scores on divergent thinking and low scores on convergent thinking were seen to be

'in angry conflict with themselves and with their school environment and are beset by feelings of unworthiness and inadequacy. In a stressfree context, however, they can blossom forth cognitively'.

Children with the opposite patern of scores

'can be described as "addicted" to school achievement. Academic failure would be perceived by them as catastrophic, so that they must continually strive for academic excellence in order to avoid the possibility of pain' (page 303).

In the 1960's great alarm was expressed about the lack of encouragement of 'creativity' in schools. Many educationalists argued that teachers undervalued pupils who were imaginative, because they were often unconventional and viewed as 'trouble-makers'. Conventional examinations were considered to encourage conformity and factual regurgitation. Research findings such as those by Wallach and Kogan, and by Getzels and Jackson, were used to justify radical reappraisals of the curriculum and teaching methods.

Bruner (1960) stressed the importance of teaching by the 'discovery method', of presenting topics in a way which allows the pupil to discover for himself important principles. Bruner considered that this approach would stimulate 'intuitive' thinking, which had been long ignored in schools. Intuition was seen as

'the intellectual technique of arriving at plausible but tentative formulations without going through the analytic steps by which such formulations would be found to be valid or invalid conclusions. Intuitive thinking, the training of hunches, is a much-neglected and essential feature of productive thinking not only in formal academic disciplines but also in everyday life. The shrewd guess, the fertile hypothesis, the courageous leap at a tentative conclusion — these are the most valuable coin of the thinker at work, whatever his line of work' (pages 13-14).

It appears that we must now accept 'intuitive', 'lateral', and 'divergent' as terms emphasizing only slightly different aspects of an important style of thinking which has to be contrasted, on the one hand with analytic, logical reasoning, and on the other with associative, rote learning. Such a three-way classification oversimplifies the rich variety of 'search strategies' used in thinking, but is a useful first step in understanding intellectual skills and seeking their educational implications.

Summary

Perhaps the best way to bring together the strands of evidence about intellectual abilities is to reconsider the problem of defining 'intelligence' and 'creativity'. We have seen that it is possible to identify three distinct types of thinking — associative, analytical, and imaginative. These are similar to the types of thinking described by James, Dewey, and Wertheimer respectively in Chapter 3, and have since been measured by a variety of psychological tests. The links between these tests and the types of thinking they are intended to measure are shown opposite.

Associative (Level I) thinking, memorizing or rote learning, describes the process described in the surface approach adopted by some students. In terms of the information processing models derived from experimental studies of the memory, we have described rote learning as the predominant use of STM and overlearning to transfer material mainly into episodic LTM.

Level II thinking is described by Jensen in terms of analytic or reasoning ability. There are, however, also tests of divergent or imaginative thinking which describe intellectual skills which are distinct from analytic skills, and

Type Of Thinking	Level III (Intelligence/Creativity)									
	Perception (Level 0)		Associative (Level I)		Analytical (Level IIA)			Imaginative (Level IIB)		
	Auditory	Visual	Auditory	Visual	Verbal	Numerical	Spatial	Verbal	Numerical	Spatial
Test Material										

which do not rely on those skills. Analytic thinking can be seen, in information processing terms, as the use of closely related areas of semantic LTM, with controlled and narrowly focussed search strategies. Imaginative thinking again makes use of semantic LTM but using diffusely related areas with wide-ranging and leisurely search strategies. Later on, the tendency to adopt predominantly one or other of these strategies will be described in terms of cognitive style. In the table above they have been described as Level IIA and IIB to indicate their distinctiveness at the same level in a hierarchy of intellectual abilities.

What, then, are 'intelligence' and 'creativity'? In everyday terms intelligence may be judged by the quickness and appropriateness of answers given to questions, or by the tendency to act decisively and effectively. We are likely to describe someone as 'creative' if they repeatedly produce ideas or artefacts which are unusual but still, in their own way, effective. Perhaps the best way to consider intelligence or creativity in relation to intellectual abilities is not to suggest that intelligence is convergent thinking and creativity is divergent thinking, but that intelligence and creativity represent higher level skills (Level III) in which people are able to *combine* any or all of the lower level skills to achieve the required outcomes. It is in the *effective use* of available skills in combination to reach the desired outcomes that intelligence or creativity are seen in action. Generally if the outcome is original or unexpected, the process is labelled 'creative', while if it is derived either logically or by judicious selection from known alternatives, 'intelligent' is the adjective applied. Similarly we might describe as 'intelligent' a person who repeatedly used an appropriate combination of intellectual skills to complete the task in hand, and reserve 'creative' for the person who not only produced effective solutions, but regularly sought original or unusual ones. In this definition it is important to recognize that the use of divergent thinking, in itself, does not imply creativity: the outcomes must also be judged as effective.

It is not suggested that these definitions overcome all the difficulties in using the terms 'intelligent' and 'creative'. The criteria for deciding whether the outcomes are effective remain, to some extent, subjective. But a more serious difficulty relates to the use of such labels to describe children, particularly where these terms are used in conjunction with scores which carry a spurious implication of precision. It is often possible to decribe the outcome of *specific tasks* as 'correct' or 'imaginative'. Labelling people, however, can be doubly misleading. It implies consistency, both over subject-matter and over time. While there is evidence from surveys for the existence of both types of consistency, there is also evidence from case studies of substantial variability and intellectual development. For teachers, assumptions of intellectual consistency might have unfortunate consequences for their approaches to teaching. The alternative conception which includes unity in diversity, and consistency allied to both variability and development, is altogether more difficult to understand. It is, however, a much safer basis from which to consider educational implications.

Finally it is important to recognize, as Thomas Reid did, that any classification schemes or models we use are simply a way of 'proceeding more methodically in our subject'. Human thought may be carried out, interchangeably, at different levels and in different modes. It is complex, flexible, and dynamic and so defeats any attempts at simple classification. Models are often a useful way of systematizing our thinking, but should not be allowed to affect the sensitivity with which individual people have a right to be treated.

CHAPTER 8

Concept Formation and Intellectual Development

Much of the research on memory processes has been carried out with student volunteers. The information processing model thus describes *adult* capacities for coding and analysing incoming perceptions. It has little to say about the gradual development of, say, search strategies in LTM. The factor analytic studies on intellectual abilities have used samples of varying ages, but again little stress has been put on the way abilities change with age. For teachers these developmental changes are of great importance, if teaching is to be adapted to the intellectual level of the child.

This chapter examines influential theories on the way children develop concepts and intellectual abilities. But this separation of cognitive development from emotional and moral development is again no more than a convenience. It allows us to simplify an otherwise impossibly complex area. The artificiality of this division can be seen by looking back at the information processing model of memory. The LTM is a storehouse not only for semantic information, but also of memories of events and of the emotions associated with those events. Memories often have a 'feeling tone' which may be painful enough to interfere with recall. Even academic knowledge is stored with links to events — when it was learned, how it was learned — and possibly with feelings of pleasure or pain also associated with those learning experiences.

The information processing model stresses the use of coding procedures in storing information in LTM. We are faced, throughout life, with a potentially overwhelming amount of perceptual information. Coping ploys of various kinds are used to limit and control the inputs from our senses. We have an attention filter to focus on one sense or on one source of information — for example, listening to a lecturer while disregarding his movements and sounds coming from outside the room. In coping with the information we do allow in perhaps the main ploy is to categorize the unfamiliar in terms of the familiar, to interpret events with reference to previous experience. And it is important to recognize that we categorize *people,* just as we might pigeon-hole information or events.

This chapter is concerned with the way a child develops ways of interpreting the world throughout childhood, using concepts and intellectual skills. Although usually described as a theory of personality, the ideas of George Kelly provide a framework for understanding our attempts at making sense of our experiences.

Personal constructs

Kelly (1955) saw human development in terms of the person's *individual* ways of interpreting the world around him. According to his theory, people act as scientists in trying to understand initially puzzling phenomena. They analyse events in terms of similarities and differences, and to do this they build up idiosyncratic sets of *personal constructs*. A construct is a device for 'construing' or interpreting perceptions and it has contrasting poles. For example, when someone is asked to select from the names of three other people (say mother, sister, and boyfriend) the two who are most similar and to say in what ways they are similar, the constructs being used can be elicited. In one example (Kelly, 1955, pages 242-3) the mother and sister were seen as 'both hypercritical of people in general', while the boyfriend was seen as 'friendly'. This person is thus using a construct with the contrasting poles of 'hypercritical' and 'friendly' to interpret differences between people. Other constructs used in this same example were 'feel inferior — self confident' and 'emotionally unpredictable — even temperament'.

Kelly stresses that these constructs help to shape behaviour, but also that the person alters constructs to make more sense of his experiences. Kelly states as a postulate that 'a person's processes are psychologically channelized by the ways in which he anticipates events'. As a corollary of that postulate he adds:

> 'a person chooses for himself that alternative in a dichotomized construct through which he anticipates the greater possibility for extension and definition of his system'.

Kelly's theory suggests that man-the-scientist feels secure only when the future becomes predictable. He uses perceived similarities and differences to interpret events, and 'reaches out to the future through the window of the present' (Pervin, 1975, page 289). He also chooses that interpretation of events which is likely to be most useful in the future. In this way the person is 'constructing his alternatives'. Again Kelly is drawing a parallel with scientific procedure. The scientist develops and modifies theories in ways which aid explanation and prediction. Kelly's ideas on motivation and personality will be considered later on, but they also provide a way of introducing research into intellectual development.

Constructs and concepts

Kelly's ideas about constructs show them to be evaluative, to have positive and negative poles, as well as to be personal. But he was mainly concerned with inter-personal behaviour. It is possible, however, to extend Kelly's image of man-the-scientist to other ways in which people try to interpret the world — through the use of concepts as well as constructs. It is not possible totally to separate these two terms, but essentially a concept is a way of grouping objects or events in terms of essential similarities. Concepts are not evaluative, nor are they as personal as constructs. In many instances it is possible to determine which characteristics are essential in defining a particular concept. For example, a mammal is 'a class of animals which suckle their young'; a bird is 'a feathered animal' (there are, of course, birds which do not fly). Eventually most people will agree about the defining characteristics of simple concepts, but abstract concepts, such as 'justice' cannot be defined in generally agreed ways. There are thus many concepts of which people have to build up their own understanding, and which thus acquire a personal meaning. Some concepts also shade into constructs where they become associated with positive or negative feelings as well as with their defining characteristics.

STOP and THINK

● Can you give examples of concepts which, for you, also carry strong emotional reactions?

● How do you set about trying to define an abstract concept, such as 'courage', or a concrete noun, such as 'mountain'?

● How do we acquire an understanding of these different types of concept?

The word 'fascist' is one with which strong emotions are often associated — a concept which often becomes a personal construct. Its dictionary definition indicates an origin as a name for a member of a political party in Italy, representing a nationalist reaction against socialism and communism, that came to power by violent means in 1922. The term has since been used, generally pejoratively, to describe attitudes and types of behaviour considered similar to those of the original 'Fascisti'. When the term fascist is being used disparagingly, the opposite pole in the personal construct might well be 'democratic' — contrasting rational persuasion with the use of force attributed to the fascists. But another person might use 'communist' as the opposite pole, and see the essential difference in terms of ideology, perhaps believing that people of both persuasions might use force to achieve their ends.

The way of building up any concept is essentially similar, it involves building up positive and negative instances — deciding which objects or events belong to the concept and which do not. The problem with building up instances of abstract concepts is both that there may be disagreement about which events can be included, and that concrete instances often have to be used before the abstract idea can be grasped.

Conceptual development

The use of concepts begins very early in childhood. The process of looking for similarity and difference, and of classifying common instances, can be found in very young children. Before they have acquired language, they may well attach their own labels to classes of objects and attempt to communicate their wants by simultaneously making these sounds and pointing. Though children may use idiosyncratic sound-labels before they can express their ideas, words are essential for the easy communications of shared meaning. Children's language develops through the combined effects of *maturation* and experience. It depends partly on the genetically determined sequence in which the child matures physiologically, and partly on opportunities for learning how to use new capabilities as they emerge. Initially babies are limited by immature speech 'mechanics'. They first have to discover how to make speech sounds and the early 'babbling' represents little more than the flexing of speech muscles. Later, infants use their own sounds to indicate objects, and parents help them to link sounds to words (moo-cow, baa-lamb). Children may, however, develop their own associations to help them draw attention to objects or events. Sometimes the traditional sound-word link may become inappropriate. For example, how could a baby be expected to find 'puffer-train' useful any longer? If an infant uses a sound to represent 'train' nowadays, it is more likely to be the two notes of a diesel engine. This example illustrates that 'baby language' has its origins in a natural tendency to label objects through symbolic sounds.

The way in which children begin to build up concepts is a good example of stimulus-response learning. William James mentioned the importance of contiguity and similarity in determining which ideas become associated. Words which are heard together or which have similar meanings become linked. It was left to behaviourist psychologists, such as Thorndike and Skinner, to explain how these associations occur, and to extend these principles to behaviour as well as thinking.

Thorndike saw as fundamental principles the laws of *effect* and *exercise*. These commonsense ideas remind us first that we are likely to repeat behaviour which leads to satisfaction or which is rewarded. Conversely punishment is likely to prevent the recurrence of actions associated with pain or humiliation. The second law indicates that repetition strengthens any stimulus-response bond — that over-learning improves performance.

These principles of learning are age-old, and not restricted to human beings. Chimpanzees use punishment, followed by reassurance, to mould the behaviour of their offsprings in ways disconcertingly similar to our own child-rearing practices (van Lawick-Goodall, 1971). Infant chimpanzees also spend much of their time in repeating actions over and over again until skills are mastered. Skinner (1953), with his research on pigeons, demonstrated the effectiveness of immediate reinforcement of correct responses. In the absence of reward (negative reinforcement) stimulus-response bonds weakened, and eventually disappeared. By appropriate 'schedules of reinforcement' Skinner was able to shape animals' behaviour, to build up complicated routines from simple component elements. Skinner saw these principles as explaining *all* behaviour, even the way children learn in classrooms. The well-known application of his theory to programmed learning will be discussed in Chapter 11. Here our concern is with the early stages of concept development, and parents clearly follow the basic outline of stimulus-response principles in correcting potentially dangerous behaviour, and in building up stimulus-response links between objects, sounds, words, and concepts. Parents often reward by immediate praise the appropriate use of words and may also criticize words wrongly applied; similarly they will show their approval of 'correct' behaviour and perhaps punish dangerous or 'bad' behaviour. At this stage parents clearly have a great influence in 'shaping' their children's behaviour and use of language. This influence, and this 'mechanical' form of learning, certainly continue throughout childhood and adolescence, but the child gradually takes over greater conscious control of his actions and learns directly from his own attempts at systematizing experience, particularly through play. Then the relative importance of stimulus-response learning markedly declines.

Alert parents are able to capitalize on the child's early use of sound labels and words, and so shape appropriate language usage and help children to acquire an understanding of concepts. Klausmeier and his colleagues (Klausmeier *et al.*, 1974) have described a developmental sequence for concept formation, which begins with a *concrete* level, similar to the process described so far.

'The discrimination of objects involves attending to distinctive features that serve to distinguish objects from one another. Thus very early the child learns to respond to gross differences in such features of objects as size, shape, colour, and texture. As the child matures, he becomes capable of making finer discriminations.

The attainment of a concept at the concrete level thus requires attending to the distinctive features of an object and forming a memory image, which represents the object as a unique bundle of features. The concept at this level may or may not be associated with the concept label, depending on whether the label has been learned and remembered, and whether it has been associated with the concept' (page 16).

To develop such concrete concepts the infant relies on physical manipulation and visual exploration of the object. The concept thus comes to be represented *enactively* (through manipulation) and *iconically* (as an image) in Bruner's (1964) terms — in other words by *sensori-motor activity* (Piaget's term).

From this earliest way of categorizing objects, Klausmeier suggests a progression to an *identity* level when objects can be recognized in spite of their orientation, the angle from which they are seen. Thus a dog is a dog, no matter whether it is seen from the front, back, or side. But children still have very uncertain concepts in these early stages of development. Initially they may well apply the same word — 'dog' — to a whole range of furry or hairy creatures with four legs. Adults shape the responses by helping the children to *discriminate,* to apply the word correctly to a restricted sub-set of hairy quadrupeds with certain distinctive features in common. Klausmeier describes as the *classificatory* level, the ability to group correctly several different instances of a concept (poodle, corgi, alsatian) without being able to explain the basis of that classification. This process of concept development is analogous to the use of personal constructs. In understanding concepts children have to decide whether a particular object fits into one concept or a slightly different one. Comparison between opposites is an essential component of the development of a construct system, while the framework of concepts is built up by repeated comparisons between instances and related concepts. Judgement of similarity and difference is common to both processes and leads to increased accuracy in codifying experience. Through understanding and interpreting present events, the future becomes more predictable.

Finally, in Klausmeier's scheme, children reach the *formal* level of concept development when they can go beyond the simple recognition of a concept and name its commonly accepted defining attributes. At this stage children are operating through Bruner's *symbolic* mode of representation to describe verbally the similarities and differences they use to include, say, poodle, corgi, alsatian in one concept and to distinguish these dogs from other concepts — cats, foxes, wolves. When asked to explain the meaning of a word, young children tend to give specific instances or examples; they do not describe it in terms of defining attributes. This ability to generalize and abstract, as we shall see, only develops fully during adolescence.

Intellectual development

So far we have considered how the main 'pigeon-holes' of LTM are built up mainly through stimulus-response associations between perceptions and semantic labels, by discriminating similarities and differences which provide cross-references between concepts or between schemata. But the child is not just forming concepts, he is also developing *mental operations* which allow the contents of LTM to be manipulated and inter-related. Over a period of fifty years, Piaget has been formulating a scheme which describes the development of intellectual skills from babyhood to adolescence.

Piaget pays little attention to stimulus-response learning. He does not deny that it occurs, but sees it as 'learning in the narrow sense'. Human thinking goes far beyond the early stimulus-response bonds. Not only are mental structures built up by associations, but also by fundamental internal rearrangements which are shown by qualitatively different approaches to situations and problems (Phillips, 1975, page 14). It is these distinctive qualitative changes in mental functioning that Piaget has described as *stages* of intellectual development. The attempts of children to come to terms with their surroundings and with other people depend on mental *organization* (such as the development of concept structures) to represent external events, and on *adaptation* — the ability to respond to those events. Adaptation, within the Piagetian scheme, takes place through two basic processes — *assimilation* and *accommodation*. The information processing model suggests in some detail how an incoming light or sound signal is transformed and stored. It is this process of changing the input to fit existing schemata which can be called assimilation. But perceptions also alter mental structure and behaviour; experience leads to learning — an accommodation to the outside world. There is an inevitable tension between these two processes. Sometimes the incoming perceptions may not fit existing schemata and a fundamental rearrangement of schemata is triggered off.

Kelly has also described a similar process in which fundamental changes occur in the way in which we construe the world. Old constructs are seen to be inappropriate or incomplete, and new constructs are introduced to allow further development. Kelly stresses that the tensions created by mismatches between new perceptions and old ways of construing events can create uncertainty and anxiety, in much the same way as Perry found students coping with a growing realization of the implications of relativistic reasoning.

In young children, however, the rearrangement of schemata is frequent and unlikely to provide anxiety. There is rarely any threat associated with this process which Piaget calls *equilibration*. He also sees this process as giving rise to a series of characteristic stages and periods.

'Piaget conceives of intellectual development as a continual process of organization and reorganization of structures, each new organization integrating the previous one into itself. Although the process is continuous, its results are discontinuous; they are qualitatively different from time to time. Because of that, Piaget has chosen to break the total course of development into units called *periods* and *stages*. Note carefully, however, that each of those cross sections of development is described in terms of the best the child can do at that time. Many previously acquired behaviours will occur even though he is capable of new and better ones' (Phillips, 1975, page 19).

Piaget based his description of the six stages which make up the *sensorimotor* period mainly on observations of his own children. Between birth and about 2 years of age, the child thinks predominantly through motor symbols, or through direct interaction with his environment. Around age 2, concrete concepts begin to give place to more elaborate classificatory concepts. Symbols are used to represent and think about the surroundings as the child enters the *pre-operational* period, which Piaget suggests is predominant up to about age 7.

Piaget explored children's reasoning through the use of a series of graded scientific experiments backed up by individual questioning. One of the best known of these involves the use of two small beakers (A1, A2) and a narrow test-tube. The two identical beakers are filled with water to the same level. One of the beakers (A1) is emptied into the test-tube and the child is asked if the remaining beaker (A2) and the test-tube each have the same amount of water or if one has more than the other. Five-year-old children will generally reply that the test-tube has more water in it because the level is higher. They have not recognized that the volume of liquid must stay the same; they are misled by the striking change in the height of the columns of liquid. They depend more on appearance than on the analysis of properties.

In another experiment a child is shown seven beads, five white, and two black. He is asked whether there are more *white beads* or more *beads*. Again five-year-olds tend to answer incorrectly. They depend on being able to *see* the relationships. They can see that there are more white beads than black ones, but they cannot simultaneously see both the whole and a part. They would require a mental operation to compare two categories of bead — all beads and white beads. Only when the period of *concrete operations* is reached will this comparison be made successfully. Then the child will also recognize the principle of reversibility; that if the water in the test-tube is poured back into the beaker (A1), the levels in the two beakers will still remain the same. Conservation of volume depends on recognizing this property of *reversibility* and also on two other operations — *compensation* and *identity*. The child has to appreciate that a tall column of liquid in a narrow tube can be the same as a short column in a wide container — that width compensates for height. Finally the recognition that nothing has been added and nothing taken away in transferring the water (identity) completes the concrete mental operations involved in this experiment.

By age 11, at least some children begin to enter the final period of intellectual development identified by Piaget — *formal operations*. The previous operations depended on recognizing simple relationships between two concrete properties, such as height and width. Other problems require a systematic strategy to uncover inter-relationships between more than two properties. For example, Inhelder and Piaget (1958) describe an experiment in which a child is presented with five flasks (A-E) containing colourless liquids. The chemical combination of A + C + E produces a yellow colour, but B is a bleaching agent which removes the colour, while D is plain water. The child is shown the colour that can be produced, but not how it is done. He is asked to discover the combination of liquids which produces the colour, and what effects are produced by liquids B and D.

'At age seven to eleven the child generally proceeds by combinations of two's and then jumps to a trial of all five together. After the age of twelve he proceeds methodically, testing all possible combinations of one, two, three, four, and five elements, and thus solves the problem' (Piaget and Inhelder, 1969, page 134).

The period of formal operations thus sees the beginning of the hypothetico-deductive method of the scientist, the use of hypotheses formulated and tested as part of a gradual elimination of alternative explanations. During this final period of intellectual development the adolescent gradually acquires the ability to consider inter-relationships between several concrete properties and also to think logically about abstract principles. These thought processes seem similar to the Level II analytic ability described by Jensen, while the early stages of concept acquisition may involve no more than Level I associative thinking. At least in a very general way, therefore, we can now accept that Level II develops much later than Level I, but as Piagetian tasks and Jensen's psychometric tests are not directly comparable, little can be said precisely about the development of either of Jensen's categories.

Although Piaget's theory has made a considerable impact, it is by no means accepted in its entirety. There are still many questions about it that need to be answered. For example,

● Is the progression through the stages and periods *always* in the same order?
● What age ranges are to be expected for the various stages?
● Can a child be operating at more than one level simultaneously?
● Do *all* children reach the level of formal operations?
● Does the appearance of the same sequence of stages imply a strong inherited component in intelligence?
● Can teaching accelerate the rate of children's progression through the stages, or must teaching methods await the maturation of appropriate intellectual skills?

Logically it seems inevitable that the progression Piaget outlines must always follow the same sequence. Formal operations depend on concrete operations and so on. Empirically there is substantial evidence that this sequence is followed in outline, although the ages mentioned by Piaget are only indicative. Piaget and Inhelder (1969) maintain that order of succession of stages and period

'is constant, although the average ages at which they occur may vary with the individual, according to his degree of intelligence or with the social milieu' (page 153).

Critics (e.g. Brown and Desforges, 1977, 1979; Flavell, 1977; Donaldson, 1978) have argued that Piaget's scheme is not fully supported by the evidence. Donaldson (1978) reports experiments using Piagetian methods in which a slight change in the instructions or the materials results in different findings.

In particular she argues that even young children can be shown to use abstract thought, although not in the restricted, formal ways incorporated into Piaget's theory.

Brown and Desforges (1977; 1979) have attacked the evidence on the distinctiveness of stages. Piaget discounts the significance of the variation in performance between tasks requiring the same level of thinking. He refers to this phenomenon as *'horizontal décalage'*. It is, however, possible to argue that the differences in level of performance between tasks are sufficiently large to throw doubt on the whole idea of stages and periods as qualitatively distinct periods of intellectual development. The *tasks* themselves may demand qualitatively distinct skills, but the intellectual processes develop gradually and at different rates in relation to different types of experience. It is not sensible to describe a stage in terms of the optimum level of thinking reached, if there are wide variations between tasks at the same level of difficulty. We should have to say, for example, that the child is using concrete operations for certain tasks or perhaps for a certain area of the curriculum, while being capable of using formal operations in other specified situations.

Although the idea of stages disintegrates if the tasks required differ substantially in content, Shayer (1979) has shown that the tasks normally used in defining Piagetian stages overlap sufficiently for these stages to be measured reliably. There remains, however, the argument that these intellectual skills will be so specific to particular types of experimental task that any generalized statement about stages, and particularly any direct implications for education are likely to be of dubious value (Desforges and Brown, 1979).

The argument here parallels the earlier dilemma we met in considering whether the results of intellectual testing are best described as showing consistency or variability. In some ways it makes good sense to describe stages of intellectual development. Certainly, as Marton (1978) has recently argued, the thinking used in solving particular problems can be described unambiguously within the Piagetian scheme, but it may be totally inappropriate to describe any individual as having reached a particular stage of intellectual development. Again such a description would imply consistency irrespective of both situation and content.

As we have seen in Raaheim's work (page 156), familiarity with the materials in a practical problem affects children's ability to reach a solution. We should thus expect children to operate contemporaneously at different stages, depending on their familiarity with the task. At the same age children may use concrete operations in one area of the curriculum and formal operations in another. We should also expect differences between children in the ages at which they begin to use abstract concepts and formal systematic thinking. Indeed it is far from clear that all adolescents are capable of formal operations. Hebron (1964) has suggested that children with an IQ of less than 110 are unlikely to reach the level of formal operations while at school. Whether the children *fail* to reach this level, or simply fail to *demonstrate* such thinking, is less clear. Gardner (1976) comments:

'Formal operations represent a level of reasoning which is reached, with effort, by most adolescents in Western society but which is not a vital part of the lives of most, and which achieves facility and full use only in those who go on into the sciences' (page 103).

As with a deep approach to learning, the evidence suggests that intention, situation and previous knowledge will all affect whether formal operations are detected. Piaget's reliance on simple scientific experiments may put non-scientists at a disadvantage and also devalue the importance, during adolescence, of the development of imaginative or intuitive thought applied to abstract notions.

Peel (1975a, b; 1976) has extended the description of adolescent thinking into a variety of curriculum areas. His work brings together ideas on conceptual development with Piaget's emphasis on the use of logical operations. For example, Peel (1976) discusses a study by de Silva (1972) which shows the difficulty adolescents have in understanding abstract economic and historical concepts. Adolescents aged 12-16 were asked to read ten short passages which introduced concepts such as 'monopoly', 'slump', 'tariff', and 'capital'. Peel (1976) uses the following example of one of the passages to illustrate differences in the ability to recognize the concept of 'capital'.

'The new trading enterprises in Tudor and Stuart times were different in many ways from the overseas enterprises of medieval times. The countries traded with were farther away than Flanders and France. The journeys to be made, therefore, were much more dangerous; the time occupied over a single journey was very much longer than had formerly been the case. Hence *ramudal* became a very important factor in these enterprises and almost the whole trade ultimately passed under the control of vast concerns.

What do you think is the meaning of the word '*ramudal*' in the above passage? Why do you think so?

The replies can be grouped into three main classes.

(A) *Logically restricted* — displaying a gross lack of comprehension of the passage, e.g. a very important thing; a high official. (B) *Circumstantially dominated* conceptualization — based on one or more pieces of evidence from the passage but lacking in total comprehension of the passage, e.g. canals, food, trading companies, exploration. (C) *Deductive conceptualizations* — where a comprehensive survey of the passage is linked with ideas originating in the testee — imagined hypothesis, inferences, etc. e.g. money, capital — supported by a reference to elements in the passage' (pages 8-9).

At age 12, 71 per cent of children gave logically restricted explanations with just over 10 per cent providing deductive responses. At age 16 there was a sharp increase in the proportion of deductive explanations, but even then 40 per cent of children remained in the lowest category.

In this experiment children were required to use analytic thinking to understand abstract concepts. Peel (1975a) argues that the ability to identify and use abstractions shows the development of formal operations in a range of subject ares. He has developed a test of generalizing and abstracting (Peel,

1978) which demonstrates differences with age, educational experience and ability level. Three words are presented in each item. Respondents are required to choose from another set of four words, the one 'which best expresses the overall meaning of the first three notions'. Some items use concrete nouns, others contain abstract concepts. The concrete examples were answered correctly by over 91 per cent of secondary school pupils, but only 63 per cent of them were successful on abstract items. With three samples — further education students, first-year undergraduates, and a combination of final year and post-graduate students — the percentages of correct responses to abstract items were 60, 71 and 82 respectively. Some of the abstract items caused considerable difficulty. Take the following example:

Murder,   aggression,   exploitation

Select from — fascism, detestable, suppression, inhumanity.
The true general term is 'inhumanity', but some 9 per cent of first-year undergraduates selected an emotional particularization 'fascism', while 8 per cent each chose either 'suppression' at the same level of generality or 'detestable' which represents a personal reaction to a 'non-essential attribute'.

As pupils begin to use abstractions, they are also able to provide more analytic and sensitive explanations of problem situations. For example, Peel (1975b) describes a study in which pupils were asked to consider a crisis situation of Maugham's *Of Human Bondage*. One of the characters is told of his mother's death; the pupils are asked to describe the person's reactions. At age 12 the comments rely largely on the *mention* of no more than two facts from the passage. By age 15, 43 per cent of the pupils *describe* facts and possibilities, but still fail to provide any *explanation*. Only 28 per cent give an 'explicit discussion of the dynamics of the crisis situation and possible consequences', while a quarter of the sample were still simply mentioning related facts.

Peel suggests that the ability to explain and judge physical problems shows a marked increase around age 13-14, but social problems cannot be dealt with in a similar way until later. The emergence of this ability to apply abstract reasoning in a sophisticated way is, as might be expected, also related to scores on verbal reasoning tests. Higher ability pupils have been found to be some two years ahead in reaching this stage than those of lower ability (Clarke, 1974).

This research on generalizing and abstracting has been described in some detail because it provides a bridge between Piaget's work and Marton's ideas on qualitatively different levels of understanding. Peel is describing the way in which the use of formal operations gradually extends from the context of simple physical experiments to complex social situations. But the characteristic categories of response he reports bear a close resemblance to the levels of 'mentioning', 'describing', and 'conclusion-orientated' identified by Marton and his colleagues (see page 76). A deep level of understanding requires the ability to abstract and generalize, besides the use of a deductive approach in relating facts to conclusion. Peel's research shows that the skills required in carrying through a deep approach to learning emerge in different content areas during adolescence, and that even the brightest pupils are unlikely to be able to use them effectively in a wide variety of situations until about age 17. The inability of some students to adopt a deep approach may thus be attributed, at least in part, to limitations in pre-requisite intellectual skills. But it is equally important to recognize that the failure to adopt a deep approach, or to use formal operational thought, may *not* reflect a deficiency in such abilities. It may, in many instances, be attributable to a lack of previous knowledge or experience, or to a low level of interest in the task presented or content-area being studied.

Heredity and experience

Piaget's ideas about the clear stages of intellectual development might suggest the influence of a genetic 'program' predetermining both the rate and sequence of development. But Piaget himself argues that both genetic and environmental influences are important.

> 'Maturation consists essentially of opening up new possibilities and thus constitutes a necessary but not in itself sufficient condition for the appearance of certain behaviour patterns. The possibilities thus opened up also need to be fulfilled, and for this to occur, the maturation must be reinforced by functional exercise and a minimum of experience' (Piaget and Inhelder, 1969, page 154).

Piaget describes the different types of experience which facilitate mental development. The child, at any early stage, uses physical manipulation of objects and later translates physical action into mental action, operating on mental images of objects rather than on the objects themselves. Piaget also recognizes the importance of social interaction and transmission in the home and school, but stresses that without active assimilation by the child such social experience will be ineffective.

What is the relative importance of heredity in affecting intellectual development? Ideological disputes between psychologists have raged over this question. Some psychologists (Burt, 1970; Jensen, 1967) have used evidence from studies of identical and non-identical twins brought up in the same and in different environments to argue that up to 80 per cent of intelligence is inherited. At the opposite extreme some behaviourist psychologists and sociologists have stressed the over-riding influence of environmental experiences. This controversy reached a head when the evidence presented by Cyril Burt was denounced as being fraudulent (Gillie, 1976). Hearnshaw's (1979) thorough evaluation of Burt's writings led to the conclusion that some of the twin data cited in Burt's later articles had indeed been fabricated, and that even the earlier data were of dubious validity. However, Vernon's (1979 a, b) well-balanced review of the literature on the relative influence of heriditary and environment on intellectual growth suggests that, even after discounting Burt's evidence, genetic effects on intelligence are still strong. Vernon estimates that 65 per cent of measured intellectual abilities can be attributed to genetic effects and some 23 per cent to environment influences. The remaining 12 per cent has been described as covariance, which 'refers to the obvious likelihood that intelligent parents who pass on superior genes to their offspring also usually provide above-average environments' (Vernon, 1979a, page 7).

While the nature/nurture debate will continue to reverberate, with each side looking for loopholes in the other's evidence and arguments, the conclusion seems inescapable that both heriditary and environment are important. Beside the twin studies, Vernon (1979a) cites other types of evidence which indicate a genetic effect:

'the fact that rats and dogs can be bred to produce bright and dull strains; the tendency for close human inbreeding to yield congenital malformations and mental defect, and the discovery that specific gene anomalies produce psychological syndromes such as Down's and Turner's' (page 8).

Vernon also comments that children often do *not* resemble their parents or siblings in intelligence. Children brought up in the same household, and therefore without grossly different environmental experiences, may show a wide range of IQ (for example, from 84 up 142 in a family of eight — Maxwell, 1969, page 180). Such a wide range is much more readily explained by genetic than by environmental effects.

The evidence *for* environmental effects is equally strong. Vernon (1979 a, b) summarizes the retarding effects of extreme environments, such as some orphanages where children had little intellectual stimulation. He estimates that a difference in IQ of up to 30 points might be attributable to extreme differences in environment but also shows that, at least up to age 7, removal from an unstimulating environment often leads to rapid increases in the levels of measured intelligence.

Other evidence of apparently strong environmental influences has been collected. For example, in a study by Burton White (White *et al.*, 1979) at Harvard the very early stages of intellectual development were examined in relation to patterns of child-rearing. Between the ages of 10 and 18 months it became possible to identify two groups of children. The 'A' group had a set of intellectual and social skills which the 'C' group lacked. The problem posed by White and his colleagues was whether there were any noticeable differences in the child-rearing behaviour of the mothers of these two groups of children. Their conclusion has been summarized by Pines (1976).

'Children change radically between ages 10 and 18 months. . . . Suddenly they can walk, move around the house, get into everything. At the same time they begin to understand language and to assert themselves. It is a stressful time for the mother, a testing time, and the way she responds then determines how her child will do by (age) 3.
    What do mothers who produce A children do during this period? Surprisingly, they don't spend a great deal of time 'interacting' with each child — they are far too busy, and some of them even have part-time jobs. Dr. White estimates that (these) mothers seldom give their undivided attention for more than 10 per cent of

his waking time. . . . Nor do they do much deliberate teaching.

However, they are superbly effective in two roles: (1) indirectly as organizers, designers, and the rulers of the child's physical environment; and (2) directly as consultants to their children "on the fly". . . .

The C mothers, on the other hand, "protect" their children (and their possessions) by ruling a large number of places out of bounds. They restrict the child's instinct to explore. . . . They may be loving, patient, and well-meaning, but they don't share their baby's excitement, they talk much less to him, and they fail to stimulate him intellectually' (Pines, 1976, page 25).

Yet in all of the research on genetic and environmental effects on intelligence, even apparently clear-cut results can be interpreted in different ways.

STOP and THINK

● Maxwell found large differences in IQ between children in the same family. White showed a clear relationship between child-rearing and intellectual ability at age 3. How would you attempt to reconcile this apparent contradiction?

● Can you think of any alternative explanations for the link between child-rearing and child's intelligence?

It is possible for 'A' mothers to have a facilitating effect on all their children, and yet for there to remain considerable variations in IQ among them. But from White's findings it seems unlikely that such differences could be as large as those found by Maxwell. On the other hand, White's research does not show whether mothers behave in similar ways with all their children. Large differences could still be found if their child-rearing patterns were inconsistent. We should also have to ask whether White's sample covered a full range of social background.

In considering the environmental effect of child-rearing patterns it is easy to ignore another facet of genetic inheritance. Although genetic effects can produce wide discrepancies between siblings, children tend, on average, to be similar to their parents. We should thus have to ask whether there were intellectual differences between 'A' and 'C' *mothers* which might have been passed on to their children, and which might also affect the mothers' child-rearing behaviour. This is another facet of the covariation effects which Vernon described. We should have to consider whether bright mothers are likely to be patient and passive. Also we should have to ask whether parents behave differently to an active, intelligent baby than an unresponsive one. It is all too easy to assume that parents are responsible for their children's behaviour, without recognizing that even a baby may affect its mother's behaviour. If intelligent toddlers are markedly more independent and able to find interest in their environment, mothers may be better able to take up the role of 'on the fly' consultants. All that we can safely say is that intelligent behaviour is likely to be a complex product of genetic predispositions, and environmental experiences and interaction. It is difficult to go further than that on the basis of the evidence we have.

The teacher is left with a dilemma. If the stages of intellectual development emerge at a pre-determined rate, must teaching methods be geared to the current stage? Or can the next stage be evoked by appropriate teaching? Piaget seems to doubt the value of trying to accelerate intellectual development, but Bruner (1960) put forward the bold hypothesis that

> 'any subject can be taught effectively in some intellectually honest form to any child at any stage of development' (page 33).

Although it would not be difficult to disprove this hypothesis by using extreme instances or to argue that the statement is too vague to be useful, it nevertheless implies an important warning to teachers not to use any genetic hypothesis as an excuse for inaction. Bruner begins the justification of his claim as follows:

> 'Research on the intellectual development of the child highlights the fact that at each stage of development the child has a characteristic way of viewing the world and explaining it to himself. The task of teaching a subject is one of representing the structure of that subject in terms of the child's way of viewing things. The task can be thought of as one of translation' (page 33).

Although Piaget would anticipate substantial limitations in Bruner's 'optimistic gospel' for teachers, they both agree on the necessity of stimulating active thought processes. Bruner (1973), like Dewey, criticizes teachers for failing to provide sufficient encouragement of hard thinking.

> 'It is an epistemological mystery why traditional education has so often emphasized extensiveness and coverage over intensiveness and depth. We have already commented on the fact that memorizing was usually perceived by children as one of the high-priority tasks, but rarely did children sense an emphasis upon ratiocination with a view to redefining what had been encountered, reshaping it, reordering it. The cultivation of reflectiveness, or what ever you choose to call it, is one of the great problems one faces in devising curricula: how to lead children to discover the powers and pleasures that await the exercise of retrospection' (page 449).

Bruner's suggestions for encouraging this mental activity in children will be discussed in the final section of the book.

Intellectual development may well depend on genetic potential, but early environment and parental encouragement to think actively are also important. Besides helping children to acquire concepts, parents may also be able to foster analytic thinking, perhaps by using verbal absurdities. If coding into semantic memory depends on the ability to discriminate similarities and differences, the use of deliberate mistakes and false categorizations, which children enjoy detecting, may well be valuable. Parents share with teachers this responsibility for stimulating children's thinking and encouraging them actively to question what they see and hear.

Summary

Children, and adults, seek to understand the world around them and hence to anticipate future events. Making sense of the welter of incoming perceptions demands endless comparisons and judgements. Kelly has explained how people develop personal constructs to understand their experiences. They also develop an elaborate system of interrelated concepts to store information and to communicate ideas.

Klausmeier describes the early acquisition of concepts in terms of a developmental sequence. Initially young children classify objects solely in terms of obvious *concrete* characteristics. The next level — *identity* — occurs when objects can readily be recognized from any angle. At the *classificatory* level, children can group correctly different instances of a concept, while at the *formal* level the basis for that classification can also be explained.

Piaget's theory describes similar developmental stages in levels of thinking, progressing from *sensori-motor,* through *pre-operational,* to *concrete operations,* and *formal operations.* Each stage results from equilibration between the basic processes of *assimilation* of experiences and *accommodation* of mental structures to fit the new experiences. However, it is now clear that children's levels of thinking are not constant at any one age. There is a developmental sequence, as formal operations are applied to different content areas — first in science and only much later in the humanities. Also children, and adults, vary in the extent to which they will *use* formal operations, even when the skills are well established. As with a deep approach to learning, the use of formal operations is likely to be dependent on previous knowledge and interest.

The effects of heredity and environment on intellectual development have been fiercely debated. The most recent estimates of relative influences attribute 65 per cent to genetic effects, 23 per cent to environment, and 12 per cent to interactions between the two. The actual percentages are still uncertain, but both inheritance and early experience have been shown to have substantial effects on intellectual development. From the teacher's standpoint it is important to recognize that intellectual stages are not physiological barriers: the genetic hypothesis cannot be an excuse for failing to encourage children to think analytically. Stages can, at least to some extent, be induced by appropriate teaching, and the effects of unfavourable early environments can be partially overcome by active intellectual stimulation and encouragement.

CHAPTER 9

Personality and Motivation: Hope for Success and Fear of Failure

In the research on how students learn we saw how differences in personality were associated with different 'paths' towards intellectual development. For example, Heath's 'hustlers', 'non-committers', and 'plungers' all moved towards the ideal of the 'reasonable adventurer', but along different routes. Each of the personality types had some of the favourable characteristics of the 'reasonable adventurer', but had to work hard to overcome an initial one-sidedness in their behaviour and ways of thinking. Heath's picturesque labels for three different types of student represent one idiosyncratic approach to describing important contrasts in people's typical behaviour. In this chapter some of the wide variety of ways to describe personality development and personality structure will be considered. Again a separation of research traditions between developmental studies and factor analytic work leaves an unsatisfactory gap between the ideas presented. Moreover there is no consensus in either area as to the most appropriate terms with which to describe personality. To avoid an overwhelming range of contradictory ideas, therefore, only a few of the theories are presented as exemplars of the many other approaches to describing personality.

STOP and THINK

Personality, like intelligence or creativity, is a word used in everyday life.

- What do *you* understand by personality?

- How would you distinguish between the terms personality, character and temperament?

In searching for a satisfactory definition of personality, Allport (1963) explored the etymological origins of the words 'personality', 'character', and 'temperament'. The Latin word *persona* originally described the painted mask which an actor held in front of his face to portray the person he was playing. The word subsequently was used to indicate the 'front' an individual presented to other people — how he wanted to be seen. It was also used to describe 'the player behind the mask, i.e. his true assemblage of inner and personal qualities' (Allport, 1963, page 25). But the original meaning persists to emphasize that personality incorporates both inner qualities and outward appearance.

In Greek, *character* meant 'engraving', and implied a pattern of traits embodied in a distinctive life-style. Later, however, this word has come to refer to moral qualities — 'He has a good character', but Allport points out that 'characteristic' remains a neutral term, synonymous with 'trait'.

Early descriptions of personality often followed the ideas of a Roman physician, Galen (150 AD), who explained human behaviour in terms of supposed bodily secretions or 'humours'. Blood became associated with a *sanguine* approach to life. An overproduction of black bile made people *melancholic,* while yellow bile was responsible for *choleric* behaviour. Finally too much phlegm led to *phlegmatic* attitudes. *Temperament* came into the English language closely linked with Galen's terminology.

'It meant then, and still means, a constitution or habit of mind, especially depending upon, or connected with, physical constitution' (Allport, 1963, page 33).

It can be taken as the genetic contribution to personality, while character is a social evaluation of a distinctive life-style.

Psychologists have concentrated on the outward, developing personality in their attempts to account for regularities in people's behaviour, and Allport (1963) put forward his own formal definition of personality as

'the dynamic organization within the individual of those psychophysical systems that determine his characteristic behaviour and thought' (page 28).

This definition draws attention to the fact that personality can change; like intelligence, it is affected by experience. The definition also indicates that personality depends on both psychological and physical attributes, which determine not only a person's characteristic behaviour, but also his thought. Finally it hints at physiological systems common to everyone, yet points to the ultimate uniqueness of the individual.

'Every man is in certain respects (a) like other men (b) like some other men and (c) like no other man' (Kluckhohn *et al.,* 1953, page 53).

In studying personality, psychologists have concentrated on identifying patterns of development followed by everyone, and on describing characteristic differences between people, or groups of people, in terms of a relatively small number of fundamental traits. The next section deals with stages associated with personality *development,* while subsequent sections introduce some of the *traits* which have been used to describe individual differences. As we have said, the emphases and research methods of these two approaches are quite different. Development has generally been described by psychotherapists on the basis of their clinical experience in treating individual patients, while traits have been identified by experiments and surveys using psychometric tests with representative samples.

Stages in personality development

The most famous description of human personality, which traces facets of adult behaviour to childhood experiences and unresolved conflicts, came from Sigmund Freud. He saw the personality as having three components — the id, the ego and the superego. The *id* was the primary source of drive and human motivation which depended on an asocial demand for instant gratification, seeking satisfaction of basic physiological needs — the *pleasure principle.* The superego was seen as the residue of parental warnings and cultural prohibitions built up during childhood. In Freud's life-time, at least, the id and the super-ego were seen as implacable opponents. Between these opposing forces of instinctual demands and social constraints, the *ego* tries to steer a course towards rational reactions to outside events. It is based on the *reality principle.*

The tension between competing tendencies is a common theme in many personality theories. Personality development is often seen as the process of achieving a temporary balance, of homeostasis, between conflicting elements. The psychoanalysists were particularly concerned about the *unconscious* influences which often disrupt rational behaviour. Kelly's image of man-the-scientist, seeking rationally to understand and predict, is shown as only one facet of the whole picture. Freud stressed the importance of suppressed sexuality in affecting later behaviour. Jung saw man in an even wider context, recognizing influences from a collective unconscious, from ways of thinking which are antediluvian remnants of mankind's adaptations to earlier environments.

> 'Modern man is in fact a curious mixture of characteristics acquired over the long ages of his mental development. This mixed-up being is the man and his symbols that we have to deal with.... Scepticism and scientific conviction exist in him side by side with old-fashioned prejudices, outdated habits of thought and feeling, obstinate misinterpretations, and blind ignorance.... The academic psychologist is perfectly free to dismiss the phenomenon of emotion or the concept of the unconscious (or both) from his consideration. Yet they remain facts to which the medical psychologist at least has to pay due attention; for emotional conflicts and the intervention of the unconscious are the classical features of his science' (Jung, 1964, pages 91, 96).

For Freud personality development depended on the ability to resolve tensions created through the repression by adults of instinctual drives. In education, the link between repression and neurosis has sometimes been used

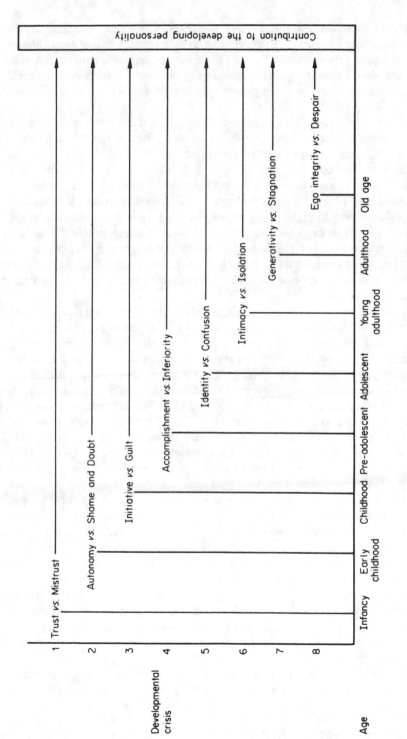

Figure 9.1 Erikson's stages in personality development (based on Gage and Berliner, 1975, page 382)

to argue that children should be free to express their emotions and to follow their immediate interests. However, this argument has often been taken too far. It is equally important in Freud's theory *not* to remove conflict altogether; a strong ego depends on the developing ability to over-rule instinctual demands, to balance the competing opposites of freedom and self-control (Fox, 1974).

Freud did describe stages in personality development in terms of children's preoccupations with various bodily functions, the oral, the anal, and the genital. Progression from one stage to the next depended on a satisfactory resolution of the conflicts created by each developmental step. This idea of conflicts, of repeated balancing of opposite tendencies, has been extended by Erikson (1963, 1968). He has developed a scheme of personality development from infancy to old age during which people pass through a succession of stages. Each stage presents the individual with a developmental task and a potential crisis. By resolving that crisis satisfactorily, the person can freely face up to the task of the next stage. If the task is not completed, an adjustment problem or inadequacy may be carried forward to the next stage and persist thereafter.

Erikson's scheme, shown diagrammatically in Figure 9.1, contains eight 'ages of man'. In each of these stages the individual has to resolve two competing tendencies. In infancy, for example, Erikson considers the predominant tension to be between trust and mistrust. The ability to build up trust, initially of the mother through feeding experiences and comfort, is an essential component of personality adjustment. The quality of later interpersonal relationships is thought to be dependent on a successful resolution of this crisis of infancy. This first stage involves dependency on others: the next crisis is the growing demand for autonomy. Patterns of child-rearing may affect the ease with which these early crises are resolved. Here overcontrol by parents emphasizes dependency and leaves the child with a feeling of shame about any wish for autonomy. Unless independence is fostered, the child may be left with a feeling that he cannot control events — the outside world or chance is responsible for what happens, not the individual himself. This feeling may also become a sense of inferiority which would make subsequent crises more difficult to face.

Later in childhood the feelings of trust and the wish for autonomy leads the child to look for scope for initiative. Again the problem for parents, and teachers is to provide firm guidance without being over-restrictive. If initiative is repeatedly blocked, independent actions later on may be accompanied by a sense of guilt. But control and guidance also help the child to decide what is right or wrong. Thus too much freedom may leave the child with an underdeveloped conscience.

As the child moves towards adolescence, during the years in primary school, Erikson describes the essential task as building up a sense of accomplishment. This pre-adolescent stage is sometimes called the 'latency period' during which the child is expected by society to acquire skills and explore capabilities in anticipation of adult life. Traditionally the child at this time had to learn the discipline of school life with its regular hours of hard, and sometimes tedious, work. Erikson (1963) comments:

'The child must forget past hopes and wishes, while his exhuberant imagination is tamed and harnessed to the laws of impersonal things' (page 258).

This particular quotation draws attention to one limitation of any developmental scheme like this. It is bound by the expectations of a particular culture and historical period. Changes in child-rearing patterns and in teaching methods may alter the nature of the crises faced by children. In the freer atmosphere of modern schools, the child will still have to develop a sense of competence, but without necessarily curbing imagination and feelings to the same extent that Erikson envisaged.

Failure to develop this sense of competence may leave the child with a continuing sense of inadequacy. But on the other hand an over-emphasis on the importance of high standards of achievement may produce a feeling that work is all-important. The 'rat-race' mentality thus fostered may distort subsequent attempts to cope with the later, and equally important, phases of life.

In adolescence the crisis involves the question 'who am I'. The young person tries to establish his identity, to determine what roles to fill in society, and to work out what aspects of life he considers most important. At this stage relationships with the opposite sex become important, but until the adolescent has a clear sense of his own identity, and confidence in it, these relationships are difficult to establish.

'(Adolescents) are now primarily concerned with what they appear to be in the eyes of others as compared with what they feel they are, and with how to connect the roles and skills cultivated earlier with the occupational prototypes of the day.... The adolescent mind is essentially a mind of the *moratorium,* a psychosocial stage between childhood and adulthood, and between the morality learned by the child, and the ethics to be developed by the adult' (Erikson, 1963, pages 262–263).

In adulthood the individual faces crises in family life and work. First, in married life, sharing has to be learned through intimacy. In both the home and work, people need the sense of what Erikson calls 'generativity' — to create, support, and nourish, whether it is a family or a developing career. Finally, the ultimate stage in Erikson's scheme involves the crisis of ego integrity *vs.* despair. Ego integrity can be described as

'the ego's accrued assurance of its proclivity for order and meaning... an experience which conveys some world order and spiritual sense, no matter how dearly paid for' (Erikson, 1963, page 268).

This ultimate stage in personality development has also been described by Jung. The term he used was *individuation*. In Jung's theory the person is again seen as trying to achieve a balance between competing facets of his personality, but also trying to resolve conflicts between social pressures towards conformity and personal needs for individuality and self-expression. Jung sees individuation as a search for a *personal* solution of the age-old 'mystery of life' — the reason for man's existence. Maslow (1954) sees a similar goal in personality development — *self-actualization*. This developmental stage, although associated with old age in Erikson's scheme, is surely anticipated in the later positions of Perry's scheme which we met in Chapter 4. When relativistic reasoning has been accepted and a commitment to a view of life has been developed, the student can be seen already to be facing up to this last of Erikson's crises. Perry's research thus serves to remind us that, as with Piaget's stages of intellectual processes, developmental steps are not entirely separate. The stages have been associated with age ranges for simplicity and convenience, but in reality few of the crises Erikson describes are ever fully resolved — they are continuing tensions in human experience. And at any one age the individual may be facing up to earlier crises which have recurred, and anticipating crises which will not be fully recognized until much later.

Personality traits

Although there is some overlap in the many different terms used by clinical psychologists in describing personality, each theorist has emphasized rather different aspects as being the most important. To some extent the research methodology which is essentially a personal integration of wide ranging clinical experience might lead us to expect subjectivity and little consensus. But these idiosyncratic ways of describing personality are also exactly what Kelly suggested as the whole basis of his theory of personality. He believed that our attempts to understand human behaviour depend on the use of *personal* constructs. Our attempts to describe other people make use of bi-polar adjectives, but the ones we use most frequently may not be commonly used by other people.

The list of adjectives from which to choose is enormous. There are at least '18,000 words (chiefly adjectives) in the English language designating distinctive forms of personal behaviour' (Allport, 1963, page 353). Each age has coined its own terms. The list thus ranges from words derived from Galen's ideas (good-humoured, cold-blooded) through the Protestant Reformation (sincere, pious, bigoted, selfish) and more recent times (social-climber, beatnik, yes-man, hippy), to the technical vocabulary of psychologists (extraversion, neuroticism, psychoticism, achievement motivation, or even Machiavellianism).

STOP and THINK

● What adjectives would you use to describe three people you know well? Use Kelly's technique of comparing two similar people with one who has different characteristics (see page 162). Decide in which way the two are similar and then choose another adjective to describe the contrasting person. Try to find as many differences as possible. The pairs of adjectives will show some of *your* personal constructs.

● In research it is often necessary to compare people in terms of the *same* dimensions of personality. How would we decide which are the most useful traits for this purpose?

● Should we expect people to show the same traits consistently or not?

The problem with using either personal constructs or general traits in describing people is that the result is oversimplification. It leads to descriptions which may become summary dismissals — lazy, ignorant, and superstitious. Allport (1963) comments

'In this case the (oversimplification) is obvious. Ascribing traits in this coarse fashion always lands us in trouble. And yet we do tend to pigeon-hole people (individuals as well as groups) with the aid of a few linguistic tags. No one is as simple and firmly structured as our labels imply... (but this does) not prove that persons are devoid of traits. (It) proves only that we should guard against our tendency to oversimplify the structure of the (other person's) personality' (page 336).

Allport stresses that the traits used in psychology are still *hypothetical constructs*. There is little direct, physiological evidence of their existence, but he also argues that some of the important traits may ultimately be traced back to such origins. Without knowledge of basic personality mechanisms how do we decide which of the 18,000 names will be useful? The answer is to identify *common* traits.

'Common traits are... those aspects of personality in respect to which most people within a given culture can be profitably compared.... The scientific evidence for the existence of a trait always comes from demonstrating by some acceptable method the *consistency* in a person's behaviour' (Allport, 1963, page 343).

The theme of consistency versus variability recurs again. A useful common trait must show the consistency of representative groups of individuals both over time and between situations. The major problem, then is to decide *how much* consistency is required to provide evidence for the existence of a trait. As we have argued in previous chapters, people's behaviour is never *entirely* predictable from one situation to another: it shows both consistency and inconsistency. Some psychologists have used this fact to argue against attempts to describe personality in terms of traits, or even against trying to measure it at all. Labelling can be seen as limiting human potentialities. Bronowski (1965) has rounded on these critics and asked them a series of awkward questions about human predictability.

'(If) a man does not want to be law-abiding; very well then, it is time to ask him the rude but searching question "Do you want to be lawless?" You refuse to be predictable as an engine is, or an animal; do you aspire to be unpredictable? And if so, are you unpredictable to yourself, the actor, as well as to me, the spectator? Do you base your claim to be a self on the proud assertion that your actions are arbitrary? (No)... a self must have consistency; its actions tomorrow must be recognizably of a piece with the actions carried out yesterday' (pages 13–15).

The extent of such consistency is an empirical question. If important traits can be measured, and if these are also found, on the whole, to be consistently related to a variety of aspects of behaviour, then their use in psychology is surely justifiable. But which traits have proved most useful in describing personality.

Jung (1938), from his clinical experience, identified what he considered to be two fundamentally different psychological types — people who viewed the world in opposite ways, the extravert, and the introvert. The extravert, as the word implies, looks outward. His behaviour is predominantly orientated towards events in the outside world and his thinking is dominated by the search for objective facts. The introvert, on the contrary, looks inward. Outside events are, of course, perceived but they tend to be judged by personal values and standards. The introvert's thinking is influenced, even obsessed, with personal interpretations and theories. Jung sees dangers in both extreme ways of thinking.

'For as in the former case the purely empirical heaping together of facts paralyses thought and smothers their meaning, so in the latter case introverted thinking shows a dangerous tendency to coerce facts into the shape of its image, or by ignoring them altogether, to unfold its phantasy image in freedom' (pages 481–482).

In Jung's theory the extraverted and introverted tendencies are *both* present in every person. Whichever characteristic becomes dominant in a person's behaviour and conscious thought, its opposite continues to be represented in the unconscious as the *shadow,* and is thought to have a continuing effect on the development of personality.

In writing about personality theories, Jung pointed out that the choice of a particular type of theory, or an emphasis within that theory, was in part a reflection of the theorist's own personality. Thus Jung's theory, with its description of extraversion and introversion in terms of ways of *thinking,* perhaps reflects Jung's own admitted introversion. He was not much concerned with outside events. In contrast Eysenck (1965) has provided descriptions of extraverts and introverts which stress differences in *behaviour*.

'(The typical extravert is) sociable, likes parties, has many friends, needs to have people to talk to, and does not like studying by himself. He craves excitement, take chances, often sticks his neck out, acts on the spur of the moment, and is generally an impulsive individual.... The typical introvert, on the other hand, is a quiet retiring sort of person, introspective, fond of books rather than people; he is reserved and distant except with intimate friends. He tends to plan ahead, "looks before he leaps", and distrusts the impulse of the moment' (pages 59–60).

Eysenck and Cattell have both used personality inventories and factor analysis in the attempt to determine which general traits are most useful in the description of personality. Both of them were students of Cyril Burt who had investigated aspects of children's personality in 1915. Burt (1965) claimed to have originally identified a general factor of emotionality, and later described two significant bi-polar factors, one of which appears to have been extraversion/introversion, while the other described the contrast between optimistic and pessimistic outlooks on life.

Cattell (1965) has identified sixteen different traits, but these overlap to some extent. A simplified description of these traits reduces the number to five: anxiety, extraversion, tendermindedness, radicalism, and conscientiousness or moral conventionality. Eysenck's research has concentrated on the first two of these dimensions. He has also described the second two traits, although he originally identified these as 'social attitudes' (Eysenck, 1970). Eysenck's most recent personality inventories (Eysenck and Eysenck, 1969) now also contain a psychoticism scale (asocial or antisocial morality) and a lie scale which measures the tendency to give conventional responses. At this descriptive level there is good agreement between the two theories, but Eysenck sees extraversion and what he calls neuroticism (similar to general emotionality) as much more basic than the other descriptions of personality.

The fundamental importance of extraversion and neuroticism, and their appearance in most personality inventories, is attributed by Eysenck to physiological and neurological concomitants. The symptoms of 'fight or flight', fear and anger, are associated with increased levels of adrenalin in the body. Adrenalin is produced by the adrenal glands near the kidney, but control of its production depends on an area of the brain called the hypothalamus. Rose (1976) describes how emotion and motivation are controlled partly by the hypothalamus and partly by diffusely located neurons called the ascending reticular activating system (ARAS). This latter system is responsible for levels of attention and alertness, cortical arousal. Incoming perceptions, analysed in the ways discussed in Chapter 6, may be interpreted as emotional stimuli, in which case the hypothalamus will be activated and adrenalin production stimulated. Or the perceptions may contain more neutral information flowing through ARAS leading to more general cortical arousal. Of course, the systems are not as separate as this simple description may imply.

Eysenck (1967) has suggested that people differ in the ease with which cortical arousal and activity in the hypothalamus can be induced. Without external stimulation Eysenck agues that introverts show greater cortical arousal than extraverts, and that people with high neuroticism scores have higher levels of hypothalamic activity than those with low scores. Most of the evidence is, however, not based directly on brain activity, but on experiments which show that introverts condition more easily, can concentrate on routine tasks for longer, and make better use of long-term memory than extraverts (Eysenck, 1970). The parallels between these findings and brain activities are strong, but as explanations they remain speculative.

Eysenck assesses levels of extraversion and neuroticism through personality inventories which are built up from a series of questions. Each question is an index of one particular personality trait, and is chosen only after it has been proved to discriminate between groups of people who are known to exhibit extraverted or introverted patterns of behaviour. Respondents are asked to reply 'yes' or 'no' to questions such as

● Can you put your thoughts into words quickly?
● Are you mostly quiet when you are with other people?
● Are you an irritable person?
● Are you troubled by feelings of inferiority?
● Have you ever been late for an appointment or work?
● Do you sometimes boast a little?

Neuroticism

		High scores	Low scores
Extraversion	High scores	*Choleric* Quickly roused Egocentric Exhibitionist Hot-headed Histrionic Active	*Sanguine* Playful Easy-going Sociable Carefree Hopeful Contented
	Low scores	*Melancholic* Anxious Worried Unhappy Suspicious Serious Thoughtful	*Phlegmatic* Reasonable High-principled Controlled Persistent Steadfast Calm

Figure 9.2 Personality types (adapted from Eysenck, 1967, page 35)

Answering 'yes to the first question and 'no' to the second question are indications of extraversion. The next two questions suggest aspects of neuroticism, while the final two items are part of a 'lie' scale designed to detect people who are trying to present themselves in a favourable light. Considerable care and ingenuity goes into the design of these personality inventories, and the strength of the various traits is determined by the number of responses given in the 'extraverted' or 'neurotic' directions. Although a person's response to any individual item may be affected by the wording, or by their mood at the time, their overall score on say 25 items remains fairly consistent over time, at least among adults.

Using the two main traits it is possible to identify four, or more, personality types in terms of their scores on these scales. In the simplest double dichotomy, the characteristic behaviour anticipated from people in these four categories is shown in Figure 9.2. The types, in fact, show considerable similarity to the age-old ideas first introduced by Galen. Research using personality inventories sometimes examines overall relationships (correlations) using scale scores, but on other occasions it is more useful to use *zonal analysis* in which 2 × 2 (as in Figure 9.2) or 3 × 3 tables are produced to examine the characteristics of personality types defined from the scale scores.

Personality and academic attainment

Predictions from Eysenck's descriptions of the contrasting behaviour of different personality types, and from the experimental findings, all point to the likely superiority of the introvert in academic work. Introverts are likely to be less distracted by their interest in social activity, to condition more readily, to maintain attention longer, and to have better long-term recall than extroverts.

The effect of neuroticism is less easy to predict. It has been argued from the 'Yerkes-Dodson law' that there might well be an inverted-U relationship (see Figure 9.3) between academic performance and neuroticism. In the original Yerkes-Dodson experiments on mice, intermediate levels of drive (hunger) led to higher levels of performance (maze running) for tasks of moderate difficulty. Anxiety is commonly seen as the equivalent spur to human behaviour, and it seemed reasonable that too much anxiety, or too little, might inhibit classroom attainment.

Some of the early studies seemed to be in line with these predictions. Furneaux (1962) found introverts to be more successful in university examinations and both Lynn and Gordon (1961) and Brown (1970) found evidence of an inverted-U relationship between neuroticism and test performance. However in the two largest British studies on school children, the predicted relationship was not obtained. In a study at Aberdeen, Entwistle and Cunningham (1968) found a *linear* relationship, with secondary children with lower neuroticism scores having consistently higher scaled marks. Among pupils in primary schools in Staffordshire, Eysenck and Cookson (1969)

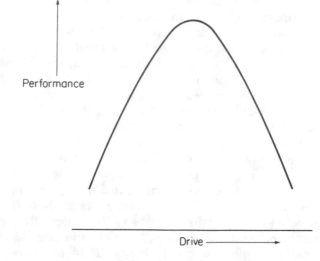

Figure 9.3 Relationship between drive and performance

reported that, if anything, the relationship was U-shaped with both high and low scores on neuroticism being associated with high attainment.

The predicted advantage for introverts has been found mainly among older pupils and students in certain areas of study. In primary schools Eysenck and Cookson found extraverts to be consistently ahead of introverts, while by age 13 no overall relationship was detected in the Aberdeen study. The analyses in this Scottish study drew attention to possible complications in the interpretation of the small correlations reported. Both sex (Entwistle and Cunningham, 1968) and ability level (Entwistle and Welsh, 1969) affected the relationships. Overall, introverted boys and extraverted girls were more successful, yet among boys in the bottom third of the ability range, extraverts reached higher levels of attainment.

The simple correlations between personality traits and attainment are low, rarely exceeding 0.2. On the other hand, with non-linear relationships anticipated, a correlation coefficient provides little information about complicated patterns which may exist in the data. Eysenck argues for the use of zonal analysis in which, say, nine personality types are created by dividing both extraversion and neuroticism into high, medium, and low categories (see Table 9.1). Then differences between extreme personality types can be up to 14 points of attainment quotient, but are more typically about half that value.

Kline (1976) uses this evidence to argue that 'the differences being discussed are so small as to be valueless from either a practical or a theoretical viewpoint' (page 57). The correlational analyses do suggest only a marginal effect, but is an average difference of 7 points of attainment trivial? Table 9.1 converts the mean scores in the Aberdeen zonal analysis into equivalent

Table 9.1 Estimated mean 'attainment ages'[a] and attainment quotients of girls aged 13 by personality types (adapted from Entwistle and Cunningham, 1968)

Neuroticism	Extraversion		
	High	Medium	Low
High	12:9 (97)	12:11 (99)	12:8 (96)
Medium	13:0 (100)	12:11 (99)	13:1 (101)
Low	13:5 (105)	13:3 (103)	13:3 (103)

[a] 'Attainment ages' were calculated by equating 11 points difference in quotient to twelve months progress, based on the norms presented in the manual.

Table 9.2. Percentage of girls aged 11 allocated to grammar school by personality type (from Eysenck and Cookson, 1969)

Neuroticism	Extraversion		
	High	Medium	Low
High	23	12	9
Medium	26	13	9
Low	25	22	22

attainment ages, using the age-allowances of 11 points per year built into the manual at the appropriate attainment level. Teachers are more familiar with differences interpreted in this way. The question about educational significance can then be reformulated. How important is it that children of different personality types may show a gap of up to nine months in their relative attainment levels?

Table 9.2 also looks at educational significance in a different way. Even if the effects of personality are slight compared with those of, say, intellectual differences, could those marginal effects still be important? In the Staffordshire study zonal analyses showed clear differences in the percentage of children of different personality types who had been selected for grammar schools. Table 9.2 shows that 23 per cent of unstable extraverts were accepted, compared with only 9 per cent of unstable introverts. Another study makes this difference even more worrying. Finlayson (1970) showed that the performance of unstable extraverts dropped markedly over the first three years of secondary school, while unstable introverts showed a continuing improvement in their performance.

Of course these simple analyses still only describe associations, or concomitant variation, they do not show that personality *causes* differences in attainment. Indeed in the research on students reported earlier, Entwistle and Wilson (1977) found that extraverts with high scores on motivation and study methods were just as successful as introverts with similarly effective study strategies. But they also showed that many more introverts than extraverts actually did work effectively. The relationship between introversion and academic performance still exists, but it may be indirect. It is also possible, however, that the differences in attainment of contrasting personality types may be paralleled by initial similar differences in ability. One study which checked on this possibility has been reported by Elliott (1972). He examined the reading ages of children aged eight. Keeping mental age constant, he still demonstrated substantial differences in reading ages in relation to scores on the JEPI*. Stable extraverts in this sample had a mean reading age of 9½ years, while unstable introverts of the same ability level were the equivalent of 2½ years behind. Primary teachers might well see this finding as having some practical significance; its implications will be considered in the final chapter.

It is thus possible to argue that at least some of the associations between personality and school attainment are worth serious consideration. But the research can be criticized on other grounds. Even if the differences *are* large enough to be important to teachers, how have they occurred, and what could be done about them? The research reported above does no more than *describe* patterns of attainment. The earliest studies sought to test personality theories and looked for *general* relationships. Later studies showed the importance of analysing separately by age, sex, and ability level, but still ignored other possible complications. The so-called age-effect could be explained as a change in performance or as a change in *personality* of children who continue to reach the same standards (Anthony, 1977). The age-effect might also be created by a change from the relatively informal methods of teaching in the primary school to greater formality in secondary school. By university level, the emphasis on independent study might also be expected to favour introverts.

More recent research, however, has tried to provide useful *explanations* of the relationships previously identified. Will a teacher's decision to adopt a particular approach to teaching affect the relationship between personality and learning in that *class*? The effects may be as specific as this: the process of teaching also needs to be considered. Entwistle and Bennett (1973) found that the move from primary to secondary school, in itself, could not explain the deterioration in the performance of extraverts, and argued that 'future research in this area would have to examine relationships between personality and attainment within defined, and contrasting, academic environments' (page 13), while Eysenck (1972) commented

'The informal 'bitty' nature of primary school instruction may suit extraverted children better; when instruction becomes more concentrated and serious, the extravert's interest begins to fade.. One unpublished study showed that in a primary school where instruction was more formal., introverts were in fact superior to extraverts' (page 48).

---

* *Junior Eysenck Personality Inventory*

The possibility of differential effects of contrasting methods of instruction on pupils of different personality types will be considered in Chapter 11. This examination of the *general* relationships between personality and attainment has shown instances where large, although unexplained, differences in attainment are involved. The question of what might be done about such differences will be tackled in the concluding chapter.

Motivation

Of all the traits used to describe differences in children's school attainment perhaps the most common is 'motivation'. The term, however, does not describe a single dimension. It is a complex concept which was analysed by Peters (1959). Some psychologists see motivation as a physiological drive pushing a person, or an animal, to behave in a certain way. Others insist that human beings act in ways which also depend on what they want to achieve. Peters accepts that it is useful to distinguish between *extrinsic* and *intrinsic* motivation. Extrinsic motivation occurs when some reward or punishment is used which lies outside the task itself — it could be the promise of a present for doing well in an examination, or the marks themselves, or the threat of teachers' or parents' disapproval for doing badly. Intrinsic motivation depends on seeing the task as relevant and interesting in its own right, but Wilson (1968) points out that intrinsic motivation can also relate to the satisfaction of an inner need, such as self-esteem or a *need for achievement*.

Another aspect of motivation is what White (1959) has called *competence* motivation. This idea is close to Erikson's idea of 'accomplishment' with the task of cultivating the ability to concentrate on work and to develop skills. Competence motivation describes the way achievement enhances future performance. Pupils come to enjoy work they can do well, even if that competence was initially developed through rote learning. Allport (1963) has referred to the 'functional autonomy' of motives, the tendency for a motive, once established, to become self-perpetuating. According to this theory achievement however fostered, will lead to self-confidence, to higher motivation, and to further effective learning. Of course, the opposite is equally true, as Holt (1964) has cogently argued. The continuing experience of failure is demoralizing, creates hostility to school, and feelings of personal humiliation.

The importance of self-confidence in learning has been emphasized by many research workers. Rogers (1969), for example, has argued that the learner's self-concept, his view of how well he can tackle the work given to him, fundamentally affects his approach and his understanding. Empirical support for Rogers' ideas has come from Coopersmith (1959) who has shown that children with positive self-concepts are likely to be academically more successful than children with less belief in themselves.

In fact this distinction between self-confidence in learning, and anxiety and uncertainty, parallels the two types of motivation which emerged in the research on students described in Chapter 5. There they were described as reflecting 'hope for success' and 'fear of failure'. These two terms have been used elsewhere in the psychological literature, as we shall see, but the idea is very much older than that. Again personality is being described as a tension between opposites and it may be salutory to recognize just how old this distinction between self-confident assertion and timid, apprehension really is.

The Hunefer Papyrus in the British Museum in London (Figure 9.4) can be seen as symbolic of an Egyptian psychological treatise. Two lions sit back to back, supporting between them a flattened disc. One interpretation of this picture (Ivimy, 1974, pages 162-3) is that the lions represented two primal forces, Shu and Tefnet. Shu looked into the future with masculine aggression fed by sexual desire. Tefnet was drawn towards the past through feminine timidity and fear of an uncertain future. The two lions are pulling in opposite directions, but their backs are weighed down, and they are restrained, by another force, Ra, represented by the flattened solar disc. This third force is reason and self-control.

Setting aside the Egyptian male chauvinism of this view, it is interesting to see echoes of the triad of opposing forces in Freud's description of the id, ego, and super-ego, and also in the more recent ideas of different types of motivation. Such an old idea is worth re-examining in the light of modern research findings. Is it possible to understand students' approaches to studying and academic work in terms of an underlying tension between competitive self-confidence and a fear of insufficiency?

Figure 9.4 Hunefer Papyrus (British Museum)

Hope for success and fear of failure

The distinction between hope for success and fear of failure was made explicit in the theory of motivation developed by Atkinson (Atkinson and Feather, 1966; Atkinson and Raynor, 1974). His work was a development of ideas on *need for achievement* (n-ach) put forward by Murray (1938) and McClelland *et al.* (1953). 'n-ach' is measured by a projective test of personality— the thematic apperception test — in which a picture is used to evoke responses which reflect characteristically different needs. One of the stimulus cards might, for example, show an adult looking over the shoulder of a child who appears to be writing. If students are asked to write about what is happening in such a situation, some of them will describe opportunities for achievement (n-ach), while others will show more concern about the impressions one person is making on another (need for affiliation). It is possible to identify, in this way, students who have contrasting needs for achievement or affiliation.

McClelland and his colleagues used a simple competitive situation to relate risk-taking and achievement motivation to success. Children were asked to toss a ring over a peg from some distance away. The variation on this old fairground game was that the pupils could choose the distance from which to throw. Of course, there were also differential rewards. More 'points' were given for success from greater distances. This simple game showed an interesting link between risk-taking and achievement motivation. Children with high 'n-ach' scores chose intermediate distances. Those with low 'n-ach' tended to stand either so close that success was inevitable although they gained few points, or so far away that success was unlikely, but failure was not humiliating.

Atkinson concentrated initially on intrinsic motivation, the motive to achieve success. He recognized that a person's actual achievement behaviour depended both on his level of n-ach, and also on how he interpreted the task presented. He described his theory as follows.

'It assumed that the strength of the tendency to achieve success (T_s), which is expressed in the interest and performance of an individual in some task... (depends on) three variables: motive to achieve success (M_s), conceived as a relatively general and relatively stable disposition of personality; and two other variables which represent the effect of the immediate environment — the strength of expectancy (or subject probability) that performance of the task will be followed by success (P_s) and the relative attractiveness of success at that particular activity, which we call the incentive value of success (I_s). In other words,

$$T_s = M_s \times P_s \times I_s'$$ (Atkinson, 1974, pages 13-14).

In later research Atkinson recognized that there was a separate tendency to avoid failure which also affected achievement-orientated behaviour. Using inventories to assess general anxiety and test anxiety, Atkinson concluded that

'whenever performance is evaluated in relation to some standard of excellence, what constitutes the challenge to achieve for one individual poses the threat of failure for another... We speak of the motive to avoid failure (MAF) and refer to a disposition which is separate and distinct from the achievement motive. It might be thought of as a capacity for reacting with humiliation and shame when one fails' (pages 16, 18).

Atkinson's most recent research thus assumes that people have both a positive interest in achievement and a negative fear of failure. Where the tendency to avoid failure is stronger than the tendency to strive towards success, achievement situations will be avoided. But students are not allowed such a simple choice. They have strong sources of extrinsic motivation which prevent them from opting out of situations in which they are continuously being evaluated against standards of excellence. The price these students pay for overcoming their tendency to avoid failure is increased anxiety.

Atkinson's theory can now be used to explain the behaviour of children in the 'ring-toss' game in terms of the competing tendencies towards success and away from failure. Where hope for success is the dominant motive, moderate risks provide the greatest satisfaction. It is important for the child to be successful *and* to receive a large number of points. Where fear of failure is stronger, situations will be preferred in which failure is either virtually impossible, or inevitable. If the task can be seen to be extremely difficult, failure is no longer so threatening: it does not involve 'loss of face'.

The different relative strengths of these motives may be, in part, constitutional, but Rosen and d'Andrade (1959) have shown that different levels of 'n-ach' are associated with child-rearing practices. In one experiment they asked boys to build towers from irregularly shaped bricks while blindfolded. Parents were allowed to help, but only through verbal instructions and encouragement. Boys who were high in achievement motivation were found to have parents who were optimistic about their child's performance and supportive. Mothers, in particular, reacted warmly to success, without withdrawing support if the towers collapsed. Elsewhere, Rosen (1959) comments that such mothers also fostered self-reliance and independence, but for the child's benefit rather than for their own convenience. These findings are reminiscent of the behaviour of 'A' and 'C' mothers in White's research (see page 174).

DeCharms (1968) has explained the origins of achievement motivation in a similar way. Children, as Erikson argued earlier, need to accept their own responsibility for what happens to them: they can then be said to have an internal '*locus of control*'. The experiences of success or failure, and praise or blame, effect people differentially. Weiner (1972) argues that where fear of failure is uppermost, success and praise are essential for supporting maximum effort. For more confident individuals, a certain amount of failure and criticism will often help to increase motivation. Experienced teachers use this principle intuitively, recognizing the damage that criticism can do to the confidence of anxious children, while spurring other children to greater efforts by 'marking them down'. High motivation can lead to improved performance, but it is important to recognize that level of performance also effects motivation. Too much success for the self-confident and too much failure for the anxious are both likely to diminish motivation.

Atkinson's predictions about the behaviour of people dominated by a fear of failure are restricted to a particular type of achievement situation, one in which external standards of performance and formal evaluation are dominant. We have already seen in the Piagetian research how performance depends, in part, on the instructions and on the particular task set. Birney, Burdick, and Teevan (1969) have found evidence of similar differences in the reactions of 'fear of failure' students. From their own studies, and from a review of previous work, they show that the inhibitory effect of fear of failure is exhibited most clearly in 'unfamiliar, complex, speeded, or competitive achievement settings'. Students with high fear of failure scores tended to be better at rote learning than comprehension tests when under time pressure. While they work more slowly, they also put more effort into the tasks and persist longer in trying to solve difficult or uncongenial problems. In academic work such effort and persistence seem to bring their reward: in spite of their poor self-image fear of failure students in the Lancaster study (page 99) had above average levels of achievement.

Birney, Burdick, and Teevan conclude a pen-portrait of a 'fear of failure' student by stating:

> 'In serious situations of achievement he seems most concerned with the social evaluation the testing authority will place on his behaviour. Conceivably this reflects his early experience, in which he was taught that such situations are very important, but punishment for failure, in the form of derogation, was much stronger than the mild rewards for success. Given this orientation he gravitates towards the channels of vocational progress that emphasize order, gradual advancement, and diffused responsibility. Here he is quite safe from the judgement that his achievement is pathological' (page 200).

Fear of failure does not necessarily interfere with academic performance, but it almost certainly does affect the way in which the work is tackled. Linking this psychological research back to the earlier research on how students learn, a more convincing argument can now be mounted for the importance of this distinction between the self-confident drive towards success and the timid, over-anxious concern about possible failure. Looking back to the factor analyses reported earlier (page 101), the study approach of 'achievement orientation' with its use of any learning strategy likely to produce good grades, seems to fit in well with these more detailed descriptions of 'hope for success'. The 'reproducing' approach similarly fits well with the likely reactions of 'fear of failure' students to competitive academic environments. Where neither of these forms of motivation is dominant, the approach to learning may be explained in terms of the relative strengths of extrinsic and intrinsic motivation. Interest in the subject, as we have seen earlier, is linked to a deep approach to studying, but if the main concern is for the qualification itself (extrinsic), then a surface approach is more likely to be adopted.

In using labels to describe students, as we have seen repeatedly before, there is a serious danger of explaining away, rather than seeking to understand sympathetically. For example, in the Lancaster interviews with lecturers described in Chapter 4, reasons for students' poor academic performance were sought. The most common explanations given were idleness and poor motivation. When students were asked similar questions the reasons they gave were incompetent or boring teaching. These 'explanations' simply seek to shift the blame: they do not really look for causes or seek to improve the existing situation.

Kelly (1964) has been particularly forthright in his condemnation of the use of 'poor motivation' or 'laziness' as an explanation of academic weakness. He asks who is responsible for the laziness. Why should we assume it is always the pupil? The student teacher quoted in Chapter 1 showed a clear insight into this problem of labelling children in this way. Remember her doubts about her treatment of Paul.

'I don't know — but his apparent failure in conventional terms has led me to... (say) that he is lazy. Perhaps it would be more truthful to say that his apparent failure hurts me too much because I recognize in it a failure in myself to communicate with him, and therefore, as my own failure is harder to accept, I am prepared to take the easy way out and say that he is lazy. What a terrible admission!'

Kelly found many experienced teachers falling back on this 'easy' explaining away, this avoiding of responsibility. He argued that these teachers had to be encouraged to think of children as naturally active. He therefore tried various ways to help teachers to avoid the labelling which had become libelling.

'One technique we came to use was to ask the teacher what the child would do if she did not try to motivate him. Often the teacher would insist that the child would do nothing — absolutely nothing — "just sit". We would ask her to observe how he went about "just sitting". Invariably the teacher would be able to report some extremely interesting goings on. An analysis of what the "lazy" child did while he was being lazy often furnished her with her first glimpse into the child's world and provided her with her first solid grounds for communication with him. Some teachers found that their laziest pupils were those who could produce the most novel ideas; others that the term "laziness" had been applied to activities that they had simply been unable to understand or appreciate' (Kelly, 1964, pages 346-347).

This note of caution has been introduced into this chapter as a warning against oversimple use of personality traits. The ideas, however, can be used in constructive ways to understand why, as we found in Chapter 5, students tackle learning tasks with characteristically different strategies. In the next chapter research into cognitive styles brings together the work on human abilities with that on personality in ways which seem to have important implications for teachers and students.

Summary

Personality development has been described by clinical psychologists in many different ways, based on their personal experience in treating their patients. One influential scheme was developed by Erikson who described eight stages, or sets of crises, facing the developing individual between infancy and old age. Each stage presents opposing tendencies, like trust and mistrust, with which the person has to wrestle to make progress — a modern version of Bunyan's *Pilgrim's Progress*. The fundamental idea common to many of these theories of development is the necessity to resolve conflicts, to achieve temporary homeostasis, in moving towards an ideal goal of 'self-actualization'. We shall meet this idea of competing opposites again in the next chapter.

The other main research tradition in describing personality relies on the use of inventories to describe common traits. It is not suggested that human personality can be adequately described by two or three scores, but the research evidence does indicate that dimensions such as extraversion and neuroticism are related to fairly consistent differences in behaviour which, in certain circumstances, may be related to school attainment, though not in any straightforward way.

Motivation is a dimension which is commonly used to 'explain' different levels of attainment. By distinguishing different types of motivation — extrinsic and intrinsic, or hope for success and fear of failure — it is possible to understand some of the reasons for pupils or students reaching different levels of success and approaching studying in contrasting ways. But it is unreasonable to use 'poor motivation' as a total explanation of failure. Low levels of attainment can cause poor motivation, and failure can be seen as an indictment of the teacher rather than a criticism of the pupil. Later chapters will explore this two-way process further.

CHAPTER 10

Styles of Thinking and Structures of Knowledge

The model of learning derived from research on students suggested the distinction between deep and surface approaches to learning. It also indicated ways in which the content and the situation might affect the approach adopted. It has subsequently become clear that not all students, and perhaps rather few school pupils, will have the necessary pre-requisites in terms of intellectual skills to carry through the deep approach successfully.

The model also drew attention to characteristically different styles of learning — comprehension and operation learning — and to versatile students who were able to operate in both modes with equal facility. The main characteristics of the operation learner, or the serialist strategy, were to process evidence successively, to prefer a narrow focus of attention, to concentrate on facts and detail, and to examine logical connections thoroughly. In contrast the comprehension learner, or the holist strategy, depends on simultaneous processing, a wide, global view of the topic, looking for wide-ranging links with other material, and making substantial use of analogies which may often be idiosyncratic.

These ideas on learning styles can now be re-examined in the light of the psychological evidence introduced in Part III. But again, to begin with, let us take a historical perspective. In Chapter 3 three early views of thinking were described. James stressed the way thinking depended on making associations between words and between ideas — an associative theory. Dewey emphasized the way problem solving, and much human thought, made use of analytic skills following a clear sequence. Wertheimer was concerned to avoid the limitations of both associative and analytic thinking by showing how productive thinking led to creative problem solving, through imaginative reconstruction.

More recent psychological theories have produced three apparently distinct types of thinking which can be described either in information processing terms, or in the terminology of psychological testing. Jensen's Level I and Level II abilities represent rote learning by strengthening the connections between associations — verbal stimulus-response learning — and analytic thinking which examines logical interconnections to reach conclusions or solutions. The third area of testing has been imaginative thinking (Level IIb). As was suggested in Chapter 7, it may be necessary also to postulate a Level III ability which involves the appropriate use of the other types of thinking. Certainly creative production may depend on varied associative links, on the ability to criticize and analyze, but beyond this on the facility with which unusual and fruitful interconnection between ideas, or a new way of interpreting ideas or perceptions, can be produced.

Similar processes are recognizable within the information processing model. At Level I we should describe the use of repeated over-learning or rehearsal strategies to strengthen associations within STM before transfer to episodic LTM. At Level II STM and episodic LTM will still be involved, but greater emphasis will be placed on effective coding into semantic LTM. Within semantic LTM there are also likely to be distinctive search strategies. Some might be fast, but limited to immediate associates of information being considered. Others, in contrast, might be leisurely and more extensive looking for remote connections. Level III thinking would then represent appropriate combinations of tight, logical searches and the more adventurous, free-wheeling explorations of semantic LTM.

This description of Level III thinking brings to mind Heath's experience with his reasonable adventurers who exhibited a

'combination of two mental attitudes: the curious and the critical. They do not occur simultaneously but in alternation. (The reasonable adventurer) at times is a "believer" but at other times he is a "skeptic". The less effective personalities may show tendencies toward one attitude or the other but may not experience the full reach of either' (see Chapter 4, page 70).

Thinking back to Pask's description of a 'versatile' student, we find that

'A student who is versatile is not prone to vacuous globetrotting; he does indeed build up descriptions of what may be known by a rich use of analogical reasoning, but subjects the hypotheses to test, and operationally verifies the validity of an analogy and the limits of its applicability' (see Chapter 5, page 94).

The review of research into cognitive development also brought distinctions in ways of thinking, showing that the complex, more abstract, forms developed after, and to some extent out of, the simpler more concrete ones. Thus Piaget's formal operations in which logical processes are applied to abstract conceptions is a stage of thinking developed successively in different content areas during adolescence. A similar process is found in conceptual development, where coding based on simple concrete properties is gradually replaced, in Klausmeier's scheme, by classification and formal definition through attributes. In developmental terms we should have to look to Perry's scheme, and some aspects of relativistic reasoning, to see echoes of Level III thinking, but the parallel is there.

In Chapter 7 two distinctive ways of thinking or *cognitive styles* were described in different terms. Hudson (1966) categorized sixth-formers in terms of the relative dominance of convergent or divergent thinking as shown by verbal reasoning and uses of objects tests. Getzels and Jackson (1962) had carried out similar analyses using contrasting test scores. But both studies had one important weakness. In looking at the dominant mode of thinking, Hudson ignored *level* of thinking. Thus a pupil with quotients of 140 on divergent and 120 on convergent thinking tests would be considered equivalent to one with scores of 120 and 100, but their capacities for creative production could be very different. Similarly Getzels and Jackson described the characteristics of pupils who scored highly on *either* convergent *or* divergent thinking tests, but said nothing about pupils who did well on *both* types of test. If comparative performance on analytic and imaginative thinking is to be the method of defining contrasting ways of thinking, then there are necessarily four categories, *not* two.

		Imaginative thinking	
		High	Low
Analytic thinking	High	Level III	Convergence (IIA)
	Low	Divergence (IIB)	Level I

Some pupils will have high scores on both types of test; others will have low scores on both. In keeping with the earlier discussion the additional categories could be called Level III and Level I thinking. But these descriptions would not normally be called styles of thinking: they represent levels of ability. The term 'cognitive style' can reasonably be used only to distinguish consistent *preferences* for a particular mode of thinking among people of similar overall intellectual capabilities.

In the literature there is still considerable confusion between cognitive style and both ability level and developmental stage. There is also confusion created by the use of many different terms to describe aspects of cognitive style, and an equivalent variety of test materials. Recent reviews by Messick (1976) and Kogan (1976) have tried to unravel this tangled skein by clarifying the meaning of 'cognitive style' and by discussing possible overlaps between the different approaches.

Messick's review provides some useful clarification.

'Although cognitive styles are viewed as habitual modes of information processing, they are not simple habits. . . . It is important to distinguish cognitive styles, which are high level heuristics that organize and control behaviour across a wide variety of situations, from cognitive strategies, which are. . . a function of the conditions of particular situations. . . .

The stability and pervasiveness of cognitive styles across diverse spheres of behaviour suggest deeper roots in personality structure than might at first glance be implied... Cognitive styles may entail generalized habits of information processing, to be sure, but they develop in congenial ways around underlying personality trends. Cognitive styles are thus intimately interwoven with affective, temperamental, and motivational structures as part of the total personality...

Cognitive styles differ from intellectual abilities in a number of ways.... Ability dimensions essentially refer to the content of cognition or the question of *what* — what kind of information is being processed by what operation in what form?

... Cognitive styles, in contrast, bear on the questions of *how* — on the manner in which behaviour occurs.... Abilities, furthermore, are generally thought of as unipolar... (and) value directional: having more of an ability is better than having less. Cognitive styles are (bipolar and) value differentiated: each pole has adaptive value... (depending) upon the nature of the situation and upon the cognitive requirements of the task in hand' (Messick 1976, pages 6-9).

It would be impossible to describe all the cognitive styles which have already been identified. Messick (1976) provides a glossary of terms, which includes nineteen different names. The descriptions do, however, imply considerable overlap. In the absence of empirical evidence about inter-relationships, choice has to be guided by educational relevance. As each cognitive style depends, to some extent, on how it is measured, the next step must be to describe several different approaches to measuring cognitive style.

Styles of processing information

Messick describes cognitive styles as 'habitual modes of information processing'. This definition provides a convenient opportunity to refer back to the model developed in Chapter 6. There it was anticipated that people might differ in the way they organize and search semantic LTM and in their reliance on episodic memory. It was argued that effective cross-referencing would depend on the existence of a large number and variety of schemata, concepts and ideas, which were distinct, clearly defined, and inter-connected. The process of concept development was described in Chapter 8. It depends on identifying important defining characteristics, and then analysing similarities and differences. Cognitive styles can be identified from both these processes. People differ both in the features they choose for classification (styles of conceptualization) and in their orientation towards similarity or difference (breadth of categorization). When faced with a piece of information which may or may not fit a defined category, some people are more ready than others to assign it to that category. They apparently use broader, more inclusive, categories.

One well-known study which used both these approaches was *Modes of Thinking in Young Children,* reported by Wallach and Kogan (1965). They investigated category breadth by defining a concept, say 'circle', and providing instances of that concept which differed to an increasing extent (round shapes, progressively flattened towards an ellipse). Children were found to differ in their willingness to accept discrepant examples.

Styles of conceptualization were investigated by showing the children pictures of fifty familiar objects and asking them to put into groups the pictures which seemed 'to belong together'. The children were also asked *why* the objects belonged together. This task was again tackled in characteristically different ways. Some children formed their groups mainly in terms of *descriptive*, concrete properties, such as 'hard objects' or 'all have knobs'. Other children made more use of *analytic* abstract properties, such as usage (for eating) or location (found outdoors). The third preference was for *relational* or thematic groupings. The objects selected were those commonly used together — for example, comb, lipstick, watch, diary, door, as a group, might be chosen because they were to do with 'getting ready to go out'. Wallach and Kogan considered that this third category of groupings would provide interesting thematic possibilities which might be useful in imaginative writing. In terms of our earlier discussion of thinking, however, this method of grouping could equally well indicate a preference for associative connections relying on the episodic LTM.

It is difficult to avoid seeing a developmental dimension in this 'style' of conceptualization — Klausmeier's work on concept development, or sensori-motor, concrete, ikonic, as opposed to symbolic, formal operations. Children have to 'construct their alternatives' before they can choose between them. As we have seen, 'style' implies a preference for, say, concrete properties even though abstract properties have also been recognized. It was not clear, however, from Wallach and Kogan's study whether children who used concrete properties were capable of more abstract conceptualizations.

In his recent review, Kogan (1976) comments on this recurring difficulty in interpreting such findings.

'The time would appear to be ripe for a reorientation of research on styles of conceptualization. Let us determine not only what the child prefers to do, but what he is capable of doing. Let us depart from a rigidly unilinear model in which styles, more or less mature, follow one another according to a developmental timetable. Instead... let us explore the balance and patterning of styles within individuals... recognizing that all the styles may be present simultaneously (although possibly differing in their level of sophistication)' (Kogan, 1976, page 115).

Styles of information processing have also been described in terms of a distinction between *cognitive complexity* and cognitive simplicity (Bieri *et al.,* 1966). The test used is similar to Kelly's Repertory Grid. Respondents are asked to name ten 'significant others' (mother, father, brother, etc.) and to rate each of them on ten predetermined constructs. Cognitive complexity is shown by the use of many dimensions in contrasting the ten people named. Messick (1976) describes cognitive complexity as a 'tendency to construe the world, and particularly the world of social behaviour, in a multidimensional and discriminating way' (page 17). Cognitive complexity depends on having a highly developed conceptual system, in which concepts are clearly differentiated, finely articulated and flexibly integrated. Unfortunately this description again suggests that cognitive complexity is more than a *style* of thinking. It seems to imply high levels of both analytic and imaginative thinking as a necessary prerequisite for cognitive complexity. It would be necessary, as Kogan argued, to separate preference from capability before accepting that cognitive complexity is also a style of thinking.

Styles of perceiving and thinking

Two of the best known cognitive styles derive from perceptual tasks — Matching Familiar Figures (Kagan *et al.*, 1964) and identifying Embedded Figures (Witkin, 1977). Figure 10.1 shows an item from one of Kogan's tests which consists of a standard drawing and six or eight variants, one of which is identical to the standard, and all of which are similar. The respondent is required to answer as quickly as possible, but has to make another attempt after each incorrect response. There is thus a pressure to find the *correct* answer, but also to decide quickly. Kogan (1976) sees the situation as building up competing anxieties towards correct, or fast, responses. The average time to answer (response latency) is measured and also the number of errors. Two cognitive styles have been detected with this test. *Impulsive* people succumb rapidly to the need to identify the matching figure: they choose hurriedly and make more mistakes. *Reflective* individuals treat the task more analytically and cautiously: they are more accurate, but slower. Among children there is again a developmental trend, as well as a cognitive style component in these measures. Fast, accurate children are often intellectually more advanced than slow, inaccurate children, but the impulsive/reflective distinction does seem to indicate an important difference in information processing strategies (Messer, 1976). With semantic material, speed and accuracy are related to intelligence, but differences in scores produced on 'speed' and 'power' tests of reasoning show that some intelligent people do *prefer* a cautious, thoughtful response.

It is interesting to compare this test with the earlier measure of category breadth. Both tests invite the respondent to accept discrepancies. Impulsive people may well also use broader categories; reflection implies caution and narrower categories. The idea of competing anxieties could also be associated with the tension between hope for success and fear of failure which was discussed in the previous chapter. But these connections must remain speculative in the absence of empirical evidence.

The final cognitive style has perhaps attracted the greatest attention. An item from an Embedded Figures Test is shown in Figure 10.2. Witkin (1976; 1977) has reviewed the extensive literature on the use of this and other methods of measuring the dimension of field dependence/field independence. In the EFT the respondent is shown a simple geometrical figure and is required to identify it in a complex figure. The task is rather similar to the children's

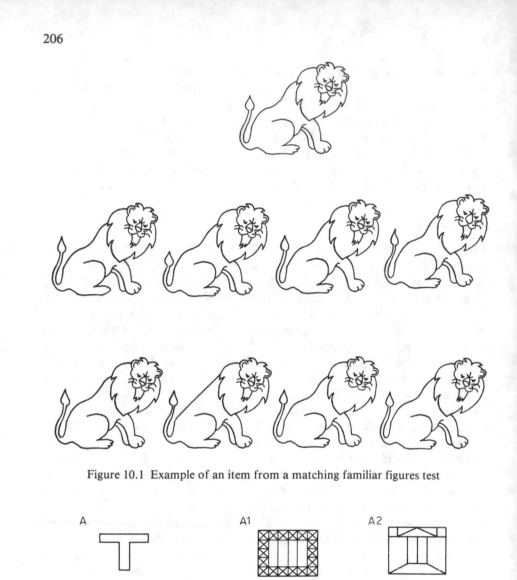

Figure 10.1 Example of an item from a matching familiar figures test

Figure 10.2 Example of an item from an embedded figures test

puzzle in which, say, a 'hidden rabbit' is discovered as part of the foliage of a tree. Some people can spot the embedded figure almost immediately: they are not distracted by the surroundings and are categorised as field-independent. Other people spend much longer even with the simple items. Witkin argues that the different scores on this test do not simply reflect perceptual skills. Like Pask he argues for the existence of underlying styles of thinking. Witkin labels these styles *articulated* (field-independent) and *global* (field-dependent), which seem, at first sight, to bear some resemblance to Pask's descriptions of operational learning and comprehension learning.

The articulated, field-independent style involves analysing and structuring incoming information; the global, field-dependent mode of operation accepts the totality of impressions. The problem in Witkin's description is that field-dependence is an *inability* to impose structure. If it is to be a *style,* a rather more positive description of 'global' thinking should be expected. At the moment its positive side can only be inferred from incidental characteristics such as tendencies to be sociable and to have an interest in other people. Field-dependent students express this interest in people by being drawn towards courses in the humanities and social sciences, and opting out of courses in science and mathematics. Field-independent students, while found predominantly in science faculties, are still capable of success in other areas of study. This facility raises the question of whether these students might be best compared with Pask's versatile learners, rather than with operation learners. But again we run up against lack of empirical evidence.

From an educational standpoint perhaps the most interesting studies reported by Witkin concern the teaching methods adopted by teachers of contrasting cognitive style. It appears that field-independent teachers or lecturers impose a tighter and more logical structure on teaching material than do 'global' teachers. They also prefer more formal approaches to teaching. Witkin argues that field-dependent students need pre-structured information, since they are less able to impose their own analytic frameworks. Hence field-dependent students ought to be more successful with teachers who have an articulated cognitive style. To date there is no evidence of differential success rates, but there is a clear indication that students prefer to be taught by teachers of the *same* cognitive style. There is thus a possible conflict here between the approach students prefer and what is considered to be most effective in helping them to learn.

There may thus be interesting differences between teachers in the way they organize the knowledge they expect students to acquire. Psychologists who have discussed the importance of structuring knowledge also differ in their prescriptions, as we shall see.

Contrasting ways of structuring knowledge

In the next chapter we shall discuss a fundamental division between educationalists in the extent to which teachers should control the learning process, define what is to be learned, and present the knowledge within a clearly defined structure.

For the time being let us assume that the teacher is expected to organize an area of knowledge into a framework which guides the student's learning, and to present ideas in a way and at a speed which is appropriate to the learner's previous knowledge and current intellectual capacity. From this assumption we can ask how best to structure knowledge and present it to pupils.

Several psychologists have used their own theories to suggest the most appropriate types of structure. Perhaps one of the best known is Skinner

(1954) whose ideas were derived from his theory of stimulus-response learning and applied to the development of programmed learning as being the result of appropriate reinforcement of 'correct' behaviour. Reinforced or rewarded behaviour persists, and it is possible to build up complex sets of behaviour out of smaller units. The principle Skinner advocated was that of building up learning in a series of small steps and reinforcing immediately each correct response by indicating its correctness.

Teaching machines present a succession of 'frames', each of which provides a small amount of information. After each frame a series of questions are used to test what has been learnt. Movement to the next frame, in the simplest type of machine, is dependent on the correct answer being given.

'The whole process of becoming competent in any field must be divided into a very large number of very small steps, and reinforcement must be contingent upon the accomplishment of each step.... By making each step as small as possible, the frequency of reinforcement can be raised to a maximum, while the possibly aversive consequences of being wrong are reduced to a minimum' (Skinner, 1954, quoted in Entwistle and Hounsell, 1975, page 35).

McKeachie (1974) has criticized the view of learning espoused by Skinner, and has argued that principles of conditioning are applicable only to the simplest forms of learning. In education, establishing simple associations between units of knowledge is rarely what is considered most important. Many teachers are likely to be repelled by the very idea of the mechanical manipulation of learning. They are more concerned with helping pupils to relate new ideas to their previous knowledge in a way which facilitates understanding.

Ausubel, as we have already seen, is one psychologist who puts great emphasis on meaningful learning. It was he who distinguished a meaningful learning set from a rote learning set (see Chapter 6, page 135) in discussing pupils' approaches to learning in schools. Ausubel (Ausubel et al., 1978) argues that the didactic method which leads to reception learning is effective and does not imply passivity on the part of the learner. Sitting still and listening, does not rule out thinking. Ausubel sees the process of active interaction between incoming information and the learner's existing cognitive structure as the 'normal' way of acquiring academic knowledge. His approach to educational psychology puts great emphasis on the *anchoring ideas* already established in a pupil's cognitive structure, and on the need to provide *organizers* which introduce the main principles of a new subject in advance (advance organizers) and indicate the main similarities and differences between the new ideas and the existing anchoring ideas (comparative organizers).

'The most important single factor influencing learning is what the learner already knows. Ascertain this and teach him accordingly.... It follows... that existing cognitive structure itself... is the principle factor influencing meaningful learning and retention.... Subject matter content... is always, and can only be, learned in relation to a previously learned background of relevant concepts, principles in a particular learner, and information that makes possible the emergence of new meanings and enhances their organization and retention'. (Ausubel *et al.*, 1978, pages 163-164.)

Ausubel is quite clear that the information presented to the learner should be organized initially by the teacher to facilitate linkages with the students' pre-existing knowledge. He is, however, equally clear that the ideas eventually stored by the learner will be unique, being the result of selective attention and interest, and the outcome of the learner's active attempts to relate new information to pre-existing concepts which necessarily have a personal, as well as a formal, meaning.

The function of advance organizers is to provide a framework within which the details presented later can be readily allocated to these guiding principles. In commenting on his two main concepts, Ausubel stresses the importance of

'(1) the availability in the learner's cognitive structure of specifically relevant anchoring ideas at an optimal level of inclusiveness, generality, and abstraction; (2) the extent to which such ideas are discriminated from both similar and different (but potentially confusable) concepts and principles in the learning material; and (3) the stability and clarity of the anchoring ideas.

Stability and clarity of the relevant anchoring ideas (which also affect their discriminability) depend on overlearning (consolidation), initial mastery within a homogeneous context before turning to more heterogeneous settings, and the use of sequentially organized learning materials....

An advance organizer is a pedagogic device that (bridges) the gap between what the learner already knows and what he needs to know if he is to learn the new material most actively and expeditiously.

Not only must (advance organizers) be more inclusive, abstract, and general than the learning material they precede, but they must also take into account relevant existing ideas in the learner's cognitive structure (so that they themselves are learnable and can also explicitly mobilize all relevant content already available in that structure)....' (Ausubel *et al.*, 1978, pages 116, 164)

This idea of learning as the interaction between pre-structured incoming information and the learner's own cognitive structure is also found in Pask's theory of understanding (Pask, 1976a; Entwistle, 1978). He has outlined a 'conversation theory' which

describes learning in terms of a conversation between two representations of knowledge. In the most familiar situation these representations reflect the cognitive structures of two people, the teacher (or subject matter expert) and the student. Learning takes place through a dialogue between the two and, in conversation theory, understanding has to be demonstrated by applying that knowledge to an unfamiliar situation.... Reproductive responses based on memory are not accepted as evidence of understanding.

Learning need not, however, involve an interaction between the cognitive structures of two people. The student may converse silently with himself in trying to understand a topic, or he may interact with a formal representation of the knowledge structure and supplementary learning materials' (Entwistle, 1978, page 255).

Pask is, in a sense, bringing together the ideas of logical sequence from programmed learning and of initial overviews from advance organizers. He has asked students to work through learning materials, following an elaborate topic map which he calls an *entailment structure*. The students are required to reach understanding of a defined target topic, but can tackle sub-topics in various orders.

Pask's entailment structure shows the sub-topics in a hierarchy, which indicates which aspects have to be understood first. Each entailment structure is developed out of discussions with subject-matter specialists, who are asked to describe all the sub-topics contained in a defined area of knowledge — say the idea of 'probability' in statistics. The specialists are then asked to explain how all these sub-topics relate to each other, and in what order the topics should be learned. They are also asked to provide concrete illustrations of any abstract relationships and concepts. For example, the idea of a 'normal curve' could be illustrated by tossing a coin and recording how often the same side occurs — once, twice, three times, and so on, in succession. The topic map provided for the student contains three sets of topics and relationships — those relating to the *real* world, those relating to its *abstract* representation which is to be learnt, and those which demonstrate the *analogies* between the concrete instances and the theoretical ideas. Figure 10.3 shows part of a simple topic map described by Robertson (1977). Topic A and B are pre-requisites for C: understanding of *both* these topics is required before topic C can be tackled. On the other hand an understanding of *either* topic D or E is sufficient for moving on to topic F. The double line linking C and F indicates that the relationship between them is analogical: topic F is the abstract analogy of topic C in the real world. The topic maps derived from normal subject matter are, of course, much more complicated, with many sub-topics and inter-relationships.

When students are faced with such a topic map, which contains various routes, they tackle the topics in different orders. Figure 10.4 shows the contrasting routes followed by two students (Robertson, 1977). One student worked his way vertically up through the hierarchy of real world topics, using

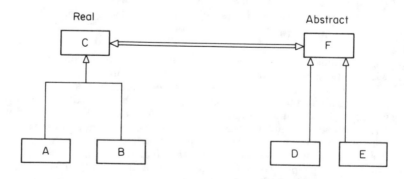

Figure 10.3 Part of a simple topic map (from Robertson, 1977)

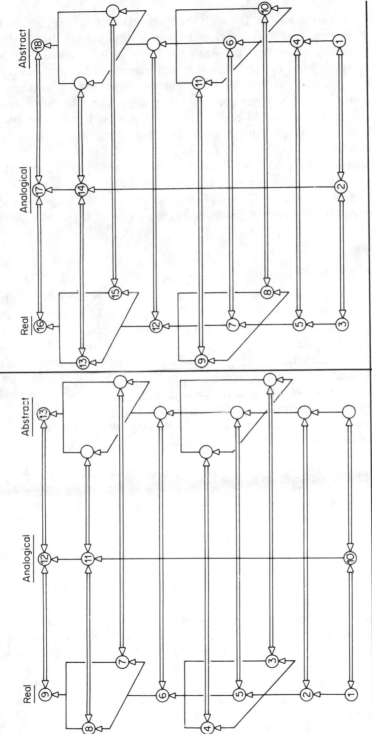

Figure 10.4 Contrasting routes through the topic map. (from Robertson, 1977, Appendix 7). Numbers indicate the order in which topics were studied

analogies only to establish a link with the final two abstract topics. The other student, in contrast, explored real and abstract topics from the beginning. These two approaches reflect the strategies likely to be adopted by students with contrasting styles of learning. The comprehension learner makes more use of the whole map, seeking to make wide inter-connections and using the analogies provided. The operation learner is more likely to move upwards through either the real world or the abstract topics with a narrow focus of attention, using analogies only when these become essential for the understanding required.

The importance of Pask's work can be seen in three ways. First the use of the topic map to aid learning; second, in showing the importance of analogy in fostering understanding; and finally, in demonstrating the different ways in which students use the same topic map. These aspects will now be explored in more detail.

The use of a topic map

Pask has used his theory to indicate deficiencies in the presentation of topics which students commonly find difficult. Text-books and teachers often follow traditional ways of organizing information. Pask has demonstrated that the framework used for organizing these troublesome topics is frequently ineffective. By encouraging subject-matter specialists to develop entailment structures which show fully all the inter-relationships between topics, and the exact links between theory and concrete examples of real-world analogies, topic maps can be provided for the students. Pask has shown that students who make use of such entailment structures reach higher levels of understanding of these difficult topics, than students taught in conventional ways (see Entwistle, 1978).

Many of the examples Pask gives of the development of entailment structures are drawn from the sciences, where more agreement is likely between specialists about structures of knowledge, and formal analogies can be readily developed. But more recently Pask has explored ways of allowing students to develop their own *entailment graphs,* which are personal concept maps. Again this device has been found useful, particularly in areas like history, where agreed hierarchies of topics and agreed interpretations are less commonly found. Figure 10.5 shows one such entailment graph developed by a student asked to explain his understanding of events in the reign of Henry VIII. This student saw these events in terms of a dialectic evolution between the politics of the Tudor dynasty and the problems of religion and divorce. The same events would, of course, be interpreted differently by other students, but the use of the entailment graph helps each student to test the logical coherence of his own interpretation. A tutor looking at such a concept map would be able to point out omissions or inappropriate links which might lead to a modified entailment graph, and a different conceptualization of the events of this period. Thus discussion of alternative ways of structuring knowledge could be

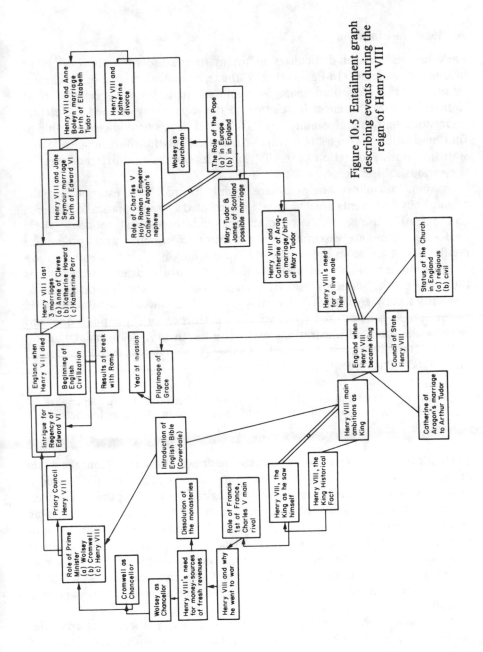

Figure 10.5 Entailment graph describing events during the reign of Henry VIII

a valuable method of teaching, particularly in the sixth form or in higher education.

Analogies in education

Pask has also traced difficulties in topics to the use of inappropriate or incomplete analogies. In Pask's theory, the term analogy is used in a technical sense, but the idea that analogies facilitate understanding only if their similarities *and* differences in relation to the topic being learned are clearly understood has general validity. In Pask's work it has often been possible to find mechanical analogies to parallel theoretical relationships in science and statistics. But in education generally, analogies are used in different ways in the various subject areas.

In some disciplines analogies are mainly formal. For example, in the sciences physical events are commonly represented as mathematical equations, and extensive use is made of diagrams and mechanical models. These analogical forms are essential in the attempt to organize and systematize regularities observed in the real world. In teaching it is also essential to use concrete illustrations to aid understanding of abstract ideas. The teacher is thus helping the pupil to use his own analogies by drawing attention to similarities between common everyday experiences and the abstractions. If such analogies are not used effectively by the teacher, or if the pupil does not see how the practical illustrations exemplify the theory, deep understanding becomes difficult, if not impossible. Dewey (1910) described the process of understanding as follows:

'Something already understood in one situation has been transferred and applied to what is strange and perplexing in another and thereby the latter has become plain and familiar, i.e. understood' (page 118).

The illustrations used in science teaching are drawn, inevitably, from the world of things, not people. They often show how an abstract principle has been *applied,* but will only have immediate pedagogical value if the pupil has a 'feel' for the practical workings of the illustration used, and already has some understanding of the principle being described. In science it is often difficult to appeal directly to previous personal experience. What is familiar must often be previous formal knowledge. Thus thorough understanding of basic concepts and ideas is of pre-eminent importance. It is this characteristic which leads science to be referred to as 'vertical': it builds on previous knowledge in a sequential way.

In the humanities, and some of the social sciences, mathematical analogies are less common. Personal experience can, however, provide a rich source of analogies and illustrations, which also provide a direct connection between abstract principles and previous understanding. Psychology makes use of a wide variety of ways of representing knowledge and aiding understanding. In this book, for example, there have been algebraic analogies, such as Atkinson's formula ($T_S = M_S \times P_S \times I_S$), while the information processing model could be described as a mechanical analogy. Information processing was also discussed with the use of less formal analogies by likening coding processes to filing research papers or to organizing a library. Finally a more picturesque analogy was presented in the previous chapter with an excursion into Egyptian mythology.

Personal experience, and particularly emotional experience, plays an important part in understanding literature and the aesthetic areas of the curriculum. An intensity of feeling in interpreting interpersonal relationships puts even greater emphasis on personal analogies. In the academic treatment of aesthetic subjects, of course, formal analysis and structure is called for, but there is little reliance on formal analogies as such.

Disciplines differ in the way analogies are used. There are also characteristic differences in use made of analogies by people with contrasting learning styles. In Chapter 5 (page 91) we saw that comprehension learners were much more ready to use analogies than operation learners, and were also likely to develop their own idiosyncratic analogies — ways of thinking which while not formally correct, were personally helpful in moving towards a more complete understanding. Pask also showed the difficulties that comprehension learners had when they were forced to learn through material which, while logical and well-organized had few illustrations, examples or analogies. We shall come to the implications of this finding later.

Styles of learning

Pask has argued that a knowledge of one's own style of learning is important in 'learning to learn'. There is a growing recognition that students cannot be expected to acquire study skills incidentally. Students often come to university without any full realization of what is required of them. They continue to use inappropriate reproductive approaches and have no awareness of the way in which their own style of learning may differ from that of other students. Pask has run 'learning to learn' seminars in which students are taught to build up and use entailment graphs, to impose structure on unstructured information, and also to recognize the implications of their own individual learning styles.

> 'The findings were most encouraging: our earlier studies gave evidence that students can learn to learn and build descriptions of unstructured materials, this study shows that the description built up by a student (his entailment graph) has distinct personal characteristics reflective of his (learning) style'. (Pask *et al.*, 1977, page 77).

By giving students feedback about their own styles of learning, and discussing the characteristic pathologies of such strategies, it is thought to be possible to help students develop a more versatile approach to learning. The essential ingredients of Pask's seminars are development of specific skills (description building through entailment graphs), increased self-awareness of personal learning style, and opportunities for practice using specially prepared materials.

Basic cognitive and learning styles

In the literature presented so far, we have met many different attempts to describe cognitive or learning styles. Are all the different terms necessary? Is it possible to present a more coherent picture based on a few more basic dimensions? Lewis (1976) is critical of the current state of research into cognitive styles.

> 'Different groups of researchers seem determined to pursue their own pet distinctions in cheerful disregard of one another... There is the impulsive versus reflective distinction, which seems to indicate something about the tempo of learning. There is the field-dependent versus field-independent distinction, the serialists and the holists, and a lot more... In my opinion, the right thing to do is to focus... on the search for individual differences which are basic, in the sense that they underlie (and to that extent, *explain*) a whole range of more readily observable differences' (pages 304-5).

The lack of firm evidence on inter-relationships between different measures of cognitive style is admitted by Kogan (1976). He comments warily that 'the cognitive styles under review are neither completely independent nor completely overlapping in their inter-relationships' (page 120). Such caution is justified. Each style, as well as each strategy, depends to a certain extent on the particular tests or tasks used to define it. To date few *consistent* inter-relationships between cognitive styles have been reported, at least among children, where style, differential ability, and developmental stages are still inextricably interwoven.

Among students, however, the picture might be expected to be clearer. In Kogan and Wallach's (1964) earlier study on *Risk Taking* among undergraduates, some interesting correlates of field-independence are reported. There is a tendency for the analytic, field-independent students to have higher mathematical than verbal ability, to be reflective, but rather rigid in their thinking. There was, however, a sex difference in relation to risk taking. Field-independent women were more cautious, while the global, field-independent women were more impulsive and took risks. The opposite was true of men, perhaps because field-independence in men was associated with 'an active "participant" attitude', as opposed to 'a passive "spectator" attitude'. Pask (1976b) found links between holism and divergent thinking, which might also imply greater category width, but here the evidence peters out.

In the absence of firm empirical relationships any attempt to summarize the meaning of these diverse cognitive styles is necessarily tentative and may lead to 'globetrotting'. Some of the connections may prove later to have been 'vacuous analogies', but at least the following descriptions provide some integration of the otherwise disparate styles discussed. *Holists* tend to be divergent thinkers, which might imply that they use wider conceptual categories and are more ready to accept thematic, as opposed to analytic, links between concepts. It might also imply that they are likely to be impulsive, emotionally uninhibited but not anxious, and to opt for courses in languages or in the humanities. *Serialists* are more convergent in their thought processes. They are thus likely to be cautious, conservative, analytic and tend to reject possible connections by using narrow categorizations. Emotionally they might be expected to be inhibited and their area of study is likely to be mathematical or scientific. *Versatile* learners are surely cognitively complex. They can vary their strategy according to the characteristics of the task, and presumably are able to withstand diversity and inconsistency.

The cognitive style literature has produced dichotomies or bi-polar constructs representing preferences towards one or other way of thinking. But there are also hints throughout, that styles have to be considered in relation to competences. People are unlikely to choose an undeveloped style; they are bound, to some extent, by the level of abilities they have acquired. If we thus return to the four-way split envisaged earlier in the chapter (page 202) — Level III, convergence, divergence, and Level I — it is worth re-examining other styles and strategies of learning to see whether these also fit into such a pattern.

STOP and THINK

Write down a list of the cognitive styles discussed in the preceding section. Can you identify similarities between these descriptions and the learning styles and personality characteristics described earlier? Which do you consider to be the most striking similarities?

Table 10.1 shows the result of such an analysis. There is no perfect fit, but it is possible to see in Style A and Style B characteristics which may be descriptive of a more general construct tapped to some extent by each of the other dichotomous categories. In several cases it is also possible to detect categories of thinking which imply hierarchically different skills (such as Level I and Level III) which are either integrative of both styles, or show evidence of their lack. The tendency to describe cognitive or learning styles in simple dichotomies may well reflect no more than our inability to cope with more complex categorizations, but the similarity in the descriptions of those dichotomies is striking. Is there any neurological parallel to modes of thinking — A, B and integrated? Ornstein (1977) has attributed different forms of consciousness to the two sides of the brain.

Table 10.1. Styles and strategies

Research area	Integrated A + B	Developed Style A	Developed Style B	Under-developed	Author
Learning strategies	Versatile	Holist or comprehension	Serialist or operation	Reproducing	Pask and Chapter 5
Levels of ability	— Intelligent (Level III)	Divergence Imaginative —	Convergence Analytic Level II	— Rote Level I	Hudson Chapter 7 Jensen
Cognitive styles	—	Broad categories	Narrow categories	—	Wallach and Kogan
	—	Thematic	Analytic	Descriptive	
	Fast and accurate	Impulsive	Reflective and (cautious)	Slow and inaccurate	Kogan
	—	Field-dependent (global)	Field-independent (articulated)	—	Witkin
Area of study	—	Arts (Personal analogies)	Science (Formal analogies)	—	
Level of understanding	Conclusion-orientated detailed	Conclusion-orientated mentioning	Description detailed	Description mentioning	Franssen and Chapter 4
Personality	Individuation (ego integ-ration)	Extravert	Introvert	—	Jung
	Reasonable adventurer	Plunger	Non-Committer	(Hustler?)	Heath

'The cerebral cortex of the brain is divided into two hemispheres, joined by a large bundle of interconnecting fibres called the *corpus callosum*. The left side of the body is controlled mainly by the right side of the cortex. When we speak of *left* in ordinary speech, we are referring to that side of the body and to the *right* hemisphere of the brain.

Both the structure and function of these two "half-brains" underlie in some part the two modes of consciousness that coexist within each one of us. Although each hemisphere shares the potential for many functions and both sides participate in most activities, in the normal person the two hemispheres tend to specialize. The left hemisphere (in those people — the majority — in which it is dominant)... is predominantly involved with analytic, logical thinking, especially in verbal and mathematical functions. Its mode of operation is primarily linear. The hemisphere seems to process information sequentially. Since logic depends on sequence and order, this mode of operation must of necessity underlie logical thought....

If the left hemisphere is specialized for analysis, the right hemisphere... seems specialized for synthesis. Its language ability is quite limited. This hemisphere is primarily responsible for orientation in space, artistic endeavour, crafts, body image, recognition of faces. It processes information more diffusely than does the left hemisphere, and its responsibilities demand a ready integration of many inputs at once. If the left hemisphere can be termed predominantly analytic and sequential in its operation, then the right hemisphere is more holistic and relational, and more simultaneous in its mode of operation' (pages 20-21).

Is cerebral dominance, then, the explanation of dichotomies in cognitive or learning style? The consequences of being left-handed are far-reaching in people's behaviour. Are we seeing similarly extensive effects in thinking created by the dominance of one or other side of the brain? All we have shown so far is that there are *parallels* between Ornstein's description of the functions of the hemispheres, and the characteristics of, say, holistic (right), serialistic (left), and versatile (integrated) learners. If this is to provide an *explanation,* we should have to show, for example, that when a person exhibits holist strategies predominant use is made of the right hemisphere of the brain. Although it is too soon to provide such clear-cut evidence, Ornstein (1977) has reported higher activity in the left hemisphere when students are asked to write a letter, while working on tests of spatial ability involved a greater use of the right hemisphere. Direct evidence of this type is, however, still sparse, and arguments by analogy are more common.

Ornstein himself draws on the teaching of Eastern philosophers to illustrate the importance of alternative forms of consciousness. He argues that traditional education over-values the logical, sequential mode and under-rates the expressive. Blakemore (1977) criticizes Ornstein and other psychologists for their 'fiery rhetoric' and for their 'curious assumption that the two hemispheres of a normal man are as divided as those of Sperry's patients' (whose corpus callosum had been cut) (page 164). Blakemore continues

'What we should be striving to achieve for ourselves and our brains is not the pampering of one hemisphere to the neglect of the other (whether right or left), or their independent development, but the marriage and harmony of the two. It so happens that the special mental territories of the minor, right hemisphere — spatial perception, pictorial recognition and intuitive thought — are not easily amenable to conventional education, nor is it clear that they would benefit from years of formal education' (page 166).

Ornstein may be guilty of over-dramatizing the differences between the normal and alternative forms of consciousness, but he is not guilty of the simplistic view attributed to him by Blakemore. He is also arguing for integration of the intellectual functions attributed to each side of the brain, but through a greater emphasis on *non-traditional* forms of education.

In describing the dominant logical mode in Western consciousness Ornstein illustrates its tendency to concentrate on parts rather than the whole by the story of the blind men who were asked to describe an elephant. They came across different parts of the animal. One man holding the trunk said 'It is long and soft and emits air'. Another feeling the legs considers it to be 'massive, cylindrical, and hard', while yet another man touching the skin reports 'It is rough and scaly'. Ornstein is, in fact, arguing for emphasis on 'education of the intuitive mode' only to restore the necessary balance which Blakemore is also advocating. A holistic view is necessary to *complement,* not to replace, logical thinking.

'The "ordinary intellect" works analytically. It operates separately on individual elements of otherwise organized wholes. If the complementary mode of operation is developed, an individual's consciousness is more complete.... The complementarity of two major modes of consciousness is hardly new. It antedates systems such as the *I Ching* (with its emphasis on the interplay of male and female, "yang" and "yin").... With a recognition of the biological basis of the dual specializations of consciousness, we may be able to redress the imbalance in science and psychology. This balance has in recent years swung a bit too far to the right (hand), to the strict insistence on verbal logic that has left context and perspective undeveloped and has ignored the existence of many basic human qualities' (Ornstein, 1977, pages 124 and 39).

Ornstein is thus arguing for an effective integration of both methods of thinking. But what form might we anticipate this integration taking. Is there a type of thinking which uses both sides of the brain simultaneously, or should we be thinking in terms of *alternation* between two distinct modes?

Chickering (1976) sees an essential part of the educational process as an alternation between what he calls differentiation and integration, which show parallels with operation and comprehension learning.

'Much significant human development occurs through cycles of differentiation and integration.... Increased differentiation occurs when one comes to see the interacting parts of something formerly seen as unitary, when one distinguishes among concepts formerly seen as similar, when one's actions are more finely responsive to individual purposes or to outside conditions, when one's interests become more varied, tastes more diverse, reactions more subtle — in short as one becomes a more complex human being.... Increasing differentiation, however, must be accompanied by increasing integration. Relationships among parts must be perceived or constructed so more complex wholes result. Concepts from different disciplines must be brought to bear on one another and connected in ways appropriate to varied tasks and problems' (Chickering, 1976, pages 81-82).

It may well be that intellectual development beyond Piaget's level of formal operations, in other words the development of what we have labelled Level III thinking, demands the ability to alternate flexibly between left- and right-sided brain functions, between the cautiously logical and the free-ranging review of remote possibilities. Pask has certainly argued that his versatile students are not only capable of selecting a style of learning appropriate to the task, they are also likely to pursue understanding beyond a simple logical conclusion and generate a distinct personal perspective (see Entwistle *et al.,* 1979b). Heath's reasonable adventurers were capable of similarly advanced thinking, and Heath was clear that this skill depended on the *alternation* of 'two mental attitudes — the critical and the curious'.

The idea of development through the tension between opposites, a synthesis out of thesis and antithesis — is found in descriptions of both society and personality. It could be seen as *the* fundamental developmental process. If, in intellectual development, the distinction between Style A and Style B thinking is in opposition (whether or not it can be attributed to laterality in the brain), it may be important in education to capitalize on this opposition in helping students towards greater flexibility or versatility in their thinking and learning. Again, if this distinction in cognitive styles is as fundamental as it now seems, we should expect to see its influence on many areas of human activity.

Such distinctions *can* be seen, although it is speculative to link these contrasts to cognitive style or laterality effects. In teaching the strongest contrast is between formal and informal methods, emphasis on control and structure or on freedom and self-expression. In writing there is an obvious difference between the sequential structure of the text-book, and the rapid changes of scene and time used by many novelists. Among research workers we have already met the fierce controversy between the proponents of a strict scientific approach and those who favour a more intuitive, holist view of the educational process.

If we are right in anticipating that integration will be no more than an appropriate alternation of Style A and Style B to the task in hand, it might be that we shall look in vain for a way of teaching, or writing, or researching which has effectively synthesized the competing alternatives. The most effective approaches may be those which use the styles in alternation, in a way which best suits the specific situation. However, it would be likely that most people would not achieve this balance, but would exhibit a pattern characteristic of whichever style they found most congenial. It is from this hypothesis that contrasting styles of teaching will be examined in the next chapter.

Summary

Table 10.1 can be used to recapitulate the different categories used to describe cognitive style. Out of these it seems possible to describe both different levels of abilities, and different styles of thinking at the same level of sophistication. The interesting parallels between the characteristics of Style A and Style B may be attributable to dominance of left or right hemispheres of the brain, but the evidence for this is sketchy. It seems likely that both styles of thinking are available to most people, although with different degrees of effectiveness. Many people, nevertheless, seem to develop a preference for one or other mode of thinking which may become apparent in their approach to learning, teaching, writing, or researching.

Various theorists have considered the need to organize knowledge in presenting it to students. Skinner has emphasized the small steps which allow regular and immediate reinforcement of correct responses. Ausubel has stressed the importance of establishing firm anchoring ideas and the use of organizers to help students process incoming information more effectively. Pask has described the use of concept maps and analogies in developing understanding. Again the contrast in views seems explicable in terms of Pask's own description of comprehension and operation learning, with Skinner and Ausubel showing distinct preferences for step-by-step, logical or serialist forms of presentation.

In education there is a need to help students become aware of the contrasting ways of thinking and their characteristic pathologies. Also many teachers may have tended to over-emphasize the importance of analytic thinking to the detriment of the imaginative and expressive modes. Ornstein has argued for a redress in this imbalance and provides this illustration (from the right-hemisphere) to make his point more strongly.

'Nasrudin sometimes took people for trips in his boat. One day a fussy pedagogue hired him to ferry him across a very wide river. As soon as they were afloat the scholar asked him if it was going to be rough.

"Don't ask me nothing about it", said Nasrudin.

"Have you never studied grammar?"

"No", said the Mulla.

"In that case, half your life has been wasted".

The Mulla said nothing.

Soon a terrible storm blew up. The Mulla's crazy cockleshell was filling with water. He leaned over toward his companion.

"Have you ever learned to swim?"

"No", said the pedant.

"In that case, schoolmaster, *all* your life is lost, for we are sinking".'

(Ornstein, 1977, page 16).

PART IV

Applications to Teaching and Studying

CHAPTER 11

Teaching Styles, Learning, and Curricular Choice

In this final section of the book, we move towards possible applications of the ideas discussed in Parts II and III to a variety of pedagogical problems. In Chapter 12 we shall look back to the model originally outlined in Chapter 5 and discuss implications for education at different age-ranges. In this chapter we examine contrasting ideas on education and teaching which can be as polarized as the distinctions met previously between Style A and Style B thinking, and consider the possible effects of alternative styles of teaching on pupils' attempts at learning.

STOP and THINK

- Try to think of instances from your own experience of teaching which you would describe as either formal or informal.

- What would you see as the likely advantages and disadvantages of each approach?

- Would it be desirable and possible to develop an integrated approach to teaching which balanced both methods, or must teachers necessarily choose one or other style?

The division in education between traditional and progressive ideas has been long-lasting (at least back to Rousseau's protest about the way education was constraining human development in the 18th century), and it remains pervasive. At the ideological level it is found in considerations about the purposes of education, and persists through discussions about the relative importance of different educational aims, down to the way in which schools are run and classes taught.

In considering the general aims of education, the main contrast seems to be between viewing the purpose of education narrowly as training which leads to vocational qualifications, or broadly as a preparation for life, a way of fostering individuality and self-expression. To some extent the narrow view accepts the existing role of education in reproducing society as it is now, while the broad view may envisage education as a way of changing society. The first philosophy reflects the importance placed on preparing children for their future roles in employment and the home. The alternative view stresses the opportunities, through education, of extending a person's potentialities and of creating a more equal society. The two extremes are essentially conflicting ideologies, and have their parallels in discussions about teaching methods.

Aims of education and methods of teaching

The narrow definition of the purposes of education leads to a concentration on ways of improving standards, of ensuring that pupils are competent and can satisfy the examiners. Proponents of this view may look towards learning theorists such as Skinner to provide appropriate ways of improving the efficiency of teaching. Skinner's theory depends on strengthening stimulus-response bonds, on shaping behaviour into predetermined patterns. The methods of teaching which are often advocated to implement this view of education emphasize control and tight structure. Control can be by teacher or by machine (programmed learning, computer assisted learning) and the structure is generally logical and sequential. Besides intellectual control, laws of learning may also be applied to pupil behaviour by applying appropriate schedules of reinforcement. Much disruptive behaviour in the classroom has its roots in pupils who want to be noticed. If a child cannot gain attention in other ways, 'bad' behaviour is certain to catch the teacher's eye. The natural reaction of the teacher is to intervene, but as this also involves 'taking notice', the unruly behaviour may be reinforced in that way. Simply ignoring the behaviour is, however, equally ineffective. The teacher needs to specify alternative types of behaviour which would allow the child to be noticed, and which are also acceptable. This 'behaviour modification' is a direct extension of Skinner's attempts to shape the movements of pigeons. As a part of the teacher's armoury it is useful, but as part of a narrow view of education, it is limiting.

Stimulus-response psychology has inspired other developments in education, notably the use of precise behavioural objectives in planning instruction. Programmed learning had this beneficial side-effect. In order to develop step-by-step sequences and appropriate tests of attainment, the writer had to decide the best logical order in which to present the topic and identify the behaviour to be tested afterwards. Conscious and careful planning of the purposes of a course must be beneficial. The specification of behavioural, or at least clearly described, objectives is also a useful first step. But again over-emphasis on the use of precise behavioural objectives can become limiting.

A more recent approach which again requires teacher control of sequencing has been called *mastery learning*. This approach has been developed out of Carroll's (1963) model of school learning and is based on the assumption that given time, and good instruction, almost all pupils will be able to 'master' what they are asked to learn. Bloom (1968) used these ideas to challenge the usual ways of describing achievement. When attainment tests are given to large groups of pupils the distribution of scores usually follows the normal curve (norm-referenced testing). Bloom comments that a normal curve would be expected *only* if school attainment were the result of a series of chance factors. If instruction is carefully planned and organized we should expect most pupils, say 80 per cent, to be able to reach certain defined criteria or levels of attainment, given time. If attainment tests are linked to these specified criteria (criterion-referenced testing) and pupils are allowed as much time as they like to reach these levels, Bloom argues that academic failure is unnecessary. If the pupil does do badly, the attainment test can be used diagnostically to show him his specific weaknesses, and that part of the course can be repeated.

Mastery learning depends on dividing the syllabus up into units, much larger than the frames within programmed learning, but shorter than conventional courses. The instructional material may involve work-books, text-books, or lectures, but these will be supplemented by individual or small-group tutorial discussions. Each instructional unit has its own diagnostic test to assess level of mastery. Thus mastery learning can be seen as containing several of the principles enunciated by Skinner, but with presentation of information and reinforcement of correct answers coming in larger blocks. Also the emphasis on unlimited time, becomes an egalitarian principle making high achievement open to all (given time).

In this model the teacher is clearly in control of pupils' activities although the pupil is given more responsibility and involvement in the process of learning. It follows Westbury's (1977) definition of teaching as

'the management of the attention and time of the students *vis-à-vis* the primary educational ends of the classroom'.

Bennett (1978) quotes this definition in support of his own argument for a model of teaching which emphasizes the role of the teacher as manager of pupil learning. Similar conclusions, as we have seen, were reached from his earlier study of pupil progress in formal and informal primary classrooms (see Chapter 2, page 28).

'The central factor emerging from this study is that a degree of teacher direction is necessary, and that this direction needs to be carefully planned, and the learning experiences provided need to be clearly sequenced and structured.... It would seem less than useful for a teacher to stand by and leave a child alone in his enquiries hoping that something will happen' (Bennett, 1976, page 162).

As we saw in the previous chapter, this emphasis on curricular planning and sequencing forms an important part of Ausubel's ideas on encouraging effective learning. Yet other psychologists have taken an almost opposite stance, arguing that freedom to explore ideas and a belief in her own abilities are the critical factors in a child's school progress. Within this broader view of education a teacher's role should be less didactic and more that of 'facilitator' of learning.

Jerome Bruner and Carl Rogers have been at the forefront of attempts to move teachers away from the narrow view of learning. Bruner (1960, 1966) has emphasized the merits of discovery learning in fostering mental activity. He has contrasted the traditional expository method of teaching with what he refers to as a hypothetical mode. Discovery learning fosters pupils' willingness to ask questions and to seek out provisional answers for themselves.

The essence of discovery learning is that the pupil is active in discovering important principles from practical examples without undue interference from the teacher.

> 'Mastery of the fundamental ideas of a field involves not only the grasping of general principles, but also the development of an attitude toward learning and inquiry, toward guessing and hunches, toward the possibility of solving problems on one's own.... To instill such attitudes by teaching requires ... a sense of excitement about discovery — discovery of regularities of previously unrecognized relations and similarities between ideas, with a resulting sense of self-confidence in one's abilities.... For if we do nothing else we should somehow give to children a respect for their own powers of thinking, for their power to generate good questions, to come up with interesting informed guesses... to make ... study more rational, more amenable to the use of mind in the large rather than mere memorizing' (Bruner, 1960, page 20; 1966, page 96).

Snelbecker (1974) sees this method as also involving less teacher control.

> 'The ... discovery learning mode requires that the student participates in making many of the decisions about what, how, and when something is to be learned and even play a major role in making such decisions. Instead of being "told" the content by the teacher, it is expected that the student will have to explore examples and from them "discover" the principles or concepts which are to be learned. Many contend that the discovery learning versus expositiory debate continues a timeless debate as to how much a teacher should help a student and how much the student should help himself' (page 425).

In fact Bruner himself did not advocate so much freedom of action, he advocated 'guided learning' within which the students were given freedom to explore ideas. At least in his earlier writing, Bruner gave the teacher an active role in organizing the curriculum to fit the pupils' level of intellectual development. He argued that the same crucial ideas should be introduced repeatedly at increasing levels of detail and abstraction to form a 'spiral curriculum'. This idea stems from one of Bruner's best-known statements (see Chapter 8, page 176) which contrasts with some of the pessimistic views about the limited capacities children have for learning.

'Any subject can be taught effectively in some intellectually honest form to any child at any stage of development' (Bruner, 1960, page 33).

Bruner puts the onus on the teacher to select material and methods of teaching appropriate to the intellectual level and maturity of the child, and believes that there are, in any area of knowledge, important, basically simple ideas which should be introduced early, and revisited regularly to strengthen grasp and 'feel' for the subject.

While Bruner emphasizes intellectual growth, Rogers (1969) is more concerned with the broadest definition of education — the development of a healthy personality which seeks 'self-actualization' (Maslow, 1973). Freedom of self-expression and the teacher's unqualified regard for the student are the linchpins of Rogers' views on education. In his influential book *Freedom to Learn,* he is strongly critical of traditional approaches to teaching which foster competition and provide experiences of failure for many children. He condemns didactic or expository methods, unless they form part of an entirely different approach to education.

'Teaching is, for me, a relatively unimportant and vastly overvalued activity.... Teaching and the imparting of knowledge make sense in an unchanging environment.... But if there is one truth about modern man, it is that he lives in an environment which is *continually changing....* We are, in my view, faced with an entirely new situation in education where the goal of education, if we are to survive, is the *facilitation of change and learning.* The only man who is educated is the man who has learned how to learn; the man who has learned how to adapt and change; the man who has realized that no knowledge is secure, that only the process of *seeking* knowledge gives a basis for security. Changingness, a reliance on *process* rather than upon static knowledge, is the only thing that makes any sense as a goal for education in the modern world' (Rogers, 1969, pages 103-4).

The criticism Rogers has about most education is that it emphasizes knowledge which soon becomes out-of-date and a useless burden in the memory — an echo of Whitehead's (1932) equally forthright views

'For successful education there must be a certain freshness in the knowledge dealt with.... Knowledge does not keep any better than fish'.

But Rogers goes further: he wants knowledge, even fresh knowledge, to be made subsidiary to the process of learning how to learn. Today's fresh knowledge is tomorrow's out-dated information. And above all Rogers wants to set the learner free from the type of experiences which crush both curiosity and self-confidence. He wants students and teachers to recognize that emotions are an essential part of learning — that is of 'significant, existential' learning.

'*Not* the lifeless, sterile, futile, quickly forgotten stuff which is crammed into the minds of the poor helpless individual tied into his seat by ironclad bonds of conformity! I am talking about LEARNING — the insatiable curiosity which drives the adolescent boy to absorb everything he can see or read about gasoline engines in order to improve the efficiency and speed of his "hot-rod"....

'We frequently fail to recognize that much of the material presented to students in the classroom has, for the student, the same perplexing, meaningless quality that the list of nonsense syllables has for us. This is especially true for the under-privileged child whose background provides no context for the material with which he is confronted. But nearly every student finds that large portions of his curriculum are for him, meaningless. Thus education becomes the futile attempt to learn material which has no personal meaning' (Rogers, 1969, pages 3-4).

In contrast Rogers wants to establish a 'community of learners', free to pursue those ideas which excite them, ideas which have intense personal meaning. He wants, above all,

'To free curiosity; to permit individuals to go charging off in new directions dictated by their own interests; to unleash a sense of inquiry; to open everything to questioning and exploration; to recognize that everything is in process of change ... (And) we know ... that the initiation of such learning rests not upon the teaching skills of the leader, ... not upon his lectures and presentations, not upon an abundance of books, though each of these might at one time or another be utilized as an important resource. No, the facilitation of significant learning rests upon certain attitudinal qualities which exist in the personal *relationship* between the facilitator and the learner' (Rogers, 1969, pages 105-6).

For Rogers these qualities are 'realness' (the teacher shows boredom, interest, anger, sympathy — is himself), 'prizing, acceptance, trust' (of the student's personal and intellectual qualities) and 'empathetic understanding' (the ability to feel how learning seems to the student).

Rogers is, without doubt, an idealist, and progressive education has been sustained by such idealists, and by the enthusiasts who find in their ideas a new and exciting way of teaching. In the final chapter we shall consider what forms such facilitation of learning may take in practice.

In the history of progressive education the justifications for 'setting the pupil free' have been varied. Freud's concern was over emotional feelings which have been repressed by excessive discipline and control, while Dewey reacted against the passivity of 'recitation' lessons in elementary schools. Another recent complaint about traditional education again touches on emotional feelings, not on the negative effects of repression, but on the lack of the positive gains to be found in building on what Maslow (1973) has termed 'peak-experiences' — 'feelings of too-much awe', transcendental or mystical experiences. Paffard (1973) has shown that many children and students have had such experiences, yet few have been encouraged to talk or think about them. The failure to capitalize on facets of human life which have profound and lasting effects on people, is to Paffard a serious indictment of current approaches to teaching.

'Education is almost exclusively concerned with man's verbalizing and conceptualizing proclivities. It develops them to a precocious and unbalanced degree and the veil of words and concepts eclipses the vividness of perception known to the innocent eye of childhood.... When it is almost exclusively intellectual, education neglects knowledge that is not propositional; meaning that is not conceptualized; thinking that is not discursive; symbols that do not function like the symbols of mathematics or science; coherence — as in a work of art — that is not the coherence of logical relations. It cannot comprehend reason of the heart as well as of the head .... One can scarcely blame education for being *verbal,* for helping children to acquire a language in which they can explore and come to terms with their environment.... But transcendental experience demands another voice.... It craves a language to express the inexpressible, a poetic, religious, extravagant language which is most effective when it is non-prosaic, non-propositional and logically odd' (Paffard, 1973, pages 226-8).

The contrasts between the narrow and the broad views of education have been based, not on putting 'progressive' ideas against the traditional, but by examining different forms of innovation. Programmed learning or computer assisted learning are both recent developments, but they represent innovations based on one particular philosophy of education. The ideas of Rogers and Pafford are a reaction against a narrowly vocational interpretation of the purposes of education. In these contrasting innovations, parallels with learning styles (serialist and holist) and with forms of consciousness (left- and right-sided thinking) can be seen. But from our previous discussion we should by now be on our guard against expecting to find general panaceas among any of these alternatives. Each opposed view of education is, in part, an expression of the theorist's own preferred way of thinking. He may be describing little more than which type of learning he himself would find most beneficial. And if we enthusiastically endorse one or other extreme method of teaching, the same might be said of us. Somehow the approach to teaching must take account of the variety of styles of learning among the learners, not just the preference of the teacher.

Empirical evidence on teaching styles

Most of the theorists who berate the excessive formality, control, and passivity of traditional teaching methods speak impressionistically from their own experience. They believe passionately that the narrow view of education is damaging to pupils, and that teaching with the broader ideas they espouse would transform the effectiveness of education. If our ideas on cognitive style do have the wide applicability suggested in the previous chapter, the failure of these idealists to support their arguments with 'hard' evidence is understandable. They are likely to have as little confidence in traditional research methodology as they have in formal methods of teaching. *Their* evidence is drawn from observation and experience, built up through anecdotes and illustrations, to demonstrate by repeated instance the efficacy of the approach they endorse. For some teachers this form of argument carries the strengths of realism and immediacy. For others, the lack of empirical data and quantitative analyses makes acceptance of the ideas difficult.

If 'hard' evidence is to be obtained about the relative strengths of different methods of teaching, the first step must be to define the contrasting approaches in an objective way. Two interesting attempts at describing teaching styles were reported independently by Bennett (1976) in Britain, and by Solomon and Kendall (1979) in the United States. Both studies were concerned with the primary or elementary schooling of 10–11-year-olds, but Bennett used a questionaire method to obtain information from the teachers about how they organized their classes, while Solomon and Kendall relied on direct observation of the classrooms. Both studies made use of cluster analyses to define what seemed to be the most distinctive patterns of classroom organization. Bennett described 12 types but later selected 7 of these as being the most clearly defined. Solomon and Kendall found that different methods of cluster analysis produced rather different results, but they were eventually

Table 11.1. Summary of the classroom types described by Solomon and Kendall, and by Bennett

Solomon and Kendall	Bennett
1 Permissive and uncontrolled with much pupil autonomy	1 Integration of subject matter, pupil choice of work and where to sit, little control of movement around classroom, little emphasis on testing
5 Warm and friendly strongly orientated toward pupil expressiveness and creativity (rather than traditional academic outcomes) and moderate with respect to teacher control and pupil autonomy	2 Integration of subject matter, teacher control low, but less freedom for pupils to choose what work to do; choice of seating and some freedom; little emphasis on testing
6 Academically orientated, with individualized teacher-pupil interaction	3 Class teaching and group work both used, but integrated subjects preferred
2 Pupil self-direction within a controlled, disciplined and somewhat impersonal setting	4 Separate subjects taught, but a good deal of freedom left to the pupils
	7 Separate subjects with an emphasis on class teaching and individual work. Little movement allowed, but also little formal assessment
3 Hostile, arbitrary and regimented, but also somewhat uncontrolled and disorganized	11 Separate subjects, class teaching, individual work, little freedom of choice or movement allowed, corporal punishment used
4 Controlled, disciplined, academically orientated and supportive	12 Extreme emphasis on formal methods and control, but with emphasis on assessment rather than punishment

able to settle on six consistent groupings. Table 11.1 summarizes the classroom types identified in these two studies, ordered from the most informal to the most formal teaching methods. The types are not identical, as different indices were used to describe the classrooms; but there are distinct similarities.

Both sets of descriptions reinforce the idea that rather few classrooms can be identified with the caricatures used to denigrate either formal or informal methods. The dimension running from teacher control to pupil-freedom certainly runs through both analyses, but in real classrooms there are few teachers who use *all* the methods associated with formal teaching, or *all* the ways in which pupil freedom and initiative can be fostered. As Solomon and Kendall concluded

'This corresponds with our initial expectation that the concepts "open" and "traditional" would prove too global, and that actual classrooms could more usefully be described in terms of observed combinations of attributes than with such (labels)':

Although Bennett reached a similar conclusion, the small sample of classrooms with which he was working forced him to examine pupil performance in relation to only three categories — formal, mixed, and informal. His results, outlined in Chapter 2 (pages 25-29), showed an apparently marked improvement in basic skills among pupils taught by formal methods, with little evidence that creativity was being fostered more effectively in the informal classes. Children in informal classes did show improving levels of motivation, but also increased anxiety.

In the American research very similar general findings can be seen with the highest levels of achievement found in the two types of class identified as controlled and disciplined, and by far the lowest level of performance in the classes which were permissive and uncontrolled. The two most controlled settings also produced high ratings on pupil creativity, but the more supportive of these classrooms also showed high levels of pupil self-esteem and quality in writing. The highest levels of creativity and curiosity were found in Type 5 classes in which there was a strong orientation towards these activities backed by moderate teacher control and pupil autonomy.

One weakness at this stage in the empirical analysis of the effects of contrasting teaching styles is that it is impossible to say with certainty that differences in teaching *caused* different levels of pupil performance. There is still the possibility, for example, that the intellectually weakest pupils were taught in the most permissive way. The next step must be to look at the effects of these contrasting environments on individual pupils.

Styles of teaching and pupil aptitudes

A new area of research (aptitude-treatment-interaction) was initiated when Cronbach (1957) criticized the separation between psychologists who studied learning and those who measured abilities. He argued that we should expect differential effects of contrasting educational 'treatments' on pupils with differing aptitudes. (Here 'aptitude' is used to describe any individual trait, whether it be an intellectual skill or a personality characteristic). Although this idea makes intuitive sense, it has proved difficult to find aptitudes on which there are consistent differential effects (Biggs, 1976; Snow, 1976; Gustafsson, 1976). More often than not the aptitudes most closely related to school learning — such as verbal reasoning — do not produce differential patterns because, whatever the 'treatment', the pupils with the highest reasoning scores also show higher levels of performance.

There is, however, some evidence to suggest that personality differences can be associated with aptitude-treatment interactions. Leith (1974) has demonstrated interesting interactions between personality, classroom organisation and teaching methods. In one study, for example, when children were asked to work in pairs, the best results came from children of the same level of extraversion, but contrasting levels of anxiety. In another study, extraverted students obtained better marks with relatively free discovery learning, while introverts were more successful with structured materials. A similar study among children in primary schools showed no interaction with extraversion, but differences in anxiety were important (Trow and Leith, 1975). Anxious pupils learned more effectively from a teacher-centred supportive strategy, while the emotionally stable children were more successful with a learner-centred exploratory approach. The pattern of results shown in such studies is shown in Figure 11.1. The 'cross-over' effect could be used to allocate pupils

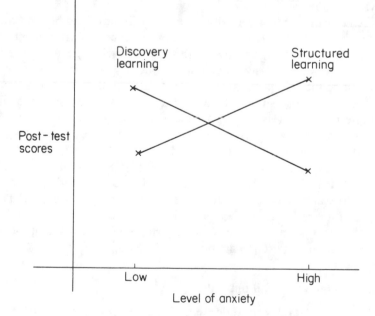

Figure 11.1 Effect of anxiety on pupil performance with contrasting teaching strategies

to treatment, although such 'streaming by personality' creates other problems and is rarely advocated. The conclusion reached by Trown and Leith was that

> 'some, but by no means all, children remember more when they are "set free" to learn. A teacher could plan to take advantage of the observed interaction by setting up exploratory situations in the classroom, but at the same time taking care to provide anxious pupils with the kind of support associated with more traditional teaching methods' (pages 138-9).

The studies reported by Leith and Trown have the advantages of experimental control and they were also carried out in classrooms, but the learning material was specially constructed and related to just one area of the curriculum. The studies by Bennett and by Solomon and Kendall categorized teaching strategies in a more general way, and related these to types of children. Besides carrying out cluster analyses to classify classrooms, they also grouped together pupils who showed similar profiles of scores. Bennett (1976) was unable to demonstrate any clear interaction between personality and teaching style in relation to pupil progress: for all but one of the personality types the formal methods were associated with the greater improvement in basic skills. There were, however, variations in the extent of the differential progress: the most motivated and least anxious pupils benefited most from the formal settings. The only exception to the pattern has already been mentioned: the least able boys improved more in the informal classrooms.

In the American study, with six contrasting classroom environments retained in the analysis, some interesting type-treatment interactions were reported for three contrasting personality types. These results are worth quoting at length

> 'More generally, the class types which appeared to be the most beneficial for the children with low initial levels of cognitive skill and motivation were those characterized by great permissiveness and variety of activities ..., and by the combination of warmth and a strong emphasis on student expressiveness ... It may be suggested that these classroom environments, which encourage the children's development of self-direction and self-expression, may have helped children to develop (or discover) motivation for task performance which may initially have been lacking. (Pupils who were)... well-motivated, with initially high levels of cognitive skill, on the other hand, generally did best in class clusters 2 and 4, both characterized by high levels of control and orderliness and relatively high levels of student initiation of activities.... The importance of controlled and orderly classes to the performance of the most proficient and motivated children was not anticipated. But, to build on the explanation presented ... (previously), it would seem that these children, being well motivated to begin with, would not require external stimulation and varied opportunities to motivate them. A controlled and orderly task orientation ... may be what they require to help them further develop from an already high level of proficiency. Furthermore, a preference for structured classrooms was one of the components making up this cluster; these children are therefore performing well in the types of class which they prefer...

The pattern of results obtained for the autonomy-preferring, expressive, non-compliant children was somewhat more varied. Perhaps the most interesting (tendency is for)... children's activity and curiosity to be maximized in the most permissive classrooms..., but creativity to be maximized... by high levels of control and orderliness. It is possible that permissive classrooms can increase the activity level and expressed curiosity of children oriented toward autonomy because the environment allows (and perhaps welcomes) what the children are inclined to do. But the development of a specific cognitive skill (such as creativity) may require that the children's expressive and autonomous inclinations be tempered somewhat. A relatively structured setting, with an orderly approach to tasks, may provide these children with a framework which they lack and may thereby help them to develop their expressive motives in productive directions' (Solomon and Kendall, 1979, pages 169-170).

Although the personality types identified in these cluster analyses are not dissimilar to several of those which were found with students (see Chapter 5, pages 96-99), in this study no account was taken of the most fundamental personality characteristics — extraversion and anxiety. In the British study these dimensions were included, but the failure to show interactions might, in part, be due to the technique of analysis. Cluster analysis is essentially atheoretical, creating combinations of characteristics which do not allow prior hypotheses to be tested. In a reanalysis of these data, Wade (1979) set out to test specific hypotheses in relation to two personality dimensions — motivation and anxiety. She was particularly interested in the performance and classroom behaviour of anxious children, who might be found to cope with their anxiety in contrasting ways — the 'approachers' who reduce anxiety by increased work activity, and the 'avoiders' whose defence mechanism might lead them to withdraw from classroom activities. She defined these groups in terms of different levels of motivation, the highly motivated being 'approachers' (HM HA) and those with low levels of motivation being seen as the 'avoiders' (LM HA). From an analysis of the previous literature, Wade predicted the academic superiority of the 'approachers'. The analyses reported by Wade examined attainment scores at the end of the school year in relation to teaching style, initial levels of attainment and sex, as well as the two personality dimensions. To simplify the pattern, Table 11.2 shows mean attainment scores for the four personality types in a zonal analysis which does not take account of sex differences.

The strongest effect, as Bennett argued, is clearly teaching style, with children taught by formal methods having higher scores in every personality type and at each ability level. There is, however, some indication of interactions between teaching style and personality type in this more controlled analysis. In formal classrooms, children with high motivation do well irrespective of their levels of anxiety. In informal classrooms, the less anxious of these motivated children do better, irrespective of their ability level. Among the less motivated children, those with the least anxiety do consistently better. In informal schools, among the brighter children, those with low scores in both motivation and anxiety reach the highest levels of attainment, perhaps

Table 11.2. Attainment scores of different personality types by attainment level and teaching style (from Wade, 1979)

	Formal		Informal	
	HM HA (approachers)	LM HA (avoiders)	HM HA (approachers)	LM HA (avoiders)
High	117.4 (74)	113.2 (37)	112.1 (43)	112.8 (19)
initial	HM LA	LM LA	HM LA	LM LA
attainment	117.6 (55)	116.6 (52)	114.4 (43)	116.0 (39)
	HM HA	LM HA	HM HA	LM HA
Low	100.3 (25)	93.2 (30)	95.5 (59)	92.3 (50)
initial	HM LA	LM LA	HM LA	LM LA
attainment	99.1 (20)	96.3 (33)	97.2 (31)	94.1 (48)

NOTE: Number of pupils in each sub-group shown in brackets.

because the competitiveness of the motivated children is not catered for in these classes.

Wade (1979, page 261) draws attention to the fact that 'approachers' (HM HA) attain more under formal methods, but also points out that there are fewer 'avoiders' (LM HA) with informal methods. She argues that the help given within an informal teaching style to anxious children to develop a more positive approach to learning could be important. However, the attainment level of the 'approachers' at both levels of ability also showed the greatest discrepancy between formal and informal methods. Thus, even if informal methods have helped children to develop a more effective way of coping with anxiety, this has not been converted into improved levels of attainment, at least in terms of the basic skills tested in this study.

Taking together the results of the various studies, there is agreement that a structured, formal but supportive, approach is likely to be most suitable for anxious children, particularly those whose anxiety is directed towards academic success. Informal methods should help the least able children and those who prefer autonomy, but an orderly approach is still required to foster creativity and a structured curriculum may be necessary to ensure greater progress in the basic skills.

Teaching styles and teacher personality

The results from the aptitude-treatment or type-treatment studies are to be expected, although the effects of personality and motivation on attainment are likely to be less strong than those of either previous attainment (including ability level) or teaching style. However there has been little research into the effects of matching or mismatching teaching with learning style — a variable which has more direct relevance to attainment than any measure of personality. The work that has been done by Pask (1976b) suggests that extreme teaching styles could be markedly disadvantageous to pupils with a mismatched learning style.

One aspect on which empirical research has so far, provided little additional information is the link between teaching style and the personality of the teacher. Are the teaching methods adopted by the teacher a reflection of his own preferences in learning? There is some evidence that teaching style is one facet of a general view about the purposes of education (Bennett, 1976; Ashton *et al.,* 1975). Formal teachers see their role in terms of the narrow view of education, in which examination results and vocational training are dominant. Informal teachers stress the pupils' enjoyment of school and opportunities for self-expression. This evidence shows consistency between educational philosophy and teaching method, but no more. Leith (1974) comments on other characteristics of formal and informal teachers

> 'Among (those who adopted) the more formal teaching methods ... teachers ... had been remarked to be conscientious, attentive to detail, impersonal and well organized, while ... (informal teachers) ... were characterized by readiness to switch attention and divert to something of immediate interest, concern for global effects rather than precise detail and dislike of tight organization schedules. The former valued orderliness, obedience to rules, attentiveness, timetable regularity, desks arranged in rows and so on, while the latter preferred spontaneity of responding, enthusiasm, individuality of contribution, no timetable limitations and informal seating' (page 16).

Although Leith did not relate these descriptions to cognitive style as such, the parallels are strong. He also drew attention to the contrast between the informal teachers' preference for providing discovery learning and the formal teachers' structured approach. The difference, from the pupils' point of view, could be seen as 'plunging into the deep end' compared with 'stepping into the shallow end of a pool' — a metaphor which could also describe holist and serialist learning strategies.

In the previous chapter the work of Witkin (1977) indicated that field-dependent teachers tended to adopt informal, discussion methods, and that field-independent teachers were more likely to prefer more structured methods of teaching. Although more direct and objective evidence is needed to mount a convincing argument, a provisional conclusion can still be reached. It is probable that a teacher's decision to adopt an extreme teaching style will be a reflection of his own preferred learning style. It is also likely that any such extreme approach to teaching, whether highly structured or fully permissive, will make learning difficult for one section of the class: it makes inevitable severe mismatches between presentation and learning style. Earlier it was argued that an important aim in education should be to help students to adopt integrated, flexible, and versatile styles of learning. Now it must be emphasized that teachers should similarly be encouraged to be equally versatile in using a variety of methods of presentation, appropriate to the subject matter being introduced. What applies to the student who is responsible only for his own learning, applies even more strongly to the teacher who is guiding the learning of many people.

Subject area differences and curricular choice

In discussing the use of analogies in education (Chapter 10, pages 214-215), it was argued that there were marked differences between disciplines in the types of analogy which were used. The sciences tended to use mathematical or mechanical analogies, whereas the humanities depended on analogies drawn from personal experience. Science also depends more on previous knowledge in building up new ideas. It emphasizes fact and detail in relation to specific experiments and creates increasingly narrow specialisms to be studied. There is thus a danger that science students may be exposed to an excessively serialist style of teaching. Certainly the most recent analyses at Lancaster of the way students perceive university departments shows that science and engineering departments are seen as more formal in their approaches to teaching than departments of social sciences, humanities, or languages (Ramsden, 1979). Earlier analyses at Lancaster (Entwistle and Wilson, 1977) of the personality characteristics of science and arts students, indicated substantial differences in the types of people who will be attracted to these fields of study (see Figure 5.1, page 97). Witkin (1979), as we saw in Chapter 10, found that field-dependent students found science courses uncongenial, and Leith (1974) has argued that both students and teachers show the personality characteristics associated with their academic discipline. Thus, as soon as pupils begin to specialize, they may move towards subjects and teachers that suit their own personality and patterns of abilities.

Hudson (1968) has shown that pupils perceive differences between subjects almost as soon as they enter secondary school. From a series of small-scale studies of children aged between eleven and seventeen, he identified a 'mythology' of arts and science. Even the youngest children believed that scientists tend to be more hard-working, puritanical, unsociable and unimaginative than arts specialists, and to be happier dealing with things than with people. Hudson, following Erikson's ideas on adolescence, sees subject choice as an important part of the adolescent's attempt to fashion an acceptable identity.

'I now envisage the choice between arts and sciences as one of the first major steps that the able adolescent takes towards his adult identity. This is often the individual's first opportunity to select and reject from among the ways of life his culture offers; his first attempt to fit a chosen style of thinking into some semblance of harmony with his more private needs' (pages 86-87).

The interplay between subject choice, personality and cognitive style becomes even closer here, because, as we have seen, Hudson (1966) had already linked science choice with convergent thinking and emotional inhibitions. Certainly the idea of the unemotional scientist has many echoes in the earlier literature. For example, Roe (1953a, b) from interviews with eminent scientists argued that a cold relationship with their parents had led to a choice of subject specialisms which would *not* involve an 'orientation towards persons'. Studies using Cattell's personality inventories have repeatedly reinforced the stereotype identified among Hudson's school children (Entwistle and Duckworth, 1977). In a recent study at Oxford (Hutchings *et al.,* 1975) found that personality differences between pupils opting for contrasting school subjects could be identified by age 13 and that by the sixth form these differences were marked.

> 'The scientists differ most significantly in being more intelligent, more dominant, more toughminded, more self-sufficient, and more controlled. They are also markedly more undemonstrative rather than excitable, and more individualist and reflective' (section 2.2.2).

Although the individual scales distinguishing arts and science students are not consistent, the overall impression is remarkably constant. Saville and

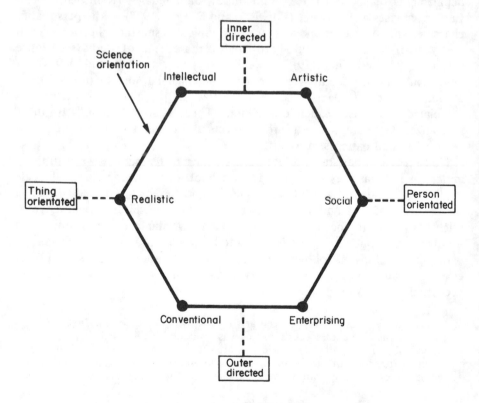

Figure 11.2 Vocational interests, values and orientations
(from Entwistle and Duckworth, 1977)

Blinkhorn (1976) pick out tough- (science) versus tendermindedness (arts) as the largest difference. Arts students also tended to be more outgoing, suspicious, imaginative, and radical, while the scientists were more socially precise and controlled. In both of these large-scale studies it is interesting to note that there are no interdisciplinary variations in level of anxiety, once sex differences are accounted for. The arts students are more emotional, but *not* more anxious.

The personality differences provide a fuller description of the arts students' 'orientation towards people'. More recently Roe has added a second dimension to help to explain occupational choice (Roe and Klos, 1972). She contrasts inner-directed, theoretical values with outer-directed, economic values and shows how certain occupations facilitate the expression of differing value systems. In fact not only have personalities been described in terms of their predominant interests (Spranger, 1928), but occupations have also been described in terms of the personalities they attract, (Holland, 1966; 1973). The similarity between the two approaches adopted by Roe and Holland can be seen in Figure 11.2. Holland uses test scores to help pupils select occupations which match their personality. But other theorists see this as too mechanical an approach. Super (1969), for example, argues that more caution is necessary: the pupil's interests develop slowly in tandem with his personality.

'Actions are determined by a person's perception of himself and of the situation in which he finds himself, by the manner in which he construes his world. In expressing a vocational preference, a person puts into occupational terminology his ideas of the kind of person he is' (Super, 1969, page 7).

Hudson (1968) links the development of subject choice both to the sense of identity, as we have seen, and also to the individual's perception of the arts/science dichotomy.

'My interest lies in the individual's capacity for choice — his freedom to select one aspect of a myth rather than another in establishing his personal identity, and in the relation of these choices to the abilities and temperamental qualities he shows.... In attempting to analyse an individual's way of life, one cannot think solely, or even primarily in terms of examinations and jobs, salaries and pension schemes; rather of the conceptual framework within which his idea of himself, his past and his future are conceived' (pages 85, 87).

Summary

The argument in this chapter has moved from the preferred learning styles shown by students to what seem to be similar differences in educational philosophies and styles of teaching. It has also been suggested, although without convincing empirical evidence, that teachers will often adopt methods of teaching which reflect their own preferences in learning. Different subject areas are also likely to differ in the relative incidence of highly structured teaching methods, partly because of the nature of the subject and partly because of the cognitive styles of the teachers who are attracted to that subject.

Even among recent innovations in teaching methods, the contrast between what may be seen as serialist and holist approaches can be found. The most narrowly focussed, step-by-step methods will be found linked to the principles of stimulus-response psychology. Programmed learning, in particular, emphasizes the importance of small steps and tightly logical sequence. The perspective adopted in mastery learning is broader, but still emphasizes control by the teacher in arranging the most appropriate sequences and materials for learning. Contrary views about teaching come from Bruner with his emphasis on discovery learning, and Rogers who endorses the broad humanistic view of education. Progressive methods have been associated with such idealistic views which ask that the pupil be 'set free to learn', although theorists give different reasons for demanding this freedom.

Evidence for the relative effectiveness of different teaching methods has only recently been presented. In interpreting their evidence, it is important to recognize that the relative importance of different outcomes will depend on the view of education espoused. If basic skills are given pride of place, an emphasis on teacher control and curriculum structure may be most important. If, however, pupil autonomy and independent learning is the main goal, the classroom environment would have to be more 'open'. But it is becoming clear that contrasting teaching styles affect pupils differentially. Thus informal methods which emphasize variety of activities and permissiveness may be valuable for the least able or the most autonomous children, but brighter, highly motivated chldren appreciate orderliness in the class and structure in the curriculum.

Besides affecting attainment, characteristically different approaches to structuring the curriculum and presenting information may also affect curricular choice. The more logical, unemotional, sequential nature of science is likely to attract the field-independent student who prefers a serialist learning strategy. The humanities are less impersonal and allow more independence in developing ideas, thus suiting field-dependent holist students.

The argument developed in this chapter leads to the conclusion that *versatility* in teaching is essential. Following the argument mounted in the previous chapter, it is likely that teachers will have to alternate between structure and freedom, providing an overall structure but allowing enough individual choice for the more autonomous pupils. This argument for versatility will be developed more fully in the final chapter. The message which has come through repeatedly is that no extreme style of teaching can be expected to be suitable for the majority of pupils.

CHAPTER 12

Applying Theory to Practice:
Primary, Secondary, and Tertiary

The main purpose of this book has been to build up an overview of educational psychology within frameworks derived from the most recent research both on how students learn and on information processing. It was argued that educational psychology has little *direct* influence on teaching methods. Its effect comes more from the way teachers individually interpret these ideas. Thus this discussion about practical applications should be taken as no more than a series of illustrations of implications that the author sees in the ideas presented earlier.

In this chapter we return to the model of learning and teaching outlined in Chapter 5 and reconsider it in the light of the psychological evidence presented subsequently. It will then be possible to provide illustrations of possible implications of the model for education at different age-levels.

Evaluating the evidence presented

Before reviewing the evidence from which the model of learning and teaching has been derived, some caveats should be noted. These take us back to the introductory section of the book, and to its main theme about styles of learning and thinking.

What type of evidence should be given the greatest weight? Should we rely entirely on empirical evidence from quantitative experiments and surveys? Or should we also take account of observations and speculative ideas? There are dangers in putting too much trust in either way of discussing education. The speculative mode of thinking can convince only through its plausibility, by appeals to our own experience and intuition. But it can look at education as a whole, and in its real setting. The quantitative analyses of empirical data provide the building blocks from which an argument can be substantiated more fully. The careful and systematic substantiation of theory is the hall-mark of 'disciplined enquiry'. Yet the inadequacies of empirical research methods in the social sciences, and the inability of such research to tackle some of the major issues which affect educators, means that a total reliance on so-called scientific methods may produce a restricted and unrealistic description of learning in schools or colleges.

The battle between empiricists and humanists was joined in the first chapter, through the opposing ideas of Kerlinger and Bantock. Similar divergencies of view have been found throughout the outline of educational psychology. Initially we had to assert the value of both approaches to education. Since then reasons why different theorists see learning or teaching in such contrasting ways have become clear. The evidence on the polarity in styles of thinking would have led us to predict these contrasts. Remember Jung's description of the ways extraverts and introverts construct their interpretations of the world.

'For as in the former case the purely empirical heaping together of facts paralyses thought and smothers their meaning, so in the latter case introverted thinking shows a dangerous tendency to coerce facts into the shape of its image, or by ignoring them altogether, to unfold its phantasy image in freedom' (Jung, 1938, pages 481-2).

As we have seen, Pask argued that understanding depends on two processes of thinking which help us first to build up a plan of the overall topic (comprehension learning or description building) and then to see how the argument is built up from the detailed arguments and facts (operation learning or procedure building). Many people prefer to use one or other of these ways of thinking more strongly than the other, and in so doing may not reach a full understanding. Failure to see important links between areas of knowledge or the way details fit into the overall picture has been described as 'improvidence'. The over-readiness to see connections between ideas or to generalize from insufficient evidence has been termed 'globetrotting'. These pathologies have been observed among students as they learn; they can also be seen among the theorists describing human behaviour.

The ability to use both processes of thinking in building up understanding has been given the name 'versatility'. Thus in trying to use evidence to substantiate the model of learning outlined earlier, we shall have to be careful to pay due attention to both 'hard' evidence and the more speculative attempts to provide an overall framework which simplifies and systematises the mass of empirical findings. The two processes cannot be used simultaneously; there needs to be an alternation of the 'curious and the critical', the overview and the detailed evidence, in the way Heath suggested.

It seems essential to start with a simple model or integrative framework, if only to proceed 'more methodically in our subject'. Yet, as Chesterton said, 'He who simplifies, simply lies'. Similarly Lewis Carroll pointed out a paradox in the use of maps. We expect a map to simplify, to provide an overall impression of the countryside. But we may also need to locate a particular landmark with great precision. The more detailed and large-scale the map becomes, the more accurate the information it provides. And yet at the same time a large-scale map fails to give an adequate overall impression. The solution, of course, is to use maps with different scales for different purposes. And in this book broad ideas and detailed evidence have been presented at different times to try to fulfil similarly different functions.

In reading the various chapters some may have seemed excessively detailed. others too superficial or speculative. The book as a whole could also be viewed in each way, but how it *is* judged will, of course, depend on the reader's own preferences, his own style of learning. The stand taken here is that our models of learning are unlikely ever to be capable of full substantiation. Our ability to understand thinking depends on our own idiosyncratic ways of thinking. This may be the psychologist's ultimate 'uncertainty principle'. If we have this limitation, then exclusive trust in empirical data is pointless. We need to be guided, but not restricted, by 'objective' evidence. As Polanyi (1968) has put it, somewhat grandly

'The discovery of objective truth in science consists in the apprehension of a rationality which commands our respect and arouses our contemplative admiration;... such a discovery, while using the experience of our senses as clues, transcends this experience by embracing the vision of a reality beyond the impression of our senses, a vision which speaks for itself in guiding us to an ever deeper understanding of reality' (pages 5-6).

A model of learning and teaching

By now it will be clear that only limited claims are being made for the three models presented earlier, after Chapter 5. There is no question of expecting 'contemplative admiration'! The models represent just three ways of organising the evidence on student learning. The summary framework (Figure B.2) was a map with a larger scale: it linked fairly closely with the detail of research evidence on approaches, process and outcomes of learning. The final model (Figure B.3 and 12.1) looked more broadly at the context of teaching and learning, and was weaker on substantiating evidence. These models did, however, provide a way of making sense of the psychological ideas introduced later. They acted as 'advance organisers' to anticipate the way in which certain concepts from psychology could have relevance to education.

The psychological evidence helped to substantiate the two main strands of the earlier models — approaches and styles. The initial small-scale experiments conducted by Marton led to the distinction between deep and surface approaches to learning. Perhaps the crucial aspect of this research was its recognition that students tackled the task of reading an academic article with different *intentions*. Some students never intended or expected to reach a deep level of understanding. The surveys conducted by Biggs and by the research group at Lancaster provide substantial confirmation that the idea of contrasting approaches to studying has important explanatory value. The orientations towards looking for meaning and towards reproducing academic material are, to some extent, consistent approaches used by students, as is the third orientation — towards achieving high grades.

The second strand in the model is the identification by Pask of marked individual differences in learning shown in holist and serialist strategies. In the Lancaster surveys hints of this distinction have come through repeatedly, but it has proved difficult to separate the deep passive approach from comprehension learning. Again, students predominantly relying on operation learning are prone also to use the techniques of memorization equated with surface processing. Thus, although the concepts of approach and style are separable in principle, there is an empirical relationship between them.

The psychological literature provided parallel descriptions of contrasting intentions (Ausubel's rote and meaningful learning sets) and of distinct learning processes, which could be described either in information-processing terms or by using findings from tests of rote-learning and reasoning. The distinctions between reasoning and imaginative thinking, together with Level III thinking as the appropriate combination of the other two, parallel Pask's three categories — operation learning, comprehension learning, and versatility. The literature on cognitive styles strongly indicated the existence of polar opposites in cognitive processes, and even hinted at a neurological basis for such dichotomies.

The model of learning and teaching (Figure 12.1) draws attention to other characteristics of the student associated with distinct approaches to learning. Biggs has argued that each of the three study orientations has an associated predominant form of motivation. A deep approach is linked with intrinsic motivation, interest in the subject in itself. A surface approach may carry with it either extrinsic motivation (concern with qualifications and course requirements) or fear of failure. Finally the orientation towards achieving has close conceptual and empirical connections with 'hope for success' or 'need for achievement'. The psychological literature on motivation provided further backing for these links, but also warned against seeing causality in one direction only. Levels of motivation are as likely to be boosted by continuing experiences of success, as is academic performance to be explained by motivation.

Personality traits also affect learning. Although the literature on the effects of extraversion and neuroticism has not provided clear-cut relationships with academic attainment, there have been interesting findings which suggest that contrasting styles of teaching or of structuring knowledge may well have differential effects on pupils' learning. A more structured approach may be more suitable for anxious children, and also for the most able and motivated. There is also some evidence that basic personality differences may be expressed in terms of contrasting ways of thinking and preferences for different subject areas.

The evidence drawn from studies on child development partly confirm the picture of learning shown in the model, but also point out some limitations. Children, as well as adults, show different levels of thinking and contrasting styles of conceptualisation. But stages of development become confounded with stylistic preferences. Alternative ways of thinking have to be developed

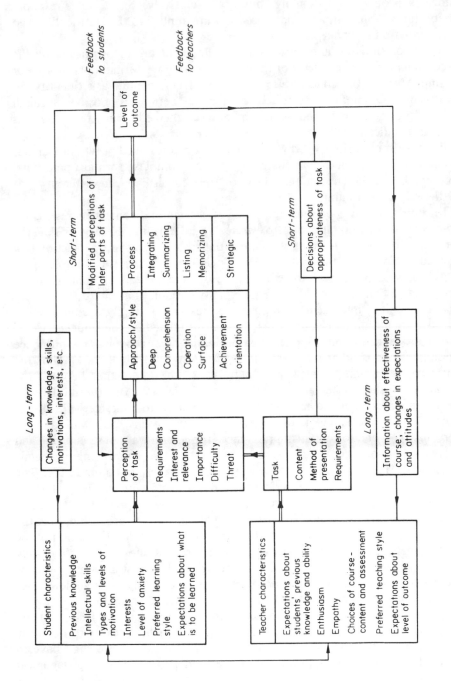

Figure 12.1 Model of factors influencing the learning process

before they can emerge as a distinctive style. Early attempts to develop concepts probably rely mainly, but not exclusively, on stimulus-response connections. Later on, analytic procedures are applied to the clarification and differentiation of concepts.

Stages of thinking and personality development are distinguished by the predominant use of one level of thinking (concrete *vs.* formal operations, for example) or by the concentration on one developmental task (identity *vs.* confusion). Development through the tension between opposites, through assimilation and accommodation, is a common theme in many theories. This idea also indicates that each stage can never exist on its own. At any stage residues of more primitive ways of thinking, or unresolved personality crises, remain. It is also clear that the ability to use complex, formal operational thinking is not shown simultaneously, or fully consistently, in different areas of the school curriculum.

Marton's emphasis on the importance of content and context represents his own way of drawing attention to *variability* in learning. He argues that the term 'approaches' to learning should be applied only to a specific reaction to a particular learning task. The term 'deep-level processor', implying a consistently deep approach to learning is considered misleading. Similarly it has been argued that styles of learning are equally variable (Laurillard, 1979), and that terms like 'intelligent', 'creative', or 'extravert' imply a stability and consistency in human behaviour which is contradicted by the evidence.

The model of teaching and learning presented here recognizes the influence of context and content on approach, by focusing on a single task. Thus the outcome of learning is explained in terms of the interaction between the intention of the learner and the demands of the task. But the model also implies a certain consistency, by drawing attention to characteristics of the learner — pre-existing knowledge, intellectual skills, motivation, and personality — and to consistent preferences for certain ways of structuring and presenting knowledge among teachers and in the contrasting academic disciplines. These consistent tendencies are, however, not immutable. The model emphasizes the way experiences from the particular task may alter the learner's characteristics or the teacher's ideas on how to present that topic in future. Although it is not explicit in the model, it is recognized that the individual differences attributed to either learner or teacher will not be consistent across all content areas or contexts. But the model deliberately contains elements of both consistency and variability, just as descriptions of intelligence have arrived at a concept of unity in diversity (a single level, but variable constituent abilities). If we are to remain sufficiently close to reality, it seems necessary to retain these, to some extent, contradictory ways of viewing learning. Again they can be seen as a way of approaching reality through the alternation of contrasting perspectives. Which is also how we shall have to proceed in considering applications of the model as a whole to pedagogical practice.

The model will not be expected to generate implications in a direct or mechanical way. Rather it will present a series of cues to provoke ideas about teaching and learning in different contexts which reflect the theoretical discussions in earlier chapters.

Theory into practice

STOP and THINK

Consider your own experiences as a teacher or student

● Select instances where you think teaching has been particularly successful. Can you explain, in terms of the model, why it was successful?

● Now select instances where teaching or learning proved difficult. Use the model to suggest how the difficulties might have been overcome.

As it has been argued that we should not expect educational research to provide direct solutions to pedagogical problems, it follows that the implications drawn from the model are not intended as general prescriptions. Rather they should be seen as illustrations of the ways in which the model might be used by the individual student, teacher or lecturer in considering his own situation, and working out his own ways of putting theory into practice.

Because teachers are generally trained to teach one of three broad age-bands of children, adolescents, or young adults, possible applications of educational psychology to primary, secondary, and tertiary education will be considered separately. The model itself is based on student learning, and so can be more readily applied to the more academic forms of learning. But the basic ideas of a deep approach, and contrasting styles can be reinterpreted in a way which is relevant to any age group. The simplest, and most insistent, message from the research literature is that there can be no single 'right' way to study or 'best' way to teach. The differences between people's abilities, cognitive preferences, and personalities are too great. However, research studies have also made it abundantly clear that the effectiveness of learning depends, in part, on the situation in which learning takes place. And the situation is the prime responsibility of the teacher. Thus the recurring question, at each age-level, will be to ask in what ways the teacher's organization and methods of teaching are likely to affect different pupils' or students' opportunities to learn.

Although readers will have a predominant interest in one age-level many of the implications can be reinterpreted at a different level. Thus each section should be followed to keep the thread of the developing argument.

Teaching children

As we have seen, class teaching can be described on a continuum between the extremes of formal and informal methods, with few teachers adopting either extreme in its entirety. Perhaps the most fundamental choice a class teacher has to make is how much freedom to allow the children. There has been a tendency recently to praise informal, open classrooms, and to criticize the more traditional direct class teaching. Such a simple choice between alternatives would not make sense within our model. Indeed it is difficult to see how such a choice ever came to be put before teachers. As Friedlander (1975) has recently argued, educationalists ought to have known better. 'Progressive' or 'open' education is no panacea.

> 'I have been in some open classrooms that seemed like the blessed ideal of what schools should be like in terms of superior, humane teaching and learning; and I have been in open classrooms that could be compared only with the back wards of an unreformed mental hospital. Likewise, I have also been in traditional classrooms that could be described in very much the same fashion, at both ends of the scale...
>
> It is a gross oversight of available knowledge in psychology to assume that looser structure in the environment of the classroom is of some benefit for all children, just because it is of great benefit for some children. It is predictable that children who have a low tolerance for ambiguity and uncertainty would find an open classroom that operates very successfully for some children, extremely threatening and anxiety-provoking. It is also predictable that personality configurations among administrators and teachers who seek out the challenge of innovation in developing the open classroom would tend to be unmindful of the valid needs for order, predictability, and specificity for persons unlike themselves.
>
> Where open classrooms are established as a school-wide policy without offering a choice, they are an invitation to disappointment. Without *individual* selection for one programme or the other, and freedom to move back and forth on the basis of experience, it can almost be forecast that there would probably be as many children who lose as there are those who gain' (pages 466-467).

The ideas discussed earlier clearly imply the use of mixed methods, but not just any mix. Informal methods may well be a way of catching interest and communicating the excitement and satisfaction that can come from learning. But what specific methods might be worth trying? The experience of one teacher is worth quoting at length.

> 'A week ago I decided to initiate a new programme in my sixth grade classroom (top juniors), based on student-centred teaching — an unstructured or non-directive approach.
>
> I began by telling the class that we were going to try an "experiment". I explained that for one day I would let them do anything they wanted to — they did not have to do anything if they did not want to.
>
> 'Many started with art projects; some drew or painted most of the day. Others read or did work in maths and other subjects. There was an air of excitement all day; many were so interested in what they were doing that they did not want to go out at recess (break) or noon!

At the end of the day I asked the class to evaluate the experiment. The comments were most interesting. Some were "confused", distressed without the teacher telling them what to do, without specific assignments to complete.

The majority of the class thought the day was "great", but some expressed concern over the noise level and the fact that a few "goofed off" all day. Most felt that they had accomplished as much work as we usually do, and they enjoyed being able to work at a task until it was completed without the pressure of a time limit. They liked doing things without being "forced" to do them and liked deciding what to do.

They begged to continue the "experiment", so it was decided to do so, for two more days. We would then re-evaluate the plan.

The next morning I implemented the idea of a 'work contract'. I gave them ditto (duplicated) sheets listing all our subjects with suggestions under each. There was a space provided for the 'plans' in each area and for checking upon completion.

Each child was to write his or her contract for the day — choosing the areas in which he would work and planning specifically what he would do. Upon completion of the exercise, drill, review, etc., he was to check and correct his own work, using the teacher's manual. The work was to be kept in a folder with the contract.

I met each child to discuss his plans... Resource materials were provided and drill materials made available to use when needed.

I found that I had much more time, so I worked, talked, and spent the time with individuals and groups. At the end of the third day I evaluated the work folder with each child. To solve the problem of grades I had each child tell me what he thought he had earned....

Some children continued to be frustrated and felt insecure without teacher's direction. Discipline also continued to be a problem with some, and I began to realize that although the children involved may need the programme more than others, I was expecting too much from them, too soon — they were not ready to assume self-direction *yet*. Perhaps a gradual weaning from the spoon-fed procedures was necessary.

I regrouped the class — creating two groups. The largest group is the non-directed group. The smallest is teacher directed.... Those who continued the 'experiment' have forged ahead.... At the end of the week they evaluate themselves in each area — in terms of work accomplished, accuracy, etc. We have learned that the number of errors is not a criterion of failure or success. Errors can and should be part of the learning process, we learn through our mistakes. We also discussed the fact that consistently perfect scores may mean that the work is not challenging enough and perhaps we should move on....

The days have fluctuated between optimism and concern, hope and fear. My emotional temperature rises and falls with each rung climbed on the ladder of our adventure.

Some days I feel confident, buoyant, sure that we are on the right track — on other days I am assailed by doubts.... I've come to realize that one must be secure in (one's) own self-concept to undertake such a programme... (and) have a clear understanding of the goals one is endeavouring to work toward....

The children developed a working discipline that respected the individual need for isolation or quiet study, yet allowed pupil interaction. There was no need for passing of notes, or 'subversive' activity, no need to pretend you were busy or interested in a task, that, in fact had no meaning to you. There was respect for meditation and contemplation as well as for overt productivity. There were opportunities to get to *know* one another — the children learned to communicate by *communicating*....

Day to day one can sense the growth in communication, in social development. One cannot measure the difference in attitude, the increased interest, the growing pride in self-improvement, but one is aware that they exist. . . .

I firmly believe that the gifted children were the ones who benefited most from this programme. They developed a keen sense of competition between one another, interest in mutual projects, and they sailed ahead, not being restricted by the slow learners. Their achievement was amazing to me.

I found that the children who had the most difficulty learning also made great progress. . . . I cannot explain what happened, but it seems to me that when their self-concept changed. When they discovered they *can*, they did! These 'slow learners' became 'fast learners'; success built upon success. . . .

(This programme) is not *the* panacea, but it is a step forward. Each day is a new adventure, there are moments of stress, concern, pleasure — they are all stepping stones to our goal of self-actualization' (Rogers, 1969, pages 12-22).

Viewed from the perspective of the model, the apparent success of this innovation is understandable. The main effort was to increase intrinsic motivation and learning that had personal meaning to the children. The enthusiastic response of many pupils would thus have been anticipated, as would the marked improvement in the quality of what had been learned. However the need some pupils show for a more ordered, teacher-controlled way of learning would also have been predicted. But this teacher was ready for this difficult challenge and responded by providing structure for those pupils who required it.

The comment that 'success built upon success' could be linked to earlier comments on the development of competency motivation and its facilitating effects on learning. Her methods also show how a move away from formal evaluation diminishes fear of failure, shifting pupils towards a more optimistic, and realistic, hope for success measured against personal, rather than absolute, standards.

The teacher who used this programme was, however, exceptional. Her comments, like those of the student-teacher at the beginning of the book, show an unusual level of awareness — an ability to question her own actions, to be self-critical without losing confidence. She soon recognized the need for detailed advance planning and for a form of structure and control — the work contracts and the close supervision of self-evaluation. She also was prepared to act on the observation that freedom was not beneficial for all children — it made some children anxious, while others took advantage of it.

Other teachers might find it difficult to maintain the pupils' high level of work activity within such an open classroom. Other pupils might have responded very differently to similar attempts to provide 'freedom to learn'. For most teachers greater control will be required, and more direct teaching of basic skills, even 'memory work'. The ethos of many informal classrooms has been one in which aesthetic productions abound, but basic skills are expected to 'emerge'. The research studies described in the previous chapter suggest strongly that in the most permissive classrooms it would be exceptional to find either good progress in the basic skills or high quality in creative work. The model shows why this should be. Effective creative production (Level III) depends on accuracy and technique, as well as on imagination — on perspiration and inspiration. Too much emphasis on creativity, without thorough preparation in basic skills and an insistence on a certain level of accuracy, may be of little value. The requirement is to alternate between providing opportunitites for self-expression and work in which precision is encouraged.

At this age-level it is also important to recognize limitations in intellectual development. Jensen has argued that some children have strong memories and weak analytic abilities. For such children, and there is no advantage in identifying them exclusively with the lowest socio-economic groups, opportunities to learn by memorization may be valuable. Successful rote-learning may have a doubly beneficial effect — success breeds success, through the development of self-confidence and competence motivation. It is also clear that for some parts of the curriculum, a certain amount of rote learning is necessary. Strong associations between number bonds, between words, or between sounds and symbols, need to be built up, through repetition in one form or another. Reading and spelling, for example, involve learning some general rules, but also the recognition of some apparently arbitrary word-forms. Repetition will be essential to build up strong associations, and probably a mixture of mechanical overlearning and seeing words in the context of meaning will be the most effective.

Two of the main approaches to teaching reading, 'look and say' and 'phonics', pick out the associative and analytic components of the skill. From time to time one or other approach has been recommended as the 'best' one. The Plowden Report (1967), however, pointed out that

'The most successful infant teachers have refused to follow the wind of fashion and to commit themselves to any one method... Children... are encouraged to try all the methods available...' (para. 584).

But is there no rationale which might suggest more precisely which combination of methods might be tried? Jensen's argument was that all children could benefit from rote learning, while only the more intelligent would initially use analytic thinking effectively. There does seem to be a strong theoretical argument for capitalizing on the strengths of rote learning in the early stages of learning to read. This suggestion in no way implies a 'second class' education for some children. The aims are the same: it is only the methods which are being varied to take account of existing intellectual differences. Once a child has begun to read even a few words, confidence is bred and competence motivation is aroused, thus encouraging the child to tackle the more difficult analytic skills in reading and synthetic skills in spelling. The deliberate use of both rote learning and analytic skills in teaching reading and spelling represents one of the 'tensions between opposites' referred to in earlier chapters. Using both appropriately to capitalize on their different strengths is preferable to an easy acceptance of one method as 'best'.

Conceptual development is clearly another aspect with which primary teachers should be familiar. The process of helping children to acquire a wide variety of basic concepts (anchoring ideas) across the curriculum will pay handsome dividends later on. As we have seen, the search processes of semantic LTM depend on a wide variety of firmly established and clearly differentiated concepts being available. It is possible to produce game-like situations which encourage pupils to examine similarities and differences between various objects (like Wallach and Kogan's test of conceptual style, see page 204). In this way it should be possible to encourage a more analytic and precise use of words and ideas. The use of 'sets' in teaching number work could well be extended to help children develop their abilities to classify objects and differentiate between concepts.

Differing levels of intellectual development have been described by Piaget, and Bruner has argued that teachers should take account of the intellectual level of the children they are teaching. It is self-evident that abstract or formal explanations could not be understood by children who are still using predominantly concrete operations. The use of concrete examples and illustrations, linked wherever possible to the children's own experience or designed to build up that experience, is essential in primary education. It is, however, important not to insist that bright children use repetitive concrete approaches, when they have already grasped the abstract principles and are ready to move on. It is also important to recognize that quite complex logical reasoning will be used on some occasions by certain pupils. Questionning remains an essential part of teaching. Children will respond to challenges and enjoy opportunities to show off and utilize knowledge they have acquired. But questions should not be limited to knowledge. Stimulating teaching and challenging ideas will help children to test out early attempts at various aspects of formal operational thought. For example, encouraging pupils to ask 'why' questions about the natural environment, and showing how simple experiments can be used to test alternative explanations, are almost certainly effective ways of stimulating analytic thinking. The use of 'absurdities' as games or in work-cards would involve logical thinking (see, for example, de Bono's (1978) ideas on teaching thinking). Searching, higher order questionning by the teacher is surely an essential stimulus for the early stages of fostering a deep approach to learning.

There is already much emphasis on the development of imaginative thinking and expression in many primary schools. The use of stimulus material, television, or out-of-school experiences to foster 'creative writing' or painting is clearly of great benefit. But again the use of games might also be considered. Wallach and Kogan (1965) suggested that the tests they used to measure divergent thinking (see page 154) could also be used to stimulate the broader search strategies which are found in imaginative thinking.

'Such tasks should from the start be perceived by the children as games which, not unlike music and art activities, are outside the academic evaluation pay-off matrix.... . The proposal, then, is to force a wedge open within the school curriculum for conducting enterprises that, although cognitive, are nevertheless free from connection with the stress of academic evaluation' (Page 324).

There seems to be great potentiality in the use of games to develop not just imaginative thinking, but also conceptual development and powers of reasoning. It is important that *processes* of learning beyond the basic skills be given due stress in early education.

Different styles of learning may be found in some children quite early, but the balance is likely to be shifting for many others. Nevertheless it may be helpful to think carefully about the way pupils characteristically behave, to identify, for example, impulsive or shy children and consider what specific help they should be given. The general principle of development as the tension between opposites, or the balancing of competing tendencies, would be one way of seeing appropriate courses of action. For example, in teaching reading it may be necessary to help children to overcome either excessive impulsivity or caution. Intelligent guessing from context, and from parts of the word to the whole, is valuable, but thoughtful analysis is also important. Impulsive children may have to be helped to be less ready to guess without analysis, while reflective children may benefit from encouragement to take the chance of being wrong.

Reading may also prove unexpectedly stressful for some anxious introverts. A study which showed the low reading ages of such children has already been described (see page 192), but the reasons were not explored. One possible explanation might be found in the daily routine of some classrooms, when children are asked to read out loud to the teacher, sometimes by the teacher's desk. This may be an ordeal for some children, which they will avoid whenever possible. Encouraging such children to be heard by parents or elder siblings at home may help to overcome such emotional difficulties.

Most class teachers nowadays have to face the challenge of teaching mixed ability classes. One way some teachers cope with this difficulty is to concentrate their efforts on helping the slower children, on the assumption that bright children look after themselves. Such an assumption is true up to a point: bright children are unlikely to fall behind. But that is not enough. If we believe in equality of opportunity, then each child deserves the help and active encouragement of the teacher to develop her full potential — not just to achieve an arbitrary 'acceptable' standard. The long-term consequences for any country of allowing the brightest children to come to the conclusion that school is boring, or that learning requires little effort or that their maximum effort is not necessary, are so serious as to demand a reappraisal of this practice. The use of 'work contracts' may be one useful way of ensuring that these children are led on to more and more demanding work.

Of course, the teacher has to provide help for the less able, and those from homes which have not provided a good base from which school learning can develop. The research described in the previous chapter suggested that informal methods might be most helpful to slow-learning children. The stimulation and variety of experiences provided by the best informal classrooms will clearly help such children. But these children will also be lagging behind in basic skills, and may also have relatively stronger memories than analytic skills. There is thus an argument, pressed by Jensen, that rote learning may be of most help to the less gifted children. Bereiter and Engelmann (1966) attracted considerable publicity when they demonstrated the improvement in basic skills which could be achieved with children from poor homes by the use of intensive over-learning procedures. This approach is certainly consistent with the theory, but *not* used in isolation. As we have said, such children also need opportunities to catch up on the variety of experiences they have missed at home, and to enjoy learning. Intensive programmes using rote learning for short periods, and providing regular opportunities for repetition within a supportive, friendly environment may be the most effective approach for these children. It is important to recognize that so-called 'disadvantaged' children need to experience early success in the basic skills, just as much as they need emotional security and opportunities for social and aesthetic development.

Other problems faced by most classroom teachers are the extent to which mistakes should be corrected and how much assessment and grading should take place. Should the standard be those of the class as a whole, or should work be judged only against the individual child's own capabilty? This was a question raised by the student teacher in Chapter 1. Reading the extract from the teacher quoted earlier in this section provides a balanced view. Correction of errors is an important part of learning, but it should not be seen as a penance. Mistakes have their own value, but if linked to formal assessment practices they may lose their educative effect. Evaluation has to strike a balance between absolute standards and personal effort and progress. Competition is valuable, but only if each child has a reasonable chance of winning whatever rewards there may be. Effort, progress, neatness, thoughtful behaviour, aesthetic and sporting skills can all be rewarded, as well as reaching high standards of work. Targets set can be tailored to the individual abilities of the child. The teacher will have to operate a 'mixed economy', if extrinsic motivation is to have beneficial effects in utilizing the child's own achievement motive, without creating detrimental anxiety. Fear of failure cannot be entirely eliminated where there is formal evaluation, but its negative effects can be minimised.

Teaching adolescents

It is impossible to separate applications into three age-ranges without substantial overlap. Many of the general principles introduced in the previous section are applicable to all ages, and some of the ideas which are discussed under the heading of 'teaching adults' will also be relevant in secondary schools.

There is no sudden change in pupils' intellectual abilities as they move from primary to secondary, or secondary to tertiary. In primary school most pupils will be using concrete operational thinking, but not *all* pupils at all times. During secondary school formal operational thought among the brightest pupils will develop rapidly, probably showing itself soonest in the sciences. But it is important to recognize that pupils should not be overloaded with abstract ideas. Clearly brighter pupils can cope with more, and at an earlier age, than those who are less intellectually advanced.

The evidence on intellectual development does not justify delaying the introduction of formal operational thinking until some predetermined stage in the curriculum. By age eleven some pupils will be using systematic and complex abstract thought. By age sixteen other pupils will still be relying mainly on concrete thinking. The task for the teacher is formidable, particularly with mixed-ability groups. Somehow pupils must be encouraged to think rigorously and abstractly to the limit of their ability, yet without being bombarded with ideas which are beyond their existing capabilities. Teachers of mixed ability classes will probably have to provide learning materials which assign pupils to different tasks carefully graded in complexity and degree of abstractness.

As pupils progress through secondary school, they will meet increasingly abstract ideas, and knowledge will be presented in more systematic and formal ways. Having selected material which is at the appropriate level, the teacher faces the problem of organizing it effectively. As we have seen, several theorists have stressed the importance of providing a clear structure and logical progression. But first it is essential that basic concepts, or anchoring ideas, are firmly established. The teacher cannot plan a course effectively without knowing the range of knowledge *and* understanding shown by the pupils. Assuming knowledge which is, in fact, only weakly grasped, is one of the most frequent causes of later learning difficulties. Time spent in providing many and varied instances of key ideas related as far as possible to personal experience will be amply repaid later. Systematic attempts to show similarities and differences between concepts, and to demonstrate how abstract ideas help to make sense of everyday experience, could be carried through more thoroughly by most teachers. It is the process which is certainly at the heart of our model of learning.

Of course in certain areas of the curriculum it will be important to recognize that rote learning is useful either as an initial strategy or to tackle areas where strong associations are necessary. But where memorization *is* required, pupils should be made aware of its specific purpose, and repeatedly helped to realize that understanding is the ultimate aim and most useful acquisition in most school subjects. We shall return to this theme of making pupils aware of how to use learning skills in the next section.

The starting point in secondary school has to be the thorough exploration, and reinforcement, of previous knowledge and skills. Carefully designed diagnostic tests, backed up by intensive question and answer sessions in class, should provide the teacher with the necessary information from which to plan his subsequent teaching strategy. The next step will then be to present new ideas within a carefully designed structure which helps pupils to link these ideas to their previous knowledge. Ausubel, as we have seen, argued that 'advance organizers' should be used for this purpose. An organizer is not just a summary of what is to come: it is a framework which emphasizes the essential principles to be justified later. Ausubel (1968) gave the following example of what might be done

> 'If the new learning material (for example, the Darwinian theory of evolution) is entirely unfamiliar to the learner, the organizer might include whatever established and relevant knowledge presumably exists in his cognitive structure that would make Darwinian theory more plausible, cogent, or comprehensible. The organizer itself (a highly general and inclusive statement of Darwinian theory) would thus be learned by... making explicit both its relatedness to generally relevant knowledge already present in the cognitive structure and its own relevance for the more detailed aspects of, or supportive evidence for, Darwinian theory (which would subsequently be presented) (pages 131-2).

The strength of advance organizers is that they provide a framework into which to fit subsequent information. But such a framework may not be suitable for certain subject areas or particular topics. A potential weakness of advance organizers is that they may be *too* logical and analytical; and too much logic may become boring. Again there is a tension between retaining coherence and maintaining interest and attention. There may be occasions when it is more important to build up evidence *before* arriving at the statement of a principle or theory. Following a historical sequence of events or the steps in an experiment builds up anticipation and maintains attention; the drama of the 'chase' has its own pedagogic value. Again, as we have seen, an analytical approach to learning may be ideal for one student and an anathema to another. There is a danger in assuming that a strictly logical order of presentation is always necessarily the most effective one to use in teaching. Careful ordering of material is essential to communication of ideas, but the different reactions of holists an serialists to step-by-step learning materials shows the danger of assuming that logical structuring is always 'best'.

Decisions on the order of presentation are inextricably bound up with other decisions. How much use to make of analogies and illustrations and what method of teaching to adopt. It is generally recognized that abstract ideas have to be illustrated by concrete examples, and that analogies or models are also helpful. But it is also true that striking illustrations can distract attention from the essential message, that analogies may be entirely unfamiliar to some pupils, and that failure to complete the links between analogy and main point, or to stress the limitations of a model, can lead to serious misunderstandings. Pask's research on 'difficult topics' (see page 212) and our own model, both show the necessity of providing first an adequate concept map to guide the pupils' own attempts to reach understanding, then sufficient detail and evidence combined with diagrams, examples and personal anecdotes to cater for contrasting styles of learning, and finally the need for teachers to explore with pupils the inadequacies and limits of the analogies used. Many text-books leave difficult concepts, which are nevertheless essential to the understanding of subsequent ideas, with a throw-away line such as 'further discussion of this topic must be delayed until university level'. If pupils are left with incomplete analogies, or with gaps in an important logical progression, understanding becomes impossible, and pupils will be thrown back on to rote learning with the implicit approval of the writer of the text-book. Enough information must be provided to make understanding possible.

Deep level understanding depends not just on adequate information, but also on the pupil's approach to learning. As we have seen repeatedly, interest and intrinsic motivation are likely to foster a deep approach, and an active search for personal meaning.

Throughout his writings on education Bruner stresses the importance of arousing interest by presenting a stimulating problem or an apparent paradox. He endorses the use of *guided* discovery in learning, not independent project work. The questions should be posed by the teacher within a predetermined framework. Too much freedom brings about inefficient learning, just as too little freedom leads to boredom. Teachers should stimulate active thinking, and no subject area should be seen as necessarily too difficult. There may be a way of presenting complex ideas in a way appropriate to the pupils' age and ability. A deep approach to learning demands independent thinking, being ready to work things out for yourself, and also being prepared to be wrong.

'Children, like adults, need reassurance that it is all right to entertain and express highly subjective ideas, to treat a task as a problem where you *invent* an answer rather than *finding* one out there in the book or on the blackboard. . . .

'Let me illustrate by a concrete instance. A fifth-grade class was working on the organization of a baboon troop — on this particular day, specifically on how they might protect against predators. They saw a brief sequence of film in which six or seven adult males go forward to intimidate and hold off three cheetahs. The teacher asked what the baboons had done to keep the cheetahs off, and there ensued a lively discussion of how dominant adult males, by showing their formidable mouthful of teeth and making threatening gestures, had turned the trick. A boy tentatively raised his hand and asked whether cheetahs always attacked together. Yes, though a single cheetah sometimes followed behind a moving troop and picked off an older, weakened straggler or an unwary straying juvenile. "Well, what if there were four cheetahs and two of them attacked from behind and two from in front? What would the baboons do then?" The question could have been answered empirically — and the enquiry ended. Cheetahs *do not* attack that way, and so we do not know what baboons *might* do. Fortunately, it was not. For the question opens up the deep issues of what might be and why it is not. Is there a necessary relation between predators and prey that share a common ecological niche? Must their encounters have a "sporting chance" outcome? It is such conjecture in this case quite unanswerable, that produces rational, self-consciously problem-finding behaviour so crucial to the growth of intellectual power' (Bruner, 1972, pages 62-63).

This example relates to a complex academic question, but other illustrations show how the same problem-finding, or problem-defining, activity can be stimulated in relation to everyday experience and in most areas of the curriculum and for most ability levels. The aim is to make pupils think for themselves (deep approach) and to create situations which are directly relevant to their experience (intrinsically motivating). Relevance in itself, without a demand for thinking up to the pupils' limit and beyond, is not educative. We must wherever possible show how knowledge relates to the real world and how it can be *applied* to solve everyday problems. As Whitehead (1932) argued

'In training a child to activity of thought, above all things we must beware of what I will call "inert ideas" — that is to say, ideas that are merely received into the mind without being utilized, or tested, or thrown into fresh combinations.... This is not an easy doctrine to apply, but a very hard one. It contains within itself the problem of keeping knowledge alive, of preventing it from becoming inert....

Let us now ask how in our system of education we are to guard against this mental dry-rot. We enunciate two educational commandments, "Do not teach too many subjects", and again, "What you teach, teach thoroughly".

The result of teaching small parts of a large number of subjects is the passive reception of disconnected ideas, not illumined with any spark of vitality. Let the main ideas which are introduced into a child's education be few and important, and let them be thrown into every combination possible. The child should make them his own, and should understand their application here and now in the circumstances of his actual life.... Education is the acquisition of the art of the utilization of knowledge. This is an art very difficult to impart' (pages v, 1-3, 6).

Promoting active thought and pointing our relevance are important parts of the teacher's task. He must also be prepared to show clearly and explicitly what type of learning is expected, how new ideas can be understood.

When I was discussing deep-level processing with a colleague, he mentioned his own experience in secondary school. At one time his homework involved the learning of Euclid's geometrical theorems. The instructions from the teacher were ambiguous, but it was clear that the theorem had to be reproduced in class the next day. To most pupils this meant learning it by heart. But this particular pupil, and a few others, discovered a trick. The theorem could be derived from its postulates! In class it was easier to build up the proof step by step, than it was to write it down from memory. This method did, however, arouse considerable guilt feelings. The pupils who used this method thought they were cheating, as the teacher had not explained that the theorems had been developed in this way. An anecdote, of course, proves nothing. But it does reinforce the warning which comes from the research evidence. Pupils will revert to rote learning when they do not see how to understand.

Formal assessment is a regular feature of most secondary schools. Within our model, feedback plays an important role in making clear what has been learned. Such information is potentially valuable to both pupil and teacher, but only if the methods of measurement produce reliable and valid assessments of performance, and pupils are shown precisely where mistakes were made and how these might be remedied. Few teachers have been trained to relate assessment to specified objectives in the systematic way used in mastery learning. Although such an approach will not be suitable in all subjects, the principles of mastery learning and criterion-referenced assessment would be worth examining to see if they could be applied.

Class tests are often given with little thought about their possible effects on students' approaches to learning. In the Gothenburg studies, we saw that even in a short experiment excessively factual questions increase the use of surface processing. Questions demanding understanding and independent thought should be included wherever possible to reinforce the idea that reproductive learning is not all that is required. Students' *perceptions* of the way marks are awarded are probably more influential on approaches to learning than any other single aspect of the school experience.

Examinations are more threat-provoking than most educational settings. The formality and time-pressures conspire with the importance of good results to shift the balance between hope for success and fear of failure firmly towards the latter. Only with highly confident pupils will the anxiety and tension enhance performance. (Remember the comments of the confident students quoted in Chapter 5). Attention will certainly be maintained, but for many pupils a pervasive fear of failure will shift the approach towards a surface strategy — a desperate urge to regurgitate facts, to show what facts are known, even when the question really demands careful selection and critical analysis. Many pupils going into an examination will still be rehearsing in STM an array of facts, formulae, and outline answers. The strain thus imposed on STM will add acutely to anxiety level. As STM is also the working memory, rehearsal has to stop once writing begins. Thus many students pour out the contents of their STM on to rough paper as soon as they possibly can, thus leaving 'thinking room' and perhaps also reducing anxiety.

It is not only *during* the examination, but throughout the revision period, that pupils may feel pushed towards memorization. One of the worst results of schooling which either deliberately or accidentally encourages reproductive learning is the long-term effects. Pupils may be left with the idea that learning *is* memorization. Although some memorized information may stay in the mind for years (like the Latin poem mentioned in Chapter 6), such fragmentary knowledge is rarely useful. A common experience of many pupils who have relied on over-learning to pass an examination is that the 'slate' is enthusiastically 'wiped clean' of the knowledge once the anxiety is removed. The knowledge has had no personal meaning, and has not been part of an organized structure of ideas within semantic LTM. The information and ideas will thus fade rapidly from memory once the need for repetition and overlearning has been removed. Also the assimilation of ideas depends on reorganizing cognitive structure, but chains of associations are firmly bound together in the order in which they are initially learned. Thus if facts are remembered through memorization, they are likely to prove difficult to reorganize in future learning.

This discussion of adolescent education has focussed on the development of high level cognitive skills and academic knowledge. Many teachers will spend much of their time teaching less able pupils or young people who have already decided that school is not for them. The principles of our model still apply, however. Effective learning depends on firmly anchored basic concepts. With less able pupils much more use will have to be made of relevant practical examples and striking illustrations. It is also important to recognize that repetition and overlearning may be particularly necessary for these pupils both in developing competency motivation, and in establishing the initial skills and knowledge on which further intellectual development depends. However, the extract from the observation study in Chapter 1 (page 13), showed how important it is for the teacher to try to see the situation from the pupils' point of view. Disruptive behaviour can be a protest against boredom, against being treated as a child, or against the lack of opportunity to express individuality. Of course, indiscipline can also reflect the all-too-logical reaction of young people who already see an inevitable future of tedious work and low pay, or even no prospect of employment at all. If such pupils see no incentive for working hard in school, if only the brightest children are singled out for commendation or responsibility, if they begin to feel themselves to be worthless, no curriculum or teaching innovation is likely to help. The whole ethos of the school would have to change first.

In this brief discussion of the teaching of adolescents, it has been impossible to give adequate consideration either to allowances for different ability levels, or to differences between subject areas. The implications of different styles of learning have been touched on, but there will be further discussion when we consider teaching at the tertiary level.

Study strategies

For those pupils who are successful in secondary school, many will go on to higher education. Perhaps the greatest contrast between schools and colleges or universities is in the degree of independence given to students. There, students are expected to know how to study on their own, and to be able to plan their own work schedules. It is also assumed that they will have mastered the basic skills of studying in their own discipline. However, if students have come from schools which have provided little experience of independent studying, or which have emphasized reproductive learning, they may find it difficult even to understand what is being required of them at college or university.

A great deal of most students' time is spent in independent reading, and yet it appears that many students use inappropriate strategies. The model of learning was developed out of the research on students. It is worth looking back to Marton's work, and applying our model of learning to the task of reading an academic article.

The model stresses initial intention. Unless the student realizes that a deep approach is required, deep level processing is unlikely to take place. But our model indicates that a student's interpretation of the task may alter even during the task. Initial perceptions of what is required, may be changed while the article is being read. It is difficult to build any sense of variability into the model itself, but reading may in practice involve varying strategies.

Put yourself in the position of someone about to start reading. What would decide your initial strategy? Presumably the first step would be to consider what seemed to be required of you. Why has the reading to be done? Is it a newspaper article you are casually glancing at, a novel or a text-book as preparation for an examination? For the first two, probably interest will be all important. If the article or novel proves to be boring you will stop reading. But with the academic article other considerations may become paramount. You may wonder first what you are expected to get out of the article. What sort of questions may come up in examination? How important is it for you to do well? The examination may be seen as a challenge through 'hope for success', or as a threat if you are more affected by fear of failure. But whichever reaction is produced, the presence of formal evaluation creates an artificial, extrinsic form of motivation, which may induce, at least at first, an anxious surface approach towards reading.

The strength of extrinsic motivation may be the most important factor governing the initial level of attention with which the article is read, but soon intrinsic and extrinsic motivation may become interwoven. Glancing over the article will indicate how familiar the content is. The initial impression of the content is probably registered in terms of familiarity, anticipated difficulty, and interest, which will again interact with each other. Familiarity, perceived relevance and interest are all likely to make a deep approach more likely. But what happens if background knowledge is inadequate, or if the article is difficult to read? The content is still potentially relevant, but how long will the student be able to maintain a high level of attention? Then the relative importance of the topic and other forms of motivation have more effect. Remember from Chapter 9, Wilson (1972) distinguishes two forms of intrinsic motivation — one deriving from interest in the subject matter, the other depending on the fostering of self-esteem. This second form of intrinsic motivation seems to cover both competence motivation and Atkinson's achievement motive. A student who hopes for, and expects, to be successful may well maintain attention in the face of difficulty. A less confident student may give up under the same circumstances, unless the importance of the topic is strong enough to hold the attention firm.

Thereafter, as reading continues and the level of interest and difficulty fluctuates, there will be a continuing variation in the level of attention, unless the combined effects of interest, hope for success and fear of failure continue to overcome dull or difficult passages in the text.

This rather long discussion of the dynamics of attention when reading an article relies a good deal on introspection, while keeping close to the general outline of the evidence described earlier. Its intention was to reinforce the idea that approach to learning depends on pre-requisite knowledge and skill, as well as on past experience of similar learning situations. It was also intended to show the way in which the balance between interest, hope for success and fear of failure may vary, even during the reading of a single article. Interest depends crucially on content or subject area, while hope for success and fear of failure are affected by prior experience of studying and by the initial perceptions of the task requirements. Such a complex set of interactions are belied by the simple model, but have to be taken into account if the research findings are to provide adequate explanations of experience.

If we think about other aspects of studying, the ideas of approach to learning is still relevant. Writing essays, writing-up practical reports or preparing for tutorials can all be carried out at different levels. A complication in understanding what is involved in a deep approach to studying is that the concept has to be re-interpreted within each separate discipline or department. 'Deep approach' carries the same general meaning, but the specific learning strategies may vary considerably. In most departments the deep approach can be defined in terms of active integration of three types — integrating what is being learned with previous experience and feeling satisfaction in making knowledge one's own, integrating components of the task into a whole, and integrating the completed learning within a wider perspective which includes seeing the purpose behind the task (Ramsden, 1979).

The way essays are written will almost certainly show the influence of individual styles of thinking. In many cases, examples of 'globetrotting' (generalizing from insufficient evidence, or writing off the point) and 'improvidence' (failure to relate evidence to the developing argument) will be criticized by tutors. There may also be comments about too great a reliance on recognizable texts (reproductive approach merging into plagiarism in extreme cases) or a failure to reach a decisive conclusion.

This final demand is for an indication that deep understanding or personal meaning has been reached. It can also be understood, as an expression of versatility, or as the characteristics of a 'reasonable adventurer' or a 'relativistic reasoner'.

Teaching adults

Certainly in higher education the demand for 'critical thinking', as we saw in Chapter 4, will be the common aim of most lecturers. It will probably be helpful for this rather vague idea to be reconceptualized within the learning model, which draws attention to the pre-requisites of deep-level understanding. Once the general purpose is clear, ways of achieving this goal can be considered. The starting point in defining the teaching situation in higher education is often the construction of the course itself. Clear aims are essential. What skills, concepts, knowledge, ideas, and levels of understanding do the students have now, and what will be expected of them at the end of the course? It is *not* sufficient simply to write the syllabus. Having decided the aims in a precise way, the students should be told what is required of them in a similarly explicit form. How else can they be expected to know what strategies of learning to use? How can they be expected to achieve what is undefined? Yet such an approach is not common even in higher education, where students might best be able to utilize such information.

In course development, once the aims have been decided, content must be carefully selected within the constraints of examination or professional training requirements. In making that selection it is important to be aware of the subconscious effects created by strong traditions in teaching that subject area. How much factual knowledge really is essential? Are alternative views of the subject being given appropriate weighting? Have enough concrete illustrations, analogies and models been included? Are the interesting topics distributed in a way designed to maintain interest throughout the course? Traditions in how a subject should be presented partly reflect the nature of the discipline, but also strong paradigms (Kuhn, 1963) or conventions about the 'right' way to think about a discipline. These conventions are sometimes overthrown by revolutionary changes in the subject, but until such time they can blinker the teaching approach in ways which may seriously affect the ease with which students learn. Lecturers may be pointing students towards the 'frontiers of knowledge', but at undergraduate level the teaching needs to show a clear recognition of the limitations in students' more 'commonsense' way of thinking about the discipline. It is dangerous for the teacher to give too much emphasis to the most advanced theoretical structures, if he thereby loses sight of his students' perspectives.

Once the content is decided, the organization first of the course, and then of each individual lecture needs careful consideration. As was mentioned in the previous section, it is important to make sure that the basic concepts and 'anchoring ideas' for the course are thoroughly understood, even if this emphasis reduces overall coverage. It is also important to show students in advance how the subject is to be tackled by providing 'advance organizers'. Of course, logical organization of the information and ideas is important, but it is also necessary to recognize that too formal a presentation may fail to hold students' attention. Effective communication demands dramatic art, as well as a clear argument.

The logic of the scientific paper or the philosophical proof can be contrasted with other organizing principles. Novelists often build up their stories in a way which avoids the obvious logical ordering of events. The use of 'flash-backs', and the switching from the activities of one character to another, builds up a satisfying whole, but in an oblique manner. It is, in fact, one of the great skills of the novelist to bring together many apparently disparate threads in interesting and surprising ways. He will also make deliberate use of unusual combinations of words, provocative language, or striking paradoxes, to maintain the reader's interest. Even academic texts may be written in a manner which is more expressive of the author's own personality, than the requirements of academic tradition. A book by Laing (1977), a radical psychologist, was recently advertised as being 'rich, disorderly, suggestive, inconclusive, and humane', thus interposing characteristic strengths and weaknesses of intuitive, holistic thinking. The use of metaphor and paradox, the interplay of connections and contrasts, perhaps, represents the 'logic' of the novel, and of the intuitive, holistic mode of thinking.

Teachers and lecturers also show their own personalities in the way they present their ideas. Careful, unemotional, logical presentation ensures accuracy and balance, while enthusiasm, humour, and overstatement provokes interest and stimulates thought. Our model of learning would demand versatility in the method of teaching to allow students of all cognitive styles to learn effectively. The lecture needs to combine a strong structure and developing argument, with appropriate illustration, anecdote or humorous aside. Each lecturer will have to develop his own characteristic balance, but an extreme style will create unnecessary difficulties for many students. Remember the contrasting styles Asimov described (page 96).

The selection of content, the order in which it is presented, and the style of teaching are all likely to affect intrinsic motivation, and thereby alter students' approaches to learning and their levels of understanding. Some lecturers seem to believe that it is none of their business to motivate the students; if they are *not* motivated, they should not be in higher education.

In interviews with lecturers (Entwistle and Percy, 1974) it became clear that poor academic progress was almost always explained in terms of lack of interest or motivation, and these were seen as faults of the student. But one lecturer did recognize a paradox in this situation.

> 'The main trouble is unwillingness to get down to work, but having said this, there is no doubt a paradox... in that at some time in the past, in order for a person to have got here, presumably he had been willing, and something is going on which diminishes this willingness'.

When students were interviewed (Entwistle, 1975), they did not see this situation as paradoxical. They had a ready explanation.

> 'So often are students bored by uninspired teaching or disenchanted by badly taught material. While university lecturers are undoubtedly knowledgeable they are totally untrained and unexamined in the art of communication.... The completely incorrect assumption is that anyone with a good degree will automatically be able to impart this knowledge to others'.

Another student drew attention to a difficulty which may not be widely recognized by lecturers.

> 'University confronts the student with rigid intellectual authority: a body of teachers with a far greater degree of knowledge challenges *and intimidates*'.

It is common for staff and students to blame each other for lack of academic progress, but it should by now be abundantly clear that such explanations are naive and simplistic. Choice of content and style of presentation by the teacher interact with the achievement motives of the student, and with the extrinsic motives induced by the learning context, to affect the level of understanding reached by the student. In a recent survey of attitudes to teaching in higher education, the Nuffield Group (Becher *et al.*, 1975) were alarmed at the gulf between staff and students.

'The "them–us" distinction was often alluded to; and it is not easily resolved. A genuine consensus of view between students and staff (rather than some form of armed neutrality) may in extreme cases prove impossible to achieve, so fundamental being the differences in life-styles and attitudes' (page 44).

Such 'armed neutrality' is not confined to the higher reaches of education; it is even more obvious in some secondary schools where pupils may reject the value of academic knowledge altogether. But throughout education the teacher surely has an obligation to present information in a lively and interesting manner, and to ensure that the aims of the course are clearly understood by the students.

When it comes to lecturing or class teaching, the information processing model from Chapter 6 can be used to draw attention to certain important skills in presenting information. Most of the points seem obvious, but are nevertheless sometimes ignored. While the teacher is talking, the student is expected to be trying to make sense of the ideas. His ability to code the information into LTM will, of course, depend on his own previous knowledge, intellectual skills, approach to learning and motivation, but also on characteristics of the teacher, such as:

- speed of delivery (pauses to allow coding)
- appropriate redundancy (provides longer for coding)
- variety of illustrations (facilitates links with previous experience)
- voice modulation (draws attention to important points)
- explanation of new concepts in terms of familiar ones
- emphasis on similarities and differences between concepts and ideas presented (facilitates accurate coding)
- structure of topic and use of advance organizers
- use of questions (maintains attention and stimulates active processing)
- use of audio-visual aids (maintains attention: allows more time for coding or note-taking).

The effect of interesting, relevant material in maintaining attention and arousing intrinsic motivation has been repeatedly stressed. But the 'psychological distance' between teacher and student, the daunting effect of formality and authority, must also be considered. Its effect is on extrinsic motivation, arousing anxiety and fear of failure. The teaching situation in a lecture hall provides a good instance.

'The whole lecture situation seems to be designed to increase psychological distance. The lecturer, typically, arrives after the students; walks to the front;

retreats behind a long bench and then behind a reading desk; opens his notes; waits for late-comers — then begins. He is the focus of attention, but the physical situation and the formality of a normal lecture delivery must create an artificial atmosphere for communication. The lecturer, unless he tries to break down psychological distance, *will* confront the student, *will* intimidate, and so will, also, unknowingly, affect the student's readiness to learn and his attitudes to studying' (Entwistle, 1975, page 145).

The use of questions, buzz sessions, eye-contact and colloquialisms, or moving closer to the class, may all help to break down some of the barriers to communication which occur in school classrooms, as well as in lecture halls. But student learning does not take place only, or even mainly, from 'teacher talk'. Learning also occurs when students are reading books, writing essays, working out problems, doing laboratory exercises or projects, discussing work with other students or tutors, or going over mistakes in examination answers. Students at school and university experience a variety of learning situations, but it is rare for a course to be conceived in a way which capitalizes on the types of learning each learning situation offers. For one thing, students are rarely offered alternative ways of learning. The wide variation in the styles of learning preferred by students indicates a need, where possible, to allow at least some choice in the mix of learning tasks undertaken. Why should all students be expected to attend the same number of lectures and tutorials? Why is guided reading not offered as an alternative to lectures, or independent projects instead of set essays?

The autonomy given to the lecturer often means that such questions need not be asked, let alone answered. The lecturer is free to choose his own approach to teaching and that, as we have seen, may reflect his own cognitive style. Even the innovations introduced in teaching in higher education seem to reflect extremes of serialist or holist styles. On the one hand there is computer managed instruction or the Keller Plan (a variant of mastery learning), while on the other hand, tutor-less discussion groups have been advocated (see Entwistle, 1976).

The decision to adopt a certain approach to teaching in higher education, as in primary education, often seems to be based on strong belief bolstered by dogmatic assertion.

'Some lecturers seem to hold, almost as an act of faith, that students only learn effectively in, say, tutorials. If a lecturer chooses to adopt just one mode of teaching, this may not be a rational matching of aims to the method, but rather an expression of his own "world view"; it could well be one facet of a humanistic philosophy which rejects the determinism and the control of others. As such a lecturer is unlikely to have chosen to specialize in a discipline which negates his world view, we should expect to find a reasonable match between the types of thinking appropriate to a discipline and the methods of instruction adopted. It is thus no accident that structured approaches are found predominantly in the sciences, where subject matter often follows a hierarchical arrangement and tough-minded attitudes are more common. If lecturers, on the whole, are adopting methods, which are effective in their discipline and congruent with their attitudes, perhaps (all is well).

Unfortunately such a simple solution is not acceptable. Individual differences have again been ignored. Students are not always successful in finding a discipline which is consonant with their outlooks on life and within most disciplines lecturers differ in their approaches to teaching. The match between subject area and teaching methods is not all that close. In the Lancaster study, although there were often substantial differences in values and attitudes between different subject areas, the range within each discipline was still large. There was also some evidence that a lack of match between students' values and their subject area was associated with poor academic performance. What we were not able to establish was whether the lack of match was with subject matter or with styles of teaching.' (Entwistle, 1976, pages 22-23).

The argument outlined earlier makes it clear that our objective in education, at whatever level, should be to help students both to utilize their own learning styles most effectively, and also to transcend the limitations which those styles carry with them. The 'improvident' serialist may look no further than the facts, while the 'globe-trotting' holist may not be prepared for the hard grind of grappling with the details which back up his ideas. We need versatile students, who are meticulous in attention to detail, yet adventurous and imaginative. This is a tall order, yet study skills are rarely taught as such: students are expected to acquire them incidentally. But the incidence of 'surface processing' among students suggests that these skills have often *not* been fully developed. There are many schemes which have been developed for improving study skills, but few of them have taken seriously the wide variation in the strategies which can be shown to be effective. The theoretical ideal may suit few students in practice. More helpful approaches are those where individual monitoring of, say, reading strategy (Thomas and Augustein, 1975) or level of attention (Ornstein, 1977) is possible.

Ornstein recommends the use of 'biofeedback' or self-regulation techniques to improve what could be taken to mean 'approaches to studying'. Students have already been trained to control anxiety states induced by learning situations through monitoring their own physiological reactions (such as sweaty palms or the absence of alpha waves in the brain). Ornstein speculates that computer-controlled learning could be extended to ensure that information would be presented to the student only when attention and emotional state were optimal. Although the more advanced applications of biofeedback may still sound implausible, the effort to raise student 'awareness' of their own approaches and strategies may be the single most effective way of raising general levels of understanding.

Teachers and educational psychology

This long final chapter has sought to integrate many of the ideas presented in earlier chapters and then to suggest some educational implications of those ideas. In all the previous chapters, research has been examined and summarized cautiously, trying to present a balanced view of each area. When it comes to educational implications, however, it is even more difficult to avoid value judgements and the pervasive effect of the author's own cognitive style and world view. In spite of stressing repeatedly that educational psychology cannot provide ready made solutions to classroom problems, the concluding sections may seem to have contradicted that view. But to derive no more than vague general implications from the frameworks would leave too much of the onus of application to the reader. There is, at least, an obligation to give illustrations of how the ideas summarized in the framework might be translated into specific suggestions. It is important to re-emphasize that these examples are indicative and no more. If the reader has come to different conclusions, so much the better. Such disagreement would already have stimulated the activity intended — using the theoretical framework in thinking about one's own experience of education. The conclusions drawn here represent one such attempt, no more.

The more important question is whether the theoretical framework itself will prove valid and useful in generating critical consideration of personal experience. The validity of the framework depends on the extent to which the ideas it summarizes help to systematize, analyse and explain people's experience of education. The strength of this framework is that it draws heavily on research conducted either within the educational system itself, or with realistically complex learning materials. The great weaknesses of educational psychology in the past have been that little attempt has been made to integrate disparate areas of mainstream psychology within its boundaries; and that the theories presented had their origins in situations which were far removed from educational settings. This book represents one attempt at selecting areas of research which seem to have direct relevance to education and which can be shown to have some coherence.

What remains is to see whether the framework developed will guide research by suggesting gaps in our knowledge where intuition had to be used to ensure coherence in the overall picture. Empirical evidence will either confirm that prediction or suggest different forms of coherence. Then the practical suggestions drawn from the framework must also be put to the test — either by teachers conducting their own classroom research into the effects of changing methods along lines suggested by the framework, or simply by observing the impact of such changes in a less controlled and systematic way.

Concluding summary

The first chapter of the book emphasized its message — a much abbreviated advance organizer. That message should also form the epilogue. The existence of widely different learning styles prevents there being any possibility of any single 'correct' way to teach or to learn. The evidence taken as a whole is strong and unequivocal. Differences in personality and cognitive style lead not only to contrasting strategies in trying to assimilate information and to distinct preferences for different ways of presenting that information, but also to characteristic styles of teaching, researching and theorizing. These styles of learning affect the levels of understanding across, if you like, a horizontal plane. They do not necessarily imply better or worse; they *do* imply qualitative differences in the 'flavour' of understanding and recall.

Levels of understanding are also strongly affected by the approach to learning. Although they are qualitatively different, there may also be a distinct hierarchy which runs from more complete to less complete understanding. A deep approach to reading, for example, involves relating facts to conclusion in an active way which should bring the reader close to the author's intended message. Students who adopt such an approach to studying in general show a greater awareness of their teachers' main educational aims. They also find their work more interesting and rewarding — in terms of both personal satisfaction and higher grades.

The approach to learning is, however, a composite dependent on previous knowledge, the range of intellectual skills available, and the balance between the student's hope for success and fear of failure. The approach can also be strongly affected by the situation, and by the student's perception of the intellectual demands being made of him. Interest and relevance enhance intrinsic motivation and favour a deep approach, while emphasis on formal evaluation and extrinsic motivation pushes the student towards surface processing. Of course these situational effects vary from student to student; they affect but do not eliminate the original individual differences. It may also be worth considering the role of humour and paradox in fostering a deep approach to learning. The unexpected and the apparently insoluble provoke an active memory search and possibly a rearrangement of previous ideas. At all levels of education, it may be important to consider ways of introducing deliberate and striking apparent or real contradictions and showing pupils or students ways of resolving them. This activity comes close to Perry's relativistic reasoning, while the most fundamental paradoxes demand personal commitment in coming to a conclusion. There may be no 'right' answers; only individual interpretations.

Building up knowledge depends on relating new information and ideas to existing cognitive structure. It is essential for teachers to ensure that basic 'anchoring ideas' are thoroughly understood and that new ideas are presented in relation to well-established previous knowledge. It is also important to provide both a clear framework and appropriate illustrations and analogies. The function of the analogy, as Dewey saw clearly, is to understand the unfamiliar through the familiar. Thus choosing analogies which are accessible to most pupils is an important, and largely unrecognized, art in teaching.

The simple dichotomies between the two approaches to learning and between two distinctive learning styles may seem implausible at first sight. Individuals show far greater variety in their learning strategies than the simple dichotomies might imply. But they remain surprisingly strong and persistent distinctions which have appeared, although with different terminology, in many studies. It has been suggested that the strength of the dichotomies in style may even reflect fundamentally different functions of the brain hemispheres. The surface/deep distinction may also be rooted in fundamental brain processes. Surface processing relies primarily on rote memorization through overlearning between STM and episodic LTM, while deep processing may initially involve some rote learning, but predominantly demands the appropriate use of a wide range of skills which were labelled, for convenience, analytic and imaginative.

The different styles by which a deep level of understanding can be reached affect choices of specialisms between the arts and science, and the way ideas are presented or learned. The plea throughout this book has been for integration and balance between a series of fundamental opposites. The creative tension between these opposites should not be destroyed by accepting too readily one extreme or the other, whether it is by adopting an introverted persona or an uncompromisingly 'informal' teaching style. By recognizing the validity of the opposite style, and by alternating between them in a thoughtful way, educational and psychological understanding can be deepened.

The alternation and tension between fundamental opposites is an essential part of education, as of life itself. It is not just the road to 'self-actualization' or 'individuation', but also towards a better understanding of the real meaning of the term 'progressive' in education. It provides a challenge to teachers and students alike to resolve a paradox, to create a new, and necessarily individual, synthesis of opposite styles of learning and teaching — the critical and the curious, the precise and the speculative, the logical and the imaginative, the emphasis on control or freedom.

'The sad truth is that man's real life consists of a complex of inexorable opposites — day and night, birth and death, happiness and misery, good and evil. . . . Life is a battleground. It always has been and always will be; and if it were not so, existence would come to an end' (Jung, 1964, page 85).

APPENDIX A

Scoring Instructions for the Inventory

The letters in the extreme right column of the inventory indicate the scale to which the item belongs. Write down each of the letters across a page as follows:

A B C D E F G

Under the appropriate letter write down the code number of each answer you gave. You should finish up with six code numbers for scales A B D and three code numbers for C E F G. Add up each set of code numbers to give a score on each scale.

The A scale gives a score out of 24 on the 'achieving' orientation which indicates well-organized study methods, competitiveness and hope for success. (See page 101 ff. for fuller descriptions.)

The B scale is also out of 24, but describes the 'reproducing' orientation of surface approaches to learning, extrinsic motivation and syllabus-boundness.

The D scale, again out of 24, is a measure of the 'meaning' dimension of deep approaches to learning, intrinsic and academic motivation.

The remaining scales are formed by adding together various totals.

Combining C and G scores gives an indication of tendency towards a comprehension learning style (out of 24).

Combining E and F scores gives a measure of the operation learning style (out of 24).

An index of a versatile approach to learning is provided by adding together D + C + E (out of 48).

An index of pathological symptoms in learning is given by combining B + F + G (out of 48).

The best prediction of overall academic success is likely to be produced by calculating the following

$$A + D + C + E + (48 - B - F - G) \text{ (out of 120)}$$

which combines the versatile approach with organized study methods and a lack of pathological symptoms.

Mean scores (and standard deviations) on this scoring system are given below for several samples of students, together with the correlation with a self-rating of academic performance.

| Scales | Mean scores and standard deviations | | | | r* |
	Arts (N = 490)	Social Science (853)	Science (865)	Overall (σ) (2208)	(2193)
Achieving (A)	12.50	12.73	13.08	12.82 (4.26)	.32
Reproducing (B)	11.98	13.65	14.26	13.51 (4.40)	− .25
Meaning (D)	15.17	14.21	13.93	14.31 (4.51)	.28
Comprehension learning	13.04	13.64	12.64	13.12 (3.63)	− .04
Operation learning	12.45	13.48	13.48	13.25 (3.70)	− .07
Versatile approach	29.58	29.65	29.64	29.63 (7.03)	.26
Learning pathologies	23.06	25.32	24.67	24.57 (7.15)	− .29
Prediction of success	67.02	65.06	66.05	65.88 (13.01)	.41

*correlation between scale score and self-rating at academic performance.

Using these provisional norms it is reasonable to consider a score which is more than half a standard deviation about the mean (eg on A a score above 15) to be 'high' and a full standard deviation above (eg 17 on A) to be 'very high'. While similar positions below the mean to be 'low' (11 on A) and 'very low' (9 on A).

APPENDIX B

Categories of Response to Questionnaire

Question 1
Examples of different levels of outcome from reading the Wertheimer article (First-year students)

A. Conclusion-orientated, detailed

The article is about the failings in traditional methods of analysing thinking, the methods of logic and association.

The article also goes on to show how lack of understanding about the thought process can have adverse effects in education, and can actually inhibit progress.

Wertheimer uses the case of a classroom situation to emphasize his point further, the fact that the children could not solve the parallelogram problem unless it was presented to them in a new way is evidence of this. Wertheimer says that in this case the wrong emphasis was being placed by the teacher i.e. the ability to get the homework problems right with no thought of whether the children really understood the theory behind it.

Children fitting shapes were then allowed to 'teach themselves' rather than being given a set formula which they would apply without thinking.

Wertheimer was showing that there was more behind the thought process than can merely be shown by performance in solving problems.

B. Conclusion-orientated, mentioning

This article was mainly about the way pupils learn. It stressed that we don't really think about what we are reading. Given a problem to solve we do not think about it but merely follow the example given so as to solve the problem. Learning in this way is repetitive — we are merely repeating what we have already been taught — we do not think about why we solve it in that way. Hence when the same problem is approached from a different angle we cannot follow the given example exactly and so are completely lost.

C. Description-orientated, detailed

Wertheimer's article was on the subject of thinking. It was attempting the question — how do we think? It provided two main areas of thought. First the classical idea of a logical progression of ideas which result in a positive answer to a particular question; and second the idea of association of thoughts, various thoughts which link together to form the answer. Wertheimer spoke of the way children think, using the example of asking children to find the area of a parallelogram with an unfamiliar position and showed that they were conditioned only to find the area of a 'normal' parallelogram. He then showed that very young children were better equipped to answer this problem — having no previous knowledge of it.

D. Description-orientated, mentioning

Article about logic principally, and what makes process of thinking meaningful — analyses traditional logic. Asks rhetorical questions about the logic of thinking — what process we use in thinking out a problem.

Article goes on to cite the example of school children learning the area of rectangles and parallelograms — how feedback experiments can show that school children may merely regurgitate mathematical formulae and methods without actually understanding them.

Note

The main difference between the two extracts which showed an emphasis on *detail* is that A brought together two main points to emphasize the author's main message, while C listed the main points without integrating them effectively. B understands the author's message but does not relate it to any evidence, while D lists a series of topics. Note that C and D follow the order in which the article presents its main points indicating more reliance on sequential memorization than on personal understanding.

Question 2

(a) Traditional logic is concerned with the criteria that guarantee exactness, validity, consistency of general concepts, propositions, inferences, and syllogisms.
(b) An efficient police manual for regulating traffic.
(c) The rules of induction; the empirical approach of collecting facts, using experimental methods and testing hypotheses.
(d) Thinking is seen as a chain of ideas or of as a series of stimuli and responses.
(e) Logic is rigorous, but is also barren, boring, empty, unproductive. Associationism has failed to distinguish between sensible and senseless

combinations of ideas; it also relies on mechanical repetition and chance to solve problems.

(f) The teacher presented the traditional proof that the area of the parallelogram was equal to the product of the base by the altitude and then asked the pupils to work out examples based on the use of that formula.

(g) The pupils could not deal with unusual examples where the formula could not be applied directly. He contrasted attempts to apply the formula blindly with children who solved these examples by imaginative reconstruction of the unfamiliar into the familiar.

(h) Wertheimer urges psychologists to understand thinking through discovering the differences between good and bad instances, as a physicist compares pure crystals with various distortions to reveal the inner nature of genuine crystallization.

Note

It is very unlikely that you would be able to remember the article in sufficient detail to give full answers to question 2. These questions were designed as caricatures of the exteme factual questions found in some examination papers and which may influence a student's subsequent approach to learning. It would, however, be possible to answer most, or all, of these questions correctly without really understanding the main message the author was trying to present.

Question 3

Examples of different categories used in classifying processes of learning will be found on pages 77-78.

References

Allport, G.W. (1963). *Pattern and Growth in Personality,* Holt, Rinehart and Winston, New York.

Anthony, W. (1977). The development of extraversion and ability: an analysis of Rushton's longitudinal data. *Br. J. educ. Psychol., 47,* 193-196.

Ashby, E. (1973). The structure of higher education: a world view, *Higher Education, 2,* 142-151.

Ashton, P., Kneen, P., Davies, F., and Holley, B.J. (1975). *The Aims of Primary Education: a Study of Teachers' Opinions,* Macmillan, London.

Asimov, I. (1968). *A Whiff of Death,* Gollancz, London.

Atkinson, J.W. (1974). The mainsprings of achievement-orientated activity. In Atkinson, J.W. and Raynor, J.O. (Eds.), *Motivation and Achievement,* Wiley, New York.

Atkinson, J.W., and Feather, N.T. (1966). *A Theory of Achievement Motivation,* Wiley, New York.

Atkinson, J.W., and Raynor, J.O. (1974), (Eds.). *Motivation and Achievement,* Wiley, New York.

Ausubel, D.P. (1968). *Educational Psychology: a Cognitive View,* Holt, Rinehart and Winston, New York.

Ausubel, D.P., Novak, J.S., and Hanesian, H. (1978). *Educational Psychology: a Cognitive View,* (2nd Edition), Holt, Rinehart, and Winston, New York.

Baddeley, A.D. (1976). *The Psychology of Memory,* Harper and Row, New York.

Ballard, P.B. (1923). *The New Examiner,* University of London Press, London.

Bannister, D., and Fansella, F. (1971). *Inquiring Man: the Theory of Personal Constructs,* Penguin Books, Harmondsworth.

Bantock, G.H. (1961). Educational research: a criticism, *Havard educ. Res., 31,* 264-280.

Becker, A.S., Geer, B. and Hughes, E.C. (1968). *Making the Grade – the Academic Side of College Life,* Wiley, New York.

Bengtsson, G., and Raaheim, K. (1976). The Family Test: an attempt to assess intelligence at work. *Reports from the Institute of Psychology,* University of Bergen, 7 (2).

Bennett, S.N. (1976). *Teaching Styles and Pupil Progress,* Open Books, London.

Bennett, S.N. (1978). Recent research on teaching: a dream, a belief and a model, *Br. J. educ. Psychol., 48,* 127-147.

Bennett, S.N., and Entwistle, N.J. (1977). Rite, but wrong: a reply to 'A Chapter of errors', *Educ. Res., 19,* 217-222.

Bereiter, C., and Engelmann, S. (1966). *Teaching Disadvantaged Children in the Preschool,* Prentice-Hall, Englewood Cliffs, N.J.

Bieri, J., Atkins, A.L., Briar, J.S., Leaman, R.L., Miller, H., and Tripodi, T. (1966). *Clinical and Social Judgement: the Discrimination of Behavioural Information,* Wiley, New York.

Biggs, J.B. (1976). Dimensions of study behaviour: another look at ATI, *Br. J. educ. Psychol.,* **46**, 68-80.

Biggs, J.B. (1978). Individual and group differences in study processes, *Br. J. educ. Psychol.,* **48**, 266-279.

Biggs, J.B. (1979). Individual differences in study processes and the quality of learning outcomes, *Higher Educ.,* **8**, 381-394.

Binet, A., and Simon, T. (1916). *The Development of Intelligence in Children,* Training School Publication, Vineland, N.J.

Birney, R.C., Burdick, H., and Teevan, R.C. (1969). *Fear of Failure,* Van Nostrand — Reinhold, New York.

Blakemore, C. (1977). *Mechanics of the Mind,* Cambridge University Press, London.

Bloom, B.S. (1977). *Human Characteristics and School Learning,* McGraw Hill, New York.

Bloom, B.S., Englehart, M.B., Frost, E.J., Hill, W.H., and Krathwohl, D.R. (1956). *Taxonomy of Educational Objectives. The Classification of Educational Goals. Handbook I – Cognitive Domain,* Longmans Green, New York.

Borg, W.R. and Gall, M.D. (1979). *Educational Research: an Introduction,* (2nd Edition), Longmans, London.

Boring, E.G. (1923). Intelligence as the tests test it, *New Republic,* **35** (June 6), 35-36.

Broadbent, D.E. (1958). *Perception and Communication,* Pergamon, London.

Broadbent, D.E. (1966). The well ordered mind, *Am. educ. Res. J.,* **3**, 281-295.

Broadbent, D.E. (1975). The magic number seven after fifteen years. In Kennedy, A., and Wilkes, A. (Eds.), *Studies in Long Term Memory,* Wiley, London.

Bronowski, J. (1965). *The Identity of Man,* Heinemann, London.

Bronowski, J. (1978). *The Origins of Knowledge and Imagination,* Yale University Press, New Haven.

Brown, G. (1970). An investigation into the relationships between performance and neuroticism, *Durham Res. Rev.,* **25**, 483-488.

Brown, G., and Desforges, C.W. (1977). Piagetian psychology and education: time for revision, *Br. J. educ. Psychol,* **47**, 7-17.

Brown, G. and Desforges, C.W. (1979). *Piaget's Theory: A Psychological Critique,* Routledge and Kegan Paul, London.

Brown, R. (1965). *Social Psychology,* Collier-MacMillan, London.

Bruner, J.S. (1960), *The Process of Education,* Harvard University Press, Cambridge, Mass.

Bruner, J.S. (1964). The course of cognitive growth, *Am. Psychol.,* **19**, 1-15.

Bruner, J.S. (1966). *Toward a Theory of Instruction,* Harvard University Press, Cambridge, Massachusetts.

Bruner, J.S. (1974). *Beyond the Information Given,* George Allen and Unwin, London.

Burt, C. (1921). *Mental and Scholastic Tests,* Staples, London.

Burt, C. (1940). *The Factors of the Mind,* University of London Press, London.

Burt, C. (1965). Factorial studies of personality and their bearing on the work of teachers, *Br. J. educ. Psychol.,* **35**, 368-378.

Burt, C. (1970). The genetics of intelligence. In Dockrell, W.B. (Ed.), *On Intelligence,* Methuen, London.

Burt, C. and Moore, R.C. (1915). The general and specific factors underlying the primary emotions, *Rep. Br. Ass. Adv. Sci.,* **84**, 694-696.

Butcher, H.J. (1968). *Human Intelligence: Its Nature and Assessment,* Methuen, London.

Carroll, J.B. (1963). A model for school learning, *Teachers College Record,* **64**, 723-733.

Cattell, R.B. (1965). *The Scientific Analysis of Personality,* Penguin Books, Harmondsworth.

Chickering, A.W. (1976). The double bind of field dependence/independence in program alternatives for educational development. In Messick, S. (Ed.), *Individuality in Learning,* Jossey-Bass, San Francisco.

Clarke, W.D. (1974). *A Study of the Development of Adolescent Judgment,* Unpublished Ph.D. thesis, University of Birmingham.

Cofer, C.N. (1975). *The Structure of Human Memory,* W.H. Freeman, San Francisco.

Cooley, W.W. and Lohnes, P.R. (1976). *Evaluation Research in Education,* Irvington, New York.

Coopersmith, S. (1959). A method for determining types of self esteem, *J. Educ. Res., 59,* 87-94.

Craik, F.I.M. and Lockhart, R.S. (1972), Levels of processing: a framework for memory research, *J. verb. Learn. verb. Behav., 11,* 671-684.

Craik, F.I.M., and Tulving, E. (1975).Depth of processing and the retention of words in episodic memory, *J. exp. Psychol. (Gen.), 104,* 268-294.

Cronbach, L.J. (1957). The two disciplines of scientific psychology, *Amer. Psychol., 12,* 671-684.

Cronbach, L.J. (1975). Beyond the two disciplines of scientific psychology, *Am. Psychol., 30,* 116-127.

Cronbach, L.J. and Suppes, P. (Eds.), (1969). *Research for Tomorrow's Schools: Disciplined Inquiry for Education,* Macmillan, New York.

Crutchfield, R.S. (1962). Conformity and creative thinking. In Gruber, H.E., Terrell, G., and Wertheimer, M. (Eds.), *Contemporary Approaches to Creative Thinking,* Atherton, New York.

Dahlgren, L.O. (1978). Qualitative differences in conceptions of basic principles in Economics. *Paper read to the 4th International Conference on Higher Education at Lancaster,* 29th August-1st September, 1978.

Dahlgren, L.O. and Marton, F. (1978). Students' conceptions of subject matter: an aspect of learning and teaching in higher education. *Studies in Higher Educ., 3,* 25-35.

Das, J.P., Kirby, J.R., and Jarman, R.F. (1975). Simultaneous and successive synthesis: an alternative model for cognitive abilities, *Psychol. Bull., 82,* 87-103.

Das, J.P., Kirby, J.R., and Jarman, R.F. (1979), *Simultaneous and Successive Cognitive Processes,* Academic Press, New York.

de Bono, E. (1971). *The Use of Lateral Thinking,* Penguin Books, Harmondsworth.

de Bono, E. (1978). *Teaching Thinking,* Penguin Books, Harmondsworth.

De Charms, R. (1968). *Personal Causation: the Internal Affective Determinants of Behaviour,* Academic Press, New York.

Desforges, C. and Brown, G. (1979). The educational utility of Piaget: a reply to Shayer, *Br. J. educ. Psychol., 49,* 277-281.

Dewey, J. (1910). *How We Think,* D.C. Heath, Boston.

Donaldson, M. (1978). *Children's Minds,* Fontana, London.

Elliott, C.D. (1972). Personality factors and scholastic attainment, *Br. J. educ. Psychol., 42,* 23-32.

Elliott, C.D., Murray, D.J., and Pearson, L.S., (1977). *The British Ability Scales,* NFER, Windsor.

Entwistle, N.J. (1968). Academic motivation and school attainment, *Br. J. educ. Psychol., 38,* 181-188.

Entwistle, N.J. (1978). Knowledge structures and styles of learning: a summary of Pask's recent research, *Br. J. educ. Psychol., 48,* 255-265.

Entwistle, N.J. and Bennett, S.N. (1973). *The Inter-relationships between Personality, Divergent Thinking and School Attainment.* Final Report to the SSRC on project MR 1346.

Entwistle, N.J. and Cunningham, S. (1968). Neuroticism and school attainment — a linear relationship? *Br. J. educ. Psychol.,* **38,** 123-132.

Entwistle, N.J. and Duckworth, D. (1977). Choice of science courses in secondary school: trends and explanations, *Stud. Sci. Educ.,* **4,** 68-82.

Entwistle, N.J., Hanley, M., and Ratcliffe, G. (1979a). Approaches to learning and levels of understanding, *Br. J. educ. Res.,* **5,** 99-114.

Entwistle, N.J., Hanley, M., and Hounsell, D.J. (1979b). Identifying distinctive approaches to studying, *Higher Educ.,* **8,** 365-380.

Entwistle, N.J., and Hounsell, D.J. (1975). *How Students Learn,* Institute for Research and Development in Post-Compulsory Education, University of Lancaster.

Entwistle, N.J., and Nisbet, J.D. (1972). *Educational Research in Action,* Hodder and Stoughton, London.

Entwistle, N.J. and Percy, K.A. (1971). Educational objectives and student performance within the binary system. In *Research into Higher Education, 1970,* Society for Research into Higher Education, London.

Entwistle, N.J. and Percy, K.A. (1974). Critical thinking or conformity? An investigation of the aims and outcomes of higher education. In Page, C.F. and Gibson, J. (Eds.), *Research into Higher Education, 1973,* Society for Research into Higher Education, London.

Entwistle, N.J. and Robinson, M. (1976). Personality, cognitive style and students' learning strategies. Paper read at the 2nd Congress of the European Association for Research and Development in Higher Education. Published in *Higher Education Bulletin,* **6,** 23-43.

Entwistle, N.J., Thompson, J.B., and Wilson, J.D. (1974). Motivation and Study Habits, *Higher Educ.,* **3,** 379-396.

Entwistle, N.J. and Welsh, J. (1969). Correlates of school attainment at different ability levels, *Br. J. educ. Psychol.,* **39,** 57-63.

Entwistle, N.J. and Wilson, J.D. (1977). *Degrees of Excellence: the Academic Achievement Game,* Hodder and Stoughton, London.

Erikson, E.H. (1963). *Childhood and Society,* (2nd Edition), Norton, New York.

Erikson, E.H. (1968). *Identity, Youth, and Crises,* W.W. Norton, New York.

Eysenck, H.J. (1965). *Fact and Fiction in Psychology,* Penguin Books, Harmondsworth.

Eysenck, H.J. (1967). *The Biological Basis of Personality,* C.C. Thomas, Springfield.

Eysenck, H.J. (1976). *The Structure of Human Personality,* Methuen, London.

Eysenck, H.J. (1972). Personality and attainment: an application of psychological principles to educational objectives, *Higher Educ.,* **1,** 39-52.

Eysenck, H.J. and Cookson, D. (1969). Personality in primary school children, I — Ability and achievement, *Br. J. educ. Psychol.,* **39,** 109-122.

Eysenck, H.J. and Eysenck, S.B.G. (1969). 'Psychoticism' in children: a new personality variable, *Res. in Educ.,* **1,** 21-37.

Eysenck, M.W. (1978). Levels of processing: a critique. *Br. J. Psychol.,* **69,** 157-169.

Festinger, L. (1957). *A Theory of Cognitive Dissonance,* Row Peterson, Evanston, Illinois.

Finlayson, D.S. (1970). A follow-up study of school achievement in relation to personality. *Br. J. educ. Psychol.,* **40,** 344-347.

Flavell, J.H. (1977). *Cognitive Development,* Prentice Hall, Englewood Cliffs, New Jersey.

Fox, S. (1974). *Freud and Education,* C.C. Thomas, Springfield, Illinois.

Fransson, A. (1977). On qualitative differences in learning IV — Effects of motivation and test anxiety on process and outcome. *Br. J. educ. Psychol.,* **47,** 244-257.

Friedlander, B.Z. (1975). Some remarks on open education, *Am. educ. Res. J.,* **12,** 465-468.

Furneaux, W.D. (1962). The psychologist and the university, *Univ. Quart.,* **17,** 33-47.

Gage, N.L. and Berliner, D.C. (1975). *Educational Psychology,* Rand McNally, Chicago.

Gagné, R.M. (1970). *The Conditions of Learning,* (2nd Edition), Holt, Rinehart and Winston, New York.

Gardner, H. (1976). *The Quest for Mind,* Quartet Books, London.

Getzels, J.W. and Jackson, P.W. (1962). *Creativity and Intelligence,* Wiley, New York.

Gillie, O. (1976). Crucial data faked by eminent psychologist, *Sunday Times,* 24th October, 1976.

Gilmartin, K.J., Newell, A. and Simon, H.A. (1975). A program modelling short-term memory under strategy control. In Cofer, C.N. (Ed.), *The Structure of Human Memory,* W.H. Freeman, San Francisco.

Gray, J. and Satterley, D. (1976). A chapter of errors: 'Teaching Styles and Pupil Progress' in retrospect, *Ed. Res.,* **19,** 45-56.

Guildford, J.P. (1950). Creativity. *Amer. Psychol.,* **5,** 444-454.

Guildford, J.P. (1967). *The Nature of Human Intelligence,* McGraw-Hill, New York.

Gustafsson, J.E. (1976). *Verbal and Figural Aptitudes in Relation to Instructional Methods,* Acta Universitatis Gothoburgensis, Gothenburg.

Hearnshaw, L.S. (1979). *Cyril Burt: Psychologist,* Hodder and Stoughton, London.

Heath, R. (1964). *The Reasonable Adventurer,* University of Pittsburgh Press, Pittsburgh.

Heath, R. (1978). Personality and the development of students in higher education. In Parker, C.A. (Ed.), *Encouraging Development in College Students,* University of Minnesota Press, Minneapolis.

Hebron, M. (1964). *Motivated Learning,* Methuen, London.

Herriot, P. (1974). *Attributes of Memory,* Methuen, London.

Holland, J.L. (1966). *The Psychology of Occupational Choice,* Blaisdell, Waltham, Massachusetts.

Holland, J.L. (1973). *Making Vocational Choices: a Theory of Careers,* Prentice Hall, Englewood Cliffs, New Jersey.

Holt, J. (1964). *How Children Fail,* Pitman, New York.

Howe, M.J.A., and Colley, L. (1976). Retroactive interference in meaningful learning, *Br. J. educ. Psychol.,* **46,** 26-30.

Hudson, L. (1966). *Contrary Imaginations,* Methuen, London.

Hudson, L. (1968). *Frames of Mind,* Methuen, London.

Inhelder, B., and Piaget, J. (1958). *The Growth of Logical Thinking from Childhood to Adolescence,* Routledge and Kegan Paul, London.

Ivimy, J. (1974). *The Sphinx and the Megaliths,* Turnstone Books, London.

James, W. (1899). *Talks to Teachers,* (1958 Reissue), W.W. Norton, New York.

Jensen, A.R. (1967). Estimation of the limits of heritability of traits by comparison of monozygotic and dizygotic twins, *Proc. Nat. Ac. Sci.,* **58,** 149-157.

Jensen, A.R. (1970). Hierarchical theories of mental ability. In Dockrell, W.B. (Ed.), *On Intelligence,* Methuen, London.

Jung, C.G. (1938). *Psychological Types,* Kegan Paul, Trench, and Truber, London.

Jung, C.G. (1964). *Man and His Symbols,* Aldus Books, London.

Kagan, J., Rosman, B.L., Day, D., Albert, J., and Phillips, N. (1964). Information processing in the child: significance of analytic and reflective attitudes, *Psychol. Monogr.,* **78** (whole).

Kelly, G.A. (1955). *The Psychology of Personal Constructs,* Norton, New York.

Kelly, G.A. (1964). Man's construction of his alternatives. In Southwell, E.A. and Merbaum, M. *Personality: Readings in Theory and Research,* Brooks/Cole, Belmont, California.

Kerlinger, F.N. (1969). Research in Education. In Ebel, R.L. (Ed.), *Encyclopedia of Educational Research* (Fourth Edition), Macmillan, New York.

Kirby, J.R. and Das, J.P. (1978). Information processing and human abilities, *J. educ. Psychol.*, **70**, 58-66.

Klatzky, R.L. (1975). *Human Memory: Structures and Processes*, W.H. Freeman, San Francisco.

Klausmeier, H.J., Ghatala, E.S., and Frayer, D.A. (1974). *Conceptual Learning and Development: a Cognitive View*, Academic Press, New York.

Kline, P. (1976). *Personality Theories and Dimensions*, (Block 2, Open University Course 201), Open University Press, Milton Keynes.

Kluckhohn, C., Murray, H.A. and Schneider, D.M. (1953). *Personality in Nature, Society and Culture*, Knopf, New York.

Koestler, A. (1964). *The Act of Creation*, Macmillan, London.

Kogan, N. (1976). *Cognitive Styles in Infancy and Early Childhood*, Lawrence Erlbaum, Hillsdale, New Jersey.

Kogan, N. and Wallach, M.A. (1964). *Risk Taking*, Holt, Rinehart, and Winston, New York.

Krathwohl, D.R., Bloom, B.J., and Masia, B.B. (1964). *Taxonomy of Educational Objectives. The Classification of Educational Goals Handbook II – Affective Domain*, David McKay, New York.

Laing, R.D. (1977). *The Facts of Life*, Penguin, Harmondsworth.

Laurillard, D. (1979). The processes of student learning, *Higher Educ.*, **8**, 395-410.

Leith, G.O.M. (1974). Individual differences in learning interactions of personality and teaching methods in *Personality and Academic Progress*, Association of Educational Psychologists, London.

Lewis, B.N. (1976). Avoidance of aptitude-treatment trivialities. In Messick, S. (Ed.), *Individuality in Learning*, Jossey-Bass, San Francisco.

Lindsay, P.H. and Norman, D.A. (1972). *Human Information Processing*, Academic Press, New York.

Lockhart, R.S. and Craik, F.I.M. (1978). Levels of processing: a reply to Eysenck, *Br. J. Psychol.*, **69**, 171-175.

Luria, A.R. (1975). *The Mind of a Mnemonist*, (Reissue) Penguin Books, Harmondsworth.

Lynn, R. and Gordon, J.E. (1961). The relation of neuroticism and extraversion to educational attainment, *Br. J. educ. Psychol.*, **31**, 194-203.

Marton, F. (1978). Describing conceptions of the world about us, Research Report from the Institute of Education, University of Gothenburg.

Marton, F. and Säljö, (1976a). On qualitative differences in learning I — Outcome and process, *Br. J. educ. Psychol.*, **46**, 4-11.

Marton, F. and Säljö, R. (1976b). On qualitative differences in learning. II — Outcome as a function of the learner's conception of the task, *Br. J. educ. Psychol.*, **46**, 115-127.

Maslow, A.H. (1954). *Motivation and Personality*, Harper and Row, New York.

Maslow, A.H. (1973). *The Farther Reaches of Human Nature*, Penguin Books, Harmondsworth.

Maxwell, J. (1969). *Sixteen Years On*, University of London Press, London.

McClelland, D.C., Atkinson, J.W., Clark, R.A., and Lowell, E.L. (1953). *The Achievement Motive*, Appleton-Century-Crofts, New York.

Macfarlane-Smith, I. (1964). *Spatial Ability: Its Educational and Social Significance*, University of London Press, London.

McKeachie, W.J. (1974). The decline and fall of the laws of learning, *Educ. Researcher*, **3**, 3, 7-11.

McNemar, Q. (1964). Lost: our intelligence? Why? *Amer. Psychol.*, **19**, 871-82.

Messer, S. (1976). Reflection-Impulsivity: a review, *Psychol. Bull.*, **83**, 1026-1052.

Messick, S., and Associates (1976). *Individuality in Learning*, Jossey-Bass, San Francisco.

Miller, G.A. (1956). The magical number seven, plus or minus two: some limits in our capacity for processing information, *Psychol. Rev.*, **63**, 81-97.

Miller, C., and Parlett, M.R. (1974). *Up to the Mark: a Study of the Examination Game*, Society for Research in Higher Education, London.

Mouly, G.J. (1978). *Educational Research: the Art and Science of Investigation*, Allyn and Bacon, New York.

Murray, H.A. (1938). *Explorations in Personality*, Oxford University Press, Oxford.

Neisser, U. (1976). *Cognition and Reality*, W.H. Freeman, San Francisco.

Neill, A.S. (1915). *A. Dominie's Log*, Herbert Jenkins, London.

Nisbet, J.D. and Entwistle, N.J. (1970). *Educational Research Methods*, Hodder and Stoughton, London.

Nisbet, J.D. and Entwistle, N.J. (1973). The psychologist's contribution to educational research. In Taylor, W. (Ed.), *Research Perspectives in Education*, Routledge and Kegan Paul, London.

Norman, D.A. and Bobrow, D.G. (1975). Active memory processes in perception and cognition. In Cofer, C.N. (Ed.), *The Structure of Human Memory*, W.H. Freeman, San Francisco.

Ornstein, R.E. (1977). *The Psychology of Consciousness* (2nd Edition), Harcourt Brace, Jovanovich, New York.

Paffard, M. (1973). *Inglorious Wordsworths*, Hodder and Stoughton, London.

Parlett, M.R. (1970). The syllabus-bound student. In Hudson, L. (Ed.), *The Ecology of Human Intelligence*, Penguin Books, Harmondsworth.

Pask, G. (1976a). Conversational techniques in the study and practice of education, *Br. J. educ. Psychol.*, **46**, 12-25.

Pask, G. (1976b). Styles and strategies of learning, *Br. J. educ. Psychol.*, **46**, 128-148.

Pask, G. and Scott, B.C.E. (1972). Learning strategies and individual competence, *Int. J. Man-Machine Stud.*, **4**, 217-253.

Pask, G., *et al.*, (1977). *Third Progress Report on SSRC Research Programme HR 2708* (see also *Fourth Progress Report, 1978*, and *Final Report, 1979*), System Research Limited, 37 Sheen Road, Richmond, Surrey.

Peel, E.A. (1972). The quality of understanding in secondary school subjects. *Educ. Rev.*, **24**, 174-182.

Peel, E.A. (1975a). Predilection for generalising and abstracting, *Br. J. educ. Psychol.*, **45**, 177-188.

Peel, E.A. (1975b). Development of intelligence and education. In Berenberg, S.R. (Ed.), *Puberty: Biological and Psychological Components*, Stenfert Kroesk, Leiden.

Peel, E.A. (1976). Language dominated thought in adolescents: some bearings on mathematical thinking. *Paper given at the Psychology of Mathematics Education Workshop*, Centre for Science Education, Chelsea College, London.

Peel, E.A. (1978). Generalising through the verbal medium, *Br. J. educ. Psychol.*, **48**, 36-46.

Perry, W.G. (1970). *Forms of Intellectual and Ethical Development in the College Years: a Scheme*, Holt Rinehart and Winston, New York.

Pervin, L.A. (1975). *Personality: Theory, Assessment, and Research* (2nd Edition), Wiley, New York.

Peters, R.S. (1959). *The Concept of Motivation*, Routledge, London.

Peterson, L.R., and Peterson, M.J. (1959). Short-term retention of individual verbal items, *J. exp. Psychol.*, **58**, 193-198.

Piaget, J. and Inhelder, B. (1969). *The Psychology of the Child*, Routledge and Kegan Paul, London.

Pines, M. (1976). A child's mind is shaped before age 2. In Dentler, R.A. and Shapiro, B. (Eds.), *Readings in Educational Psychology: Contemporary Perspectives*, Harper and Row, New York.

Phillips, J.L. (1975). *The Origins of Intellect: Piaget's Theory* (2nd Edition), W.H. Freeman, San Francisco.

The Plowden Report (1967). *Children and their Primary Schools,* H.M.S.O., London.

Polanyi, M. (1958). *Personal Knowledge,* Routledge and Kegan Paul, London.

Popper, K. (1957). *The Poverty of Historicism,* Routledge and Kegan Paul, London.

Popper, K.R., and Eccles, J.C. (1977). *The Self and its Brain,* Springer International, London.

Raaheim, K. (1974). *Problem Solving and Intelligence,* Universitetsforlaget, Bergen-Oslo-Tromso.

Raaheim, K. (1976). Do we need convergent thinking? *Paper presented at the 21st International Conference of Psychology,* Paris, July, 1976.

Raaheim, K., and Kaufmann, G. (1974). Is there a general problem-solving ability? *J. Gen, Psychol.,* **90,** 231-236.

Ramsden, P. (1979). Student learning and perceptions of the academic environment, *Higher Educ.,* **8,** 411-428.

Reid, T. (1785). *Essays on the Intellectual Powers of Man,* Republished in 1969 by M.I.T. Press, Cambridge, Massachusetts.

Robertson, I.T. (1977). An investigation of some relationships between learning and personality, *Unpublished Ph.D.,* Open University, Milton Keynes.

Roe, A., and Klos, D. (1972). Classification of occupations. In Whiteley, J.M. and Resnikoff, A. (Eds.), *Perspectives on Vocational Development,* American Personnel and Guidance Association, Washington D.C.

Rogers, C.R. (1969). *Freedom to Learn,* Merrill, Columbus, Ohio.

Rose, S. (1976). *The Conscious Brain* (Revised Edition), Penguin Books, Harmondsworth.

Rosen, B.C. (1959). Race, ethnicity, and the achievement syndrome, *Amer. Soc. Rev.,* **26,** 574-585.

Rosen, B.C., and d'Andrade, R. (1959). The psychosocial origins of achievement motivation, *Sociometry,* **22,** 185-218.

Saville, P., and Blinkhorn, S. (1976). *Undergraduate Personality by Factored Scales,* N.F.E.R., Slough.

Saljo, R. (1975). *Qualitative Differences in Learning as a Function of the Learner's Conception of the Task,* Acta Universitatis Gothoburgensis, Goteborg. (Also reported in Marton and Saljo, 1976b).

Saljo, R. (1979). Learning about learning, *Higher Educ.,* **8,** 443-451.

Sharp, A. (1978). Motivation and vocabularies of motive: an inter-disciplinary analysis of pupils' attitudes to school and their classroom behaviour. *Unpublished Ph.D. Thesis,* University of Lancaster.

Shayer, M. (1979). Has Piaget's construct of formal operational thinking any utility? *Br. J. educ. Psychol.,* **49,** 265-276.

Skinner, B.F. (1953). *Science and Human Behaviour,* Macmillan, New York.

Skinner, B.F. (1954). The science of learning and the art of teaching, *Harvard educ. Rev.,* **24,** 88-97.

Smith, H. (1975). Teaching spelling, *Br. J. educ. Psychol.,* **45,** 68-72.

Snelbecker, G.E. (1974). *Learning Theory, Instructional Theory, and Psychoeducational Design,* McGraw Hill, New York.

Snow, R.E. (1976). Aptitude-treatment interactions and individualised alternatives in higher education. In Messick, S. (Ed.) *Individuality in Learning,* Jossey-Bass, San Francisco.

Solomon, D., and Kendall, A.J. (1979). *Children in Classrooms: An Investigation of Person-Environment Interaction,* Praeger Publishers, New York.

Spearman, C.E. (1904). 'General intelligence' objectively determined and measured, *Amer. J. Psychol.* **15,** 72-101.

Spearman, C. (1923). *The Nature of Intelligence and the Principles of Cognition,* Macmillan, London.

Spearman, C. (1927). *The Abilities of Man: their Nature and Measurement,* Macmillan, London.

Spranger, E. (1928). *Types of Men: the Psychology of Ethics and Personality,* Max Niemeyer Verlay, Halle (Saale) (Reprinted by Johnson, New York, 1966).

Super, D.E. (1969). Vocational development theory: persons, positions and processes, *Couns. Psychol.,* **1,** 2-9.

Svensson, L. (1977). On qualitative differences in learning III — Study skill and learning, *Br. J. educ. Psychol.,* **47,** 233-243.

Thomson, G.H. (1924). *Instinct, Intelligence and Character,* George Allen and Unwin, London.

Thomson, G.H. (1951). *The Factorial Analysis of Human Ability* (5th Edition), University of London Press, London.

Thurstone, L.L. (1938). Primary mental abilities, *Psychometr Monogr.,* No. 1.

Townsend, M.A.R., and Keeling, B. (1976). An investigation of Level I and Level II cognitive processes in the learning and recall of factual and inferential information, *Br. J. educ. Psychol.,* **46,** 306-317.

Trown, E.A. and Leith, G.O.M. (1975). Decision rules for teaching strategies in primary schools: personality — treatment interactions, *Br. J. educ. Psychol.,* **45,** 130-140.

Tulving, E. (1972). Episodic and semantic memory. In Tulving, E. and Donaldson, W. (Eds.), *Organisation of Memory,* Academic Press, New York.

Tyler, L.E. (1976). The intelligence we test — an evolving concept. In Resnick, L.B. (Ed.), *The Nature of Intelligence,* Lawrence Erlbaum, Hillsdale, N.J.

van Lawick-Goodall, J. (1971). *In the Shadow of Man,* Collins, London.

Vernon, P.E. (1950). *The Structure of Human Abilities,* Methuen, London.

Vernon, P.E. (1970). Intelligence. In Dockrell, W.B. (Ed.), *On Intelligence,* Methuen, London.

Vernon, P.E. (1979a). Intelligence testing and the nature/nurture debate, 1928-1978: what next?, *Br. J. educ. Psychol.,* **49,** 1-14.

Vernon, P.E. (1979b). *Intelligence: Heredity and Environment:* W.H. Freeman, San Francisco.

Wade, B. (1979). Anxiety and achievement motivation in relation to the cognitive attainment and behaviour of pupils in formal and informal classrooms, *Unpublished Ph.D. Thesis,* University of Lancaster.

Waismann, F. (1968). *How I See Philosophy,* Macmillan, London.

Wallach, M.A. and Kogan, N. (1965). *Modes of Thinking in Young Children,* Holt, Rinehart and Winston, New York.

Ward, J. (1926). *Psychology Applied to Education,* University Press, Cambridge.

Watts, I. (1810). *The Improvement of the Mind,* Gale and Curtis, London.

Weiner, B. (1972). *Theories of Motivation: From Mechanism to Cognition,* Markham, Chicago.

Wertheimer, M. (1945). *Productive Thinking,* Harper, New York.

Westbury, I. (1977). The curriculum and the frames of the classroom, Paper presented to the 1977 AERA Conference (quoted by Bennett, 1978).

White, C.D., Murray, D.J., and Pearson, L.S. (1979). *The Origins of Human Competence,* D.C. Heath: Lexington, Massachusetts.

White, R.W. (1959). Motivation reconsidered: the concept of competence, *Psychol. Rev.,* **66,** 297-333.

Whitehead, A.N. (1932). *The Aims of Education,* (Paperback Edition, 1962), Benn, London.

Wilson, J. (1968). *Philosophy and Educational Research,* N.F.E.R., Slough.

Wilson, J.D. (1969). Predicting levels of first year university performance, *Unpublished Ph.D. Thesis,* University of Aberdeen.

Witkin, H.A. (1976). Cognitive style in academic performance and in teacher-student relations. In Messick, S. (Ed.), *Individuality in Learning,* Jossey-Bass, San Francisco.

Witkin, H.A., Moore, C.A., Goodenough, D.R., and Cox, P.W. (1977). Field-dependent and field-independent cognitive styles and their educational implications, *Rev. educ. Res.,* 1-64.

Index